marques vickers

TWISTED TOUR GUIDE
NORTHERN VIRGINIA: Alexandria-Fredricksburg-Richmond
SHOCKING HISTORY, DISCOVERIES and SCANDALS

AF434745

1

TWISTED TOUR GUIDE NORTHERN VIRGINIA:

Alexandria-Fredericksburg-Richmond

SHOCKING HISTORY, DISCOVERIES AND SCANDALS

By Marques Vickers

MARQUIS PUBLISHING
BAINBRIDGE ISLAND, WASHINGTON

Version 1.1

Published by Marquis Publishing
Bainbridge Island, WA
TwistedTourGuides.com

Vickers, Marques, 1957

Twisted Tour Guide
Northern Virginia:
Alexandria-Fredericksburg-Richmond
Shocking History, Discoveries and Scandals

Dedication: To my daughters Charline and Caroline. Many thanks to my sister Lisa and brother-in-law Adrian and Bianca for hosting me.

TABLE OF CONTENTS

A Fiery Interruption For A Doomed Bride
The Thorny Continued Existence Of A Confederate
Tombstone
A Spiritual Center For The Earliest Black Congregation
A Racially Motivated Lynching Absent of Due Process
Clem's Stroll With A Bloody Razor Seeking Revenge
The Silent Sentinels and Their Passion For Equal Rights
An Unsolved Murder of an Aspiring Police Sergeant
A Masonic Pilgrimage Honoring George Washington
A Non-Violent Library Sit-In Fuels Early Civil Right
Advocacy
A Presidential Legacy Doomed By His Predecessor
George Washington Slept Here While On Business or Play
A Spy Plane Shot Down Over Russia Triggers An
International Incident
A Supreme Court Landmark Decision Reaffirming The
Right To Marry Freely
A Tainted Murder Site Scorched By A Concealing Fire
An Idiotic Afternoon Robbery and Pointless Murder
Glacial Justice For A Violent Defilement and Shooting
Unsolved Break-In and Vicious Stabbing in Affluent Old
Town
A Drug Debt Retrieval Resulting In Three Lost Lives
A National Trail of Tears Originating From Mount Vernon
A Publicly Recognized Serial Killer and Failed Political
Candidate
A Contract Killing Concluding A Clouded Past
A Buried Maritime Past Prompts Cargo Questioning
A Congressional Baseball Practice Tainted By Gunfire
A Symbol of Defiance and Defeat Removed Amidst
Changing Times

FAIRFAX:
The Civil War Battle of the Fairfax Courthouse
The Final Execution Of A Serial Rapist Following Due
Process

The Accumulation of Hostilities Between Motorcycle Gang
Rivals
The Christmas Tree Lady's Mysterious Farewell
The Spy Fished Out From The Cold
A Fairfax Mayor Who Squandered His Public Credibility

FREDERICKSBURG:
An Episcopal Church Bearing Witness To Three Centuries
of Local Trauma
The Esteemed Mother of The Father of Our Country
A Debt Of Honor Tainting An Aristocratic Family's
Reputation
The Most Excessive Carnage From A Civil War
Engagement
An Empathic and Controversial Creator of Verse Leading
By Example
An Embezzlement Scandal That Tainted Fredericksburg's
Knox Family
A Former Slave Escaping To Tell A Shackled Narrative
The Acknowledgement of Free Religious Protection
A Serial Killer's Shocking Violence During A More
Innocent Era
A Police Department Renowned For A Dunking Stool and
Burglary Ring
The Profound Darkness of John Muhammad's Soul
The Insanity Behind A Deliberate and Disturbing Murder
Insuring For A Squandered Future

RICHMOND:
An Orator's Famous Demand For Liberty…For Some
The Chief Justice Who Shaped The Philosophy of the
Supreme Court
A Consuming Fire Destroying the Richmond Elite
A Washington D.C. Equivalent Executive Mansion in
Richmond
Downtown Canal Walk Tracing Historic Richmond

SOURCES AND ARCHIVES SOURCED:

FBI.gov, The Guardian.com, Nola.com, WashingtonPost.com, Wikipedia.org, OffbeatNova.com, BoundaryStones.weta.org, WUSA9.com, NBCWashington.com, WTOP.com, WAFB.com, CNN.com, Richmond.com, USAToday.com, Alamy.com, StyleWeekly.com, Battlefields.org, AlexandriaLivingMagazine.com, Jay.typepad.com, AlexandriaGhosts.com, GravesstoneStories.com, StMaryOldTown.org, Hmdb.org, Smithsonianmag.com, VirginiaPlaces.org, OurHistoryMuseum.org, Alexandriava.gov, Sites.Lib.jmu.edu, Alexandria Gazette, WashingtonExaminer.com, NPS.gov, FXVA.com 20.state.nj.us , ConnectionNewspapers.com, Media.alexandriava.gov, Law.Justia.com, Vadoc.virginia.gov, OldTownCrier.com, Murderpedia.org, UTC.iath.virginia.edu, Frozentropics.blogspot.com, Alexandriava.gov, DCGhosts.com, Britannica.com, InmateLocator.cor.pa.gov, MountVernon.org, OldTownHome.com, Expedia.com, FXVA.com, TampaBay.com, Alexandria.com, NPS.gov, EncyclopediaVirgina.org, NOVAParks.com, PurpleHeart.org, LeeFendallHouse.org, VirginisBusiness.com, WoundedWarrior.marines.mil, Blackbird.VCU.edu, TheClio.com, FindAGrave.com, Alexandria.org, OffbeatNOVA.com, Alxnow.com, Rocketwerks.tumblr.com, HFFI.org, MetMuseum.org, Washington City Paper, Sports Illustrated, Fredericksburgva.gov, History.state.gov, NPSFRSP.wordpress.com, TheInnAtKenmoreHall.com, Patch.com Web.archive.org, RichmondHillVa.org, ArlingtonMagazine.com, GoHikeVirginia.com, VentureRichmond.com, Poets.org, SerialKillerCalendar.com, LeoLofland.com, NewYorkTimes.com, RichmondTourGuys.com,

RichmondMagazine.com, PBS.org, DHR.Virginia.gov, Baltimore.org, TheValentine.org, PoeMuseum.org, BMTITUS.com, PoeInBaltimore.org, HistoricStJohnsChurch.org, HollywoodCemetery.org, WTVR.com, WVPublic.org, GeorgiaEncyclopedia.org, ShelteringArmsInstitute.com, Richmond.com, ArlingtonCemetery.mil, DailyMail.co.uk, Arlingtonva.us, Fredericksburg.com, AlBennettandSonFuneralHome.com, Virginia.org, StGeorgesEpiscopal.net, Sah-archipedia.org, VirginiaHistory.org, Washingtonian.com and HistoricFairfax.org.

Photography shot during 2022-2023. Some of the locations may have altered with time and ownership changes. Many of the locations are still privately inhabited. Please don't disturb the residents.

PREFACE:

Evade the Tourist Herds and Enter Into An Insider's
Northern Virginia

Known and unknown history, hidden delights and
fascinating stories pervade the history of Northern Virginia.
This kaleidoscope of discovery, personalities, egos,
scandals, conflict framed by sheer beauty creates a vivid
tapestry defining over three centuries.

This guide transports you geographically and
photographically to the precise famous and infamous
locations where history occurred. The scenes may
sometimes appear ordinary, weird, but often illuminate the
physical background and descriptions behind events. Many
of the narratives defy believability, yet they are true.

This Twisted Tour Guide is your alternative to conventional
travel. It accommodates the restless visitor, tourist and
resident seeking a unique and different perspective to
traditional tourism. Northern Virginia remains one of the
most beguiling, historic and enchanting cities within the
Unites States.

Welcome to one on the most useful, eclectic and
enlightening introductions to Northern Virginia.

ARLINGTON

Intuitive Thinking Saves The Declaration of Independence From Destruction Pimmit Run:

North Glebe Road (State Highway 120) and 41st Street, Arlington

The British Army's sacking of Washington D.C. ranks as one of lowest points in American history. On August 24, 1814, the invasion of the Capitol materialized despite military officials certainty to the contrary.

Stephen Pleasonton, a State Department clerk had grave doubts regarding their confidence. He gathered together the Declaration of Independence, correspondence from George Washington and other documents of importance and hid them in a gristmill adjacent to Pimmir Run in Arlington. Once the chaotic evacuation began, his foresight proved timely. The British forces torched all government buildings including the White House.

The gristmill was located where the Chain Bridge Road and Glebe Road coincide under the current George Washington Parkway overpass. The documents only remained inside the mill a single evening. They were then relocated to Leesburg the next day to insure their survival.

Pimmit Run is a 7.8-mile stream that originates from Fairfax County running into the Potomac River. The stream parallels Chain Bridge as it bisects the Arlington Bluff. The gristmill has long ago disappeared. Thousands of motorists pass the site daily. Stephen Pleasonton faded into historical obscurity following his action. His initiative saved the original copies of some of America's most precious historical documentation.

A Purloined Enemy Estate Become A National Treasure
Arlington National Cemetery
1 Memorial Avenue, Fort Meyer

Confederate General Robert E. Lee's family had their Arlington Estate confiscated following a questionable and unethical property tax dispute during the Civil War.

George Washington Parke Custis was the son of Martha Dandridge Custis Washington through her first marriage. When his natural father John Parke Custis died, George moved to his mother's Mount Vernon residence where he resided with her and new husband George Washington. The couple raised him as their own son.

Custis later began building the Arlington House on land that he had inherited from his natural father. The construction was completed in 1818. He intended the residence to become his home and a memorial to his foster father. He married Mary Lee Fitzhugh in 1804 and they had four children. Only one, Mary Anna Randolph Custis survived and would marry Robert E. Lee.

Arlington House was given to Mary Lee in her father's will with the stipulation that allowed her to live and operate the Arlington Estate for the rest of her life. She was not authorized to sell any portion of it.

Upon Virginia seceding from the Union following the commencement of the Civil War, Robert E. Lee resigned his military commission on April 20, 1861. He would assume command of the armed forces of Virginia, later becoming commander of the Confederate Army of Northern Virginia.

On May 7, 1861, troops from the Union's Virginia militia

occupied Arlington. General Winfield Scott gave orders to clear the region of all troops not loyal to the United States. Mary Lee was reluctant to leave, but assumed that her house would soon be captured by federal troops. She buried many of her family treasures on the grounds and departed to live on her sister's estate at Ravensworth in Fairfax County. Arlington Estate became occupied without opposition on May 24.

Civil War dead overwhelmed the military cemeteries located in Washington D.C. and Alexandria by 1863. The demand for burial space became heightened following the *Battle of the Wilderness* staged on May 5-7, 1864 in Spotsylvania County, Virginia. The Arlington Estate was designated as the most suitable potential burial site within the District of Columbia region. The grounds were aesthetically pleasing, elevated and free from flooding, and boasted a view of the Capitol city.

Arlington Estate was also the legal property of the military head of the opposition army. Depriving Lee of his residence became a popular rationale for possession. Mary Lee had sent an agent to pay the $92.07 property tax bill in a timely manner. The government turned away her agent refusing to accept her payment. The estate was foreclosed. The government acquired the property at a tax sale in 1864 for $26,000.

The first military burial on site was William Henry Christmas on May 13, 1864 near the current northeast gate in Section 27. Burials were not officially authorized until the following month.

Following the war's conclusion in 1874, heir Curtis Lee would sue the United States claiming his ownership of the estate as stipulated in his grandfather's will. On December

9, 1882, the U.S. Supreme Court ruled 5-4 in his favor determining that the Arlington Estate was confiscated without due process. Congress returned the property to him. On March 3, 1883, he sold it back to the government for $150,000 during a signing ceremony with Secretary of War, Robert Todd Lincoln. The land was then converted into a military reservation.

The cemetery has since expanded into 639 acres through land acquisitions. Nearly 400,000 individuals are buried inside including some of the most famous American political and military leaders. All burials were segregated by race and military rank until President Truman desegregated the military in 1948.

Periodic scandals have embarrassingly revealed that cemetery officials had formerly placed the wrong headstones on tombs, buried coffins within shallow graves, and stacked bodies on top of one another. In 2005, the cemetery gradually imposed increasing restrictions on media coverage.

The cemetery is divided into 70 sections designated by casualty themes. *The Tomb of the Unknown Soldier* is part of the Arlington Memorial Amphitheatre that has hosted state funerals and Memorial and Veterans Day ceremonies. The tomb consists of seven pieces and was completed and opened to the public on April 9, 1932. Additional memorials include the *USS Main* Mast, Space Shuttle Challenger, Lockerbie Cairn, Cross of Sacrifice and Laos Memorial. President John F. Kennedy's tomb features an accompanying eternal flame and is the most frequently visited.

Other notable burial sites include Robert, Ted and Jacqueline Kennedy, President William Howard Taft,

Astronauts Gus Grissom, Roger Chaffee and John Glenn, Military leaders General John J. Pershing, Field Marshall Sir John Dill and Major General Philip Kearny. Fourteen Supreme Court Justices including most recent Ruth Bader Ginsburg are accompanied by than 400 Medal of Honor recipients.

TOMB OF THE UNKNOWN SOLDIER

PRESIDENT KENNEDY'S GRAVE

A Clandestine Love Nest For A Controversial 1920s Seductrice
Gulf Branch Nature Center and Park:
3608 Military Road, Arlington VA

Silent film star Pola Negri (born Nee Apolonia Chalupac) radiated sexual energy on stage and screen during the 1920s. She achieved prominence in Warsaw and Berlin before immigrating to the United States. Her initial American success was a role in *Passion* (1922) followed up by over twenty films for Paramount Pictures. She parlayed her exotic beauty into roles casting her as a flirt and a manipulative woman, who could induce men through her charisma to do what she wished.

Her screen roles mirrored her public and private persona. Her two most prominent lovers included actors Charlie Chaplin and Rudolph Valentino. Critics and the viewing public panned her excessively melodramatic behavior at Valentino's funeral. Her screen downfall became her inability to adapt her strong Polish accent into a successful transition to talking films. She returned to Germany and spent the 1930s acting in Berlin-based films choreographed by Nazi directors and censors. By 1941, her roles and appeal had dimmed and she retired to Los Angeles followed by San Antonio, Texas. She lived in obscurity there until her death in 1987 at the age of 90 from a combination of a brain tumor and pneumonia.

During her American acting prominence, she briefly lived in an Arlington stone bungalow. Her hideaway was rumored to be a love nest for clandestine trysts with Valentino and Hollywood style pool parties.

The building would eventually become the Gulf Branch Nature Center featuring a vernal pond, pollinator gardens and a restored 19th century log cabin. Gulf Branch stream flows adjacent emptying into the Potomac River. Hiking trails route visitors from the center along Gulf Branch traveling through a designated conservation area.

Racist Agitators Bonded By Hatred
Former American Nazi Party Headquarters Sites:
928 North Randolph Street, Arlington
2507 N. Franklin Road, Arlington
George Lincoln Rockwell Death Site:
Dominion Hills Shopping Center: 6011-6035 Wilson
Boulevard, Arlington

Racist activist George Lincoln Rockwell was brazen and often foolhardy in his quest for publicity covering his fringe movement. During a June 25, 1961 *Freedom Rally* event staged by Elijah Muhammad's Black Muslim movement at the Uline Arena in Washington D.C., he attended with a dozen of his American Nazi party *stormtrooper* degenerates. Prominently seated towards the front of the stage, the Neo-Nazis were provocatively dressed in clownish uniforms representing military figures. They listened respectfully and silently to a speech by Malcolm X.

Rockwell and Elijah Muhammad shared a profound respect for each other bonded by racial hatred.

On February 25, 1962, Rockwell was a guest speaker at a Black Muslim event in the International Amphitheatre in Chicago featuring both leader Elijah Muhammad and Malcolm X. He referred to Muhammad as *The Black People's Hitler* and praised his black separatist movement. Malcolm X would eventually have an epiphany against the movement and abuses imposed by Elijah Muhammad. He would separate from the movement. His decision would result in his assassination on February 21, 1965 in Manhattan.

Rockwell would represent a leadership symbol whose beliefs, strategies and writings parodied the white supremacy movement. He was an ardent admirer of Adolf Hitler despite serving in the United States Navy. He was trained as a pilot and served in World War II and the Korean War in non-combat roles. He would become honorably discharged in 1960 upon the radicalization of his divisive viewpoints.

Rockwell's political philosophy and politics became gradually more vocal during the 1950s. He publicly denied the Holocaust and became fiercely anti-Semitic. He founded the American Nazi Party (ANP) in March 1959 and later established the organization's headquarters out of his home in Arlington.

The party never established credible traction politically, but Rockwell attracted media attention for his bombastic and extreme views. His organization was more posturing than violent. He ran as a write-in candidate during the 1964 presidential election receiving 212 votes. He maintained a pattern of copying the manners of other iconic leaders and disruptive publicity stunts.

His polarizing tactics would conclude badly. On August 25, 1967, he was leaving a laundromat located only yards away from his residence. John Patler, who'd recently been expelled by Rockwell from the ANP the previous March, gunned him down from the shopping center rooftop. Patler had attempted to inject Marxist ideals into the party publications.

The killing astonished few individuals including Rockwell's father. Even fewer mourned. Patler was convicted of murder and sentenced to twenty years in prison. He served eight and than an additional six following a parole violation.

Rockwell left his organization with 300 active members and reportedly 3,000 marginal financial supporters. His parents wanted his private burial in Maine. The Neo-Nazi's wanted a military burial at Culpeper National Cemetery due to his honorable discharge status. The cemetery insisted that no Nazi insignias could be displayed. His fifty gathered mourners blatantly ignored the policy creating a blockage at the entrance. The cemetery would be closed amidst a five-hour standoff. The limousine with his casket was nearly sideswiped by a passing train. The next day, Rockwell's body was secretly cremated.

**The Enduring Fractured Trust Prompted By The
Watergate Scandal
Watergate Office Building:
2600 Virginia Avenue NW, Suite 610, Washington D.C.
Deep Throat Parking Garage:
1816 N Nash Street, Arlington VA**

Making sense and perspective of the Watergate Scandal a half-century afterwards requires an understanding of the prevalent expectations most citizens shared towards their Executive branch then. For nearly two and a half centuries, many Americans have harbored a healthy distrust and caution towards political institutions.

This angst and divisiveness was heightened during the early 1970s, particularly following the conclusion of the Vietnam War. Ridicule towards the assumption of political propriety has inflamed dialogue beginning with the presidential tenure of George Washington.

The Watergate scandal distanced itself in severity from precedent improprieties. In the past, national leaders may have misled or misrepresented facts, but never had they been caught and exposed so flagrantly. The scandal pricked an artery of American trust towards an essential presumed truth in public disclosure. This violation of that trust required public accountability and ultimately a change in leadership.

The genesis of President Richard Nixon's administration unraveling began on January 27, 1972 when G. Gordon Liddy, then the Finance Counsel for the Committee for the Re-Election of the President (CRP) presented an intelligence plan to three members of the administration's staff. These three included Attorney General John Mitchell, Presidential Counsel John Dean and acting CRP chairman

Jeb Magruder. The project involved extensive illegal activities against the Democratic Party.

The crux of the plan involved burglarizing the Democratic National Committee's headquarters located in the Watergate Complex in Washington D.C. The intent was to photograph campaign documents and wiretap telephones within the office. The break-in occurred on May 28th with two telephones targeted to be wiretapped. The plan seemingly worked flawlessly until it was determined that the listening devices were defective. A second burglary to correct the flaw was planned for three weeks later.

The second break-in attempt would launch the operation into infamy. Shortly after midnight on Saturday, June 17th, a Watergate security guard noticed tape covering the latches on some of the complex's doors leading from the underground parking garage to several offices. He removed the tape and shortly afterwards, noted that upon his return later the locks had been re-taped. He telephoned police.

A series of missteps by the burglars followed. Three plainclothes policemen arrived in an unmarked vehicle. The burglar's spotter watching from across the street at a Howard Johnson's Motel Lodge failed to observe their arrival in front of the Watergate building. The officers advanced to the sixth floor and the Democratic National Committees suite of 29 offices. They would apprehend five men and impound lock picking tools, film, two cameras, three pen-sized tear gas guns and $2,300 in cash.

There was no evidence to suggest that Nixon was cognizant of the operation. His administration team began immediate efforts the following morning to cover-up both the crime and any direct linkage to the CRP.

Nixon's initial error occurred during a conversation with his chief of staff, H. R. Haldeman on June 23rd when he was informed about the break-in. He expressed ignorance regarding the operation to Haldeman, but ordered him to the have the CIA impede the FBI's investigation into the financial sources behind the burglary.

Days afterwards, Ron Ziegler, Nixon's press secretary publicly described the arrests as a *third-rate burglary attempt*. On August 29th, Nixon addressed the issue with a news conference. He indicated that John Dean, his presidential lawyer had fully investigated the incident concluding that no one employed by the White House or administration had any involvement with the operation. The problem with his pronouncement was that Dean hadn't conducted an investigation. Worse, he was amongst the initial three administration members aware of the plan.

On September 15th, a grand jury indicted the five office burglars along with G. Gordon Liddy and former CIA officer E. Howard Hunt on charges of conspiracy, burglary and violation of federal wiretapping laws. Following a juried trial, on January 30, 1973, all seven either pled guilty or were convicted by a jury.

The case might have ended with their sentencing. Nixon was easily re-elected on November 7th in one of the largest landslides in electoral voting history, 520-17. His opponent George McGovern only won the state of Massachusetts and the District of Colombia.

The break-in from the outset was entirely needless. The revelations to follow the election were only just beginning.

The journey through the labyrinth of darken financing, dirty political tricks and ethically absent perpetrators proved unsettling to the American public palette,

Over the next eighteen months, the scandal would evolve into arguably the worst political scandal in American history. The sustained and accurate accounts by *Washington Post* reporters Bob Woodward and Carl Bernstein revealed that the Watergate break-in was an element of a much larger campaign of political spying and sabotage employed by the Nixon re-election campaign. Their chief anonymous informant was William Mark Felt, Sr., nicknamed *Deep Throat*, deputy director of the FBI. Woodward met clandestinely with Felt at an underground parking garage in Rosslyn, Virginia between June 1972 until January 1973.

As public disclosure regarding the extent of the CRP's activities widened, Nixon's administrative team were ensnared in a web of duplicity. Their efforts to deny guilt or destroy incriminating evidence heightened public distrust of Nixon and his effectiveness as a national leader. Many observers felt that his concealment of the trust was a betrayal that undermined the election process and democracy.

Unable to effectively govern under an enormous weight of suspicion, Nixon resigned as President on August 9. 1974. His desperate action preceded the certainty that he would be impeached by the House of Representatives and removed from office by the Senate. He had increasingly fewer allies defending his actions publicly.

One month later, he was pardoned by his successor, Gerald Ford. Public resentment over the pardon limited Ford's tenure as President to only the conclusion of Nixon's term.

Jimmy Carter would defeat him in the 1976 election. Sixty-nine individuals would be indicted during the follow-up investigation with 48 being convicted. Many of these individuals were the highest-level members of the Nixon administration.

Viewing the scandal in hindsight, the magnitude of actual events involved with the cover-up appear comparatively subdued to subsequent scandals.

Two later Presidents, Bill Clinton and Donald Trump have been impeached. Trump twice. Clinton admitted an extra-marital relationship with a Capitol intern. Trump was impeached first for an inappropriate extortion request with the Ukrainian government and second for inciting an attempted Coup d'Etat on the Capitol steps. Both were narrowly spared conviction by the Senate because their political parties held a narrow majority.

Impeachment remains an aggressive and retaliatory threat towards a sitting President. In the future, such an action will doubtlessly be employed when an opposition party holds a majority in the House of Representatives and US Senate. The ghost of Watergate still haunts the American political legacy. The event merely substantiated a fractured public faith that may never heal within our philosophically divided country.

DEEP THROAT GARAGE

The Unexplainable Evil Behind The Southside Strangler Motives
Murder Sites:
Debbie Dudley Davis, 4520 Devonshire Street, Richmond
Dr. Susan Hellams, 514 West S1st Street, Richmond
Diane Cho, Porter Street, Chesterfield County (Near Richmond)

Carolyn Jean Hamm, 4921 S. 23rd Street, Arlington

Timothy Wilson Spencer would become publicly acknowledged as a serial killer during the fall of 1987. He began as a prolific burglar, escalating his criminal activity into three rapes and murders within Richmond and one in Arlington. He would become the first perpetrator within the United States to be convicted of a murder solely based on DNA evidence.

Spencer's crimes followed a pattern of breaking into residences between September 18-November 27, 1987. He raped the lone female occupant and then strangled her to death. His victims ranged between 15 and 44 years of age. As his crimes escalated in notoriety, he began being labeled the *Southside Strangler*.

His Arlington killing of Susan Tucker inside her condominium finally resulted in his arrest as investigating officers traced his movements from Richmond. He was spending Thanksgiving 1987 with his mother, who lived only a mile from Tucker's residence. The similarity of the killings linked him with the earlier Richmond murders.

During the course of his subsequent trial, DNA evidence was introduced enabling Spencer's conviction for the murder, rape and burglaries of Susan Tucker, Debbie Davis and Susan Hellams. He was sentenced to death. He was not tried for his involvement in the death of 15 year-old Diane Cho, a high school student.

One of the surprises emerging from Spencer's trial resulted when his DNA sample was compared to others found at unresolved murder sites. His DNA was traced to evidence collected during the 1984 Arlington homicide of Carolyn Jean Hamm, a Washington D.C. based attorney inside her home.

Investigators were puzzled why there existed a three-year gap between this killing and his 1987 crime spree. They determined that Spencer had been incarcerated for burglary during that period. Another man, David Vasquez had been found erroneously guilty for Hamm's murder. He was already serving his prison term following conviction. His release would become the first national exoneration through DNA evidence. Spencer would not be tried for this murder since he was already condemned to death.

He would be executed by electrocution at the age of 32 on April 27, 1994 at 11:13 p.m. at the Greenville Correctional Center. His response towards his condemnation disappointed many of the 100 spectators in attendance. He walked eight short steps from his deathwatch cell to the execution chamber not betraying any emotion, guilt or remorse.

The warden asked him if he had any final words. He responded with *Yeah, I think...* but never completed his sentence. A leather death mask was fitted over his face. Afterwards, he turned both of his thumbs in an upward direction.

According to a witness: *After the first lethal dose of electricity was introduced, his body became swollen and lurched forward against the restraints securing him to the chair. A second jolt prompted his body to swell as smoke began to rise from his head and leg. The electricity was switched off and his body slumped. Five minutes later, the prison doctor placed a stethoscope against his chest confirming his death.*

Spencer would expire in eerie silence offering no explanation behind his actions. Sometimes evil simply eludes elocution.

**The Final Breaking Point Of An Arkansas Lawyer
Vincent Foster Suicide Location:
Fort Marcy Park, 700 George Washington Memorial
Parkway, McLean VA**

Vincent Foster had constructed a credible professional reputation within the Arkansas legal establishment. When his boyhood friend Bill Clinton was elected President in the 1992 election, he welcomed the opportunity to assist him during his transition period before assuming office.

Foster learned abruptly and painfully that the rigors and pressures of Washington D.C. were far more invasive and destructive than Little Rock, Arkansas. During the transition period when Foster was vetting a number of top appointees, he began complaining to his personal physician over feelings of depression and anxiety. He experienced panic attacks that had the effect of gutting his soul.

There was no one able or capable of consoling or shielding him once the intense media and political attacks began. The Clinton administration transition faced early snafus including an Attorney General nominee that had failed to pay taxes for nanny services. Shortly following, a financial impropriety scandal tainted the White House travel office. *Travelgate* resulted in seven firings, negative press and the threat of a Congressional investigation.

Foster shouldered the blame, but likely prematurely. The *Travelgate* storm had been blown enormously out of proportion. It withered into insignificance. The escalating fears that Foster internalized convinced him that his own professional reputation was near ruin. Returning back to a legal practice in Arkansas had ceased to become a legitimate alternative.

Foster, like many who have suffered the debilitating effects of depression, could not envision simply waiting out the imminent crisis. His concerned sister arranged for him to speak with a psychiatrist and also suggested two additional confidential practitioners. His fear towards compromising his security clearance tempered his follow-up. He telephoned one contact, but hung up when he only got an answering machine.

Politics is a dangerous arena for the emotionally vulnerable. Character assassination is bloodsport. Media commentators and rival political partisans sniff weakness and often attack without discretion. Foster couldn't shake his obsession over the damage of a potential Congressional inquiry. He spent the weekend of July 17-18, 1993 accompanying his sister to the Maryland shore for rest and recuperation.

On Monday, July 19th, no one realized that he was formulating a personal exit strategy. He spent the day reportedly in his office with the door closed wrapping up legal and family matters, his father's estate details and sending out thank-you notes.

The next morning should have brightened his perspective. Supreme Court nominee Ruth Bader Ginsburg and FBI head Louis J. Freeh were breezing through their confirmation hearings, certain to be appointed. He no longer cared judging by his response of the news to a colleague.

He ate his lunch alone on the couch of his office. Around 1:00 p.m., he picked up his suit coat and strolled to his car. He informed his office staff that he'd be returning, but didn't carry his briefcase with him. He folded his suit jacket neatly on the front passenger seat and drove out to Fort Marcy Park. There were no eyewitnesses to his activities. Did he hesitate over this next act?

Fort Marcy Park was a Civil War fortress constructed to protect the Chain Bridge approach to Washington D.C. Foster mounted a diminutive trail to arrive at a cannon near a grouping of park benches. He likely reflected before lifting an old revolver into his mouth. He fired once. His body would be discovered at approximately 5:30 p.m. resting on a hillside slope near the canon.

His personality collapse was rumored, but his abrupt, isolated and unforeseen death suggested the possibility of murder. An exhaustive inquiry involving 125 witnesses, DNA tests, physicians, lawyers and FBI agents followed. Their findings confirmed that his actions constituted a legitimate suicide.

His death would become another scandal attached to the Clinton administration only six months old.

Suicide proved insufficient and counterproductive for conspiracy theorists and presidential critics. With his death, Foster became fingered as *the man who knew too much*. He was maliciously linked with a succession of accusations including the Whitewater scandal, a romance with Hillary Clinton and a litany of constructed insider abuses. None would later be substantiated nor proven.

Vincent Foster opted by his self-destruction to cease the personal attacks and character assassination levied against him. The depth of his desperation would be acknowledged posthumously, but not to the satisfaction of Clinton detractors. He would not become the last tragic casualty on the grounds of Fort Marcy.

On January 25, 2022, Kevin Ward, the mayor of Hyattsville, Maryland killed himself with a self-inflicted gunshot wound. Political life on any level is capable of darkening the perspective of the soul.

The Spy Trapped By The End of the Soviet Union
Ames Couple Residence:
2512 North Randolph Street, Arlington, VA
CIA Headquarters:
1000 Colonial Farm Road, Langley, VA

The 1989 fall of the Berlin Wall and subsequent dissolution of the Soviet Union was the worst thing that had ever happened to Aldrich Ames. He was a 31-year veteran of the Central Intelligence Agency (CIA), but infamously became known as spying for the Russians since 1985.

Ames was a CIA case officer whose initial assignment had been in Ankara, Turkey. He also had worked in New York City and Mexico City. In April 1985, he was assigned to the CIA's Soviet and Eastern Union Division at CIA Headquarters in Langley, Virginia. He spoke Russian and specialized in Russian intelligence services. That same year he married his deputy, Maria del Rosario Casas. Two years earlier he had divorced his first wife.

The new position became a lucrative opportunity for Ames that he promptly exploited. He voluntary sought out KGB officers at the Soviet Union Embassy in Washington D.C. His *ideal* job placement earned him a comfortable salary of $50,000. He yearned for more.

During the summer of 1985, Ames met frequently with a Soviet diplomat passing on confidential information about CIA and FBO contacts. Amongst his most valued information was identifying technical operations targeting the Soviet Union. Several of the Russian operatives that Ames had identified were subsequently arrested and reportedly executed.

Ames' motivation for betraying secrets was not ideology. He was compensated handsomely and continued his activities even following the collapse of the Soviet Union. He was reportedly paid $1.88 million during the first four years of his spying activities.

Ames' newfound wealth raised attention within the CIA. A ten-month investigation was begun in May 1993. The monitoring included intensive physical and electronic surveillance of his activities. Ames was unaware that he was under microscopic observation. He had planned to meet with his Russian handler in Bogotá, Columbia followed by a planned visit to Moscow.

Fearing Ames might abruptly disappear within Russia, Ames was arrested along with his wife on February 21, 1994. He protested his innocence, but at his trial he pled guilty to spying for the Soviet Union and subsequently the Russian Federation. Ames admitted that his information had compromised virtually every Soviet agent within the CIA. Officials indicated that over 100 intelligence operators had been identified and at least ten executed.

The remorseless Ames confessed that he never feared being caught by the FBI or CIA. Instead, he feared Soviet defectors who might finger him. His plea bargain deal spared him the death penalty. He was sentenced to life imprisonment without the possibility of parole. He was ordered to forfeit his entire assets. His wife received a modest five-year prison sentence for tax evasion and conspiracy to commit espionage.

The CIA was roundly criticized for not monitoring Ames' activities sooner. CIA Director James Woolsey refused to dismiss or demote any of Ames' peers or supervisors. Woolsey irrationally bargained on the furor subsiding. His gamble failed and he later resigned under pressure.

Ames remains incarcerated, rotting away and forgotten within the Federal Correctional Institution in Terre Haute.

One of America's Darkest Days: 9/11
The 9/11 Pentagon Memorial:
1 N Rotary Road, Arlington VA

American Airline flight #77 departed from Dulles International Airport on the morning of September 11, 2001 bound for Los Angeles. Less than 35 minutes into the flight, five Saudi passengers affiliated with the al-Qaeda movement stormed the cockpit. They forced the 58 passengers, pilots and crew members to the rear of the aircraft. One of the hijackers, trained as a pilot, took over control of the plane.

His intended destination was nearby. The hijackers were counting on the element of abrupt surprise, as their intended target was the Pentagon building. Contrary to their expectations and demands, passengers aboard the plane relayed the news of their hijacking to their friends and family via their cell phones. The doomed victims could do nothing to prevent the inevitable.

The Saudi pilot steered the plane towards the western side of the facility. At 9:37 a.m., the fully fueled Boeing 757 slammed into the Pentagon building igniting an explosion and fire that would require several days to fully extinguish. A section of the building collapsed into rubble. All aboard the plane were killed. One hundred and twenty-five additional victims including emergency workers on the ground would be added to the fatality count.

The horror of that collision would only be numerically exceeded by the damage and carnage inflicted upon the World Trade Center Buildings in New York City. The grim sequence of events became a dark day in American history.

The damaged sections of the Pentagon would be rebuilt in

2002 with employees returning to those sectors in August.

During the immediate aftermath following the attack, a temporary memorial was established on a hill at the Navy Annex overlooking the Pentagon. People would solemnly visit and pay tribute to the 184 who died and others who were injured on the ground. One year later, the *Victims of Terrorist Attack on the Pentagon Memorial* was dedicated at Arlington National Cemetery.

Architects Julie Beckman and Keith Kaseman submitted the winning design for the 9/11 Pentagon Memorial. The effect is a brilliant example of conceptual design. The layout consists of 184 illuminated benches, arranged according to the victim's ages over a 2-acre plot. Each bench is engraved with the name of a victim. The benches representing the interior Pentagon fatalities are arranged facing the building's south façade. A shallow lighted pool of flowing water is positioned under each memorial bench. A wall along the edge of the Memorial begins at a height of 3 inches rising to 71 inches. This height represents the age range of the victims starting at 3 years old to 71 years old.

The Memorial was officially opened on September 11, 2008, exactly seven years following the tragedy. Each year an American flag is hung on the section of the Pentagon struck by American Airlines Flight #77. This section of the building is lit up in blue lights.

It is often thought and hoped for that such Memorials reminding visitors of tragic events, may one day end their reoccurrence. Sadly, successive generations add their own defining stories. Washington D.C. is a town littered with monuments, history and memories.

The December 7, 1941 attack on Pearl Harbor was once

coined *a day that will live in infamy*. As veterans of World War II increasingly expire and relations with Japan have long ago stabilized, the day has lessened in significance for many younger citizens. September 11th, 2001 currently remains a reminder of national vulnerability and tragedy. The harsh lesson learned should never be downplayed or worse, someday forgotten.

**The Hot Cash Sting That Froze A Congressman's
Legacy
Money Transfer: Ritz Carleton Hotel Parking Lot
1250 South Hayes Street, Arlington VA**

Democratic Congressman William Jefferson updated an old tactic of concealing *hot* money inside a domestic residence. Instead of hiding the cash under a mattress, he chose his freezer. In August 2005, the FBI raided Jefferson's home and freezer discovering $90,000 in tracked currency. The currency was divided into nine bundles and wrapped in aluminum foil inside pie crust containers.

The stash was part of a staged $100,000 bribe destined for Atiku Abubaker, then the vice president of Nigeria. This first installment was designed to enlist Abubaker's help in gaining approval from the country's telecommunications authority. Jefferson's influence and position was a key role to a deal that Virginia businesswoman Lori Mody was financing. Mody and Jefferson had formed a temporary alliance over this project. Jefferson was due to earn a significant cut.

In 2005, Jefferson was a sitting member of the House Ways and Means Committee. He was an ideal conduit for facilitating grayscale commerce. Jefferson was parlaying his committee position and clout to arrange African business deals. Mody's project was simply one additional deal that he was navigating through the perilous waters of rogue transactions.

Mody and Jefferson met in the parking lot of the Arlington Ritz Carlton Hotel on July 30. She transferred a briefcase to him stocked with traceable bills. The transaction was completed seamlessly. Jefferson was very guarded in his remarks towards her. He neither examined the contents of the briefcase nor acknowledged its purpose.

Unknown to Jefferson was that Mody had been a cooperating witness for the FBI since March. The transfer was being filmed on five different cameras as evidence. The FBI provided the money and car that Mody was driving.

The confirmation video footage and Mody's sworn statements enabled the FBI to raid Jefferson's Congressional offices in May 2006. Undaunted by the mounting pressure, he narrowly won re-election despite being named as the subject in a corruption probe. Voter turnout for the election was barely over 16%. He would be relieved of his House Ways and Means committee post afterwards.

Thirteen months later, he was indicted on sixteen felony charges related to corruption, racketeering, conspiracy, money laundering, obstruction of justice and other offenses. In 2008, he once again sought re-election despite the indictments. He lost narrowly to Republican candidate Anh *Joseph* Cao.

At the conclusion of his late 2009 trial, he was found guilty on eleven of the sixteen corruption charges. He was sentenced to thirteen years in prison, the longest ever for a member of Congress.

On May 2012 he began serving his sentence at the federal prison facility in Beaumont, Texas. He appealed his case following a U.S. Supreme Court ruling on similar issues. On October 5, 2017, he was ordered released after a U.S. District Judge dismissed seven of ten charges against him. He would ultimately only serve five and a half years in prison.

Jefferson's riches to rags fall marred an impressive career trajectory. He spent his formative years working alongside his father on their family farm. He earned his law degree from the Harvard Law School before entering politics as a legislative assistant.

He unsuccessfully lost twice in elections for Mayor of New Orleans and once for governor of Louisiana. His election to Congress came in 1990 following the retirement of 10-term incumbent Lindy Boggs.

Jefferson would serve nine-terms and become the state's first black congressman since the end of Civil War Reconstruction. Little of that distinction will be remembered once his legacy was permanently iced during 2005 inside his freezer.

ALEXANDRIA

**A Woman of Substance During An Era of Intolerance
Jones Point Park:
Jones Point Drive, Alexandria**

Margaret Brent was a remarkable and substantive woman, far ahead of her time. She became too competent due to difficult circumstances and headstrong to tolerate the male domination of the era.

In 1638, she sailed with her sister and two brothers from England, arriving at St. Mary's, Maryland on November 22nd. She was 37 and unmarried. The principal family landholder was her eldest brother.

In Maryland, the Brent family secured large land grants and in October 1639, Margaret became the first colony female landowner of 70 acres. She and her sister Mary established the *Sisters' Freehold* in St. Mary's and an adjacent 50 acres titled *St. Andrews'*. Their initial entitlement was enlarged to 800 acres per sister. He brother Giles Brant later transferred a 1,000-acre land track on Kent Island to Margaret as payment for a debt. He continued to manage the property as a trading post.

By the mid-1640s, an English Civil War spilt over to into Maryland. Protestant sea captain Richard Ingle raided the predominantly Catholic colony and burned down numerous structures including Giles Brent's trading post. Governor Leonard Calvert recruited armed men from the nearby colony of Virginia for assistance. The British raiders were repulsed, but colony was reduced to only 100 residents. Calvert became ill before paying the mercenaries and appointed Margaret Brent as his executor. His advice to her was: *Take All, Spend All.*

Brent liquidated his estate to pay the soldiers who'd saved the colony. Her designated status put her into conflict with Calvert's surviving brother, Lord Baltimore. He had traditionally managed his Colonial estate and assets from England. He had appointed his brother as governor to manage his holdings and was outraged when Brent had acted without his direct authority. Ironically, until he could appoint a male successor to Calvert, she collected his rents and paid his debts using her role as his temporary attorney.

Baltimore, a Catholic, was navigating a slippery course with the new English protestant government. Brent had followed Calvert's advice and employed his proceeds to feed the hungry mercenaries with corn. Soon afterwards, his financial resources were drained and she was obliged to sell Baltimore's cattle to pay the soldier's wages. The fighting men had no intention of leaving Maryland until they were duly compensated.

The issue became increasingly thorny as Lord Baltimore became suspicious of Brent's motives in managing his assets. He doubted the severity and threat of the earlier attack against the colony.

Margaret Brent had demanded from the Maryland General Assembly the right to two votes based on her being an independent landowner and Lord Baltimore's attorney. Governor Thomas Greene refused her petition citing voting privileges for women were reserved only for queens. The growing hostility between Lord Baltimore and the Brent family prompted the latter's relocation in 1649 to Virginia's Northern Neck.

Margaret diversified her estate by investing in property within Alexandria, Fredericksburg and Mt. Vernon. Her property within Alexandria consisted of a rectangular tract of land on the Potomac River above Hunting Creek. This parcel would be located at the confluence of the Potomac and Fort Washington Point. It would later be renamed Jones Point.

The territory would become the site of a lighthouse operated between 1856-1926. The structure was designed as a navigational aid to assist ships avoid shifting underwater shoals on the Potomac and aid the development of the maritime economy of the region. In 1918, a massive shipyard was constructed at Jones Point to build ships for World War I. The facility obscured the lighthouse's beacon illumination. In 1926, an automated light tower replaced the manually operated lighthouse to reduce expenses. Today, Jones Point Park is a popular recreation center split by the elevated 495 Freeway that interchanges with the Richmond Highway 1 leading to Mount Vernon.

Margaret Brent would outlive her sister Mary by fifteen years. She inherited her land holdings upon her death. Margaret died at the approximate age of seventy in 1671. Neither sister would ever marry predicated on a suspected vow of celibacy each had sworn at Mary Ward's Institute in England. During their time residing in the American colonies, men outnumbered women six to one.

The combined women's estate would be divided between her nephew James Clifton and their brother Giles and his children. British soldiers burned much of the Brent family estate documentation during the Revolutionary War and the War of 1812. Union troops vandalized the Brent family graveyard during the Civil War. The remaining gravestones were acquired and preserved by a local church in Stafford County.

An Uncomfortable Legacy and Ultimate Private Savior Mount Vernon Estate:
3200 Mount Vernon Memorial Highway, Mt. Vernon

The uncomfortable realization that George Washington was a slave owner has tainted his legacy over two hundred years since his death. His acknowledged providing for slave's emancipation upon his wife's death is accurate, but far from straightforward.

In his will, written several months before his untimely death at 67, Washington left directions for the emancipation of all the slaves who *belonged to him*. Three hundred and seventeen slaves managed his Mount Vernon estate. One hundred and twenty-three individuals belonged to him. Under the terms of his will, this contingent was designated to become freed upon the death of his wife Martha. She would die three years after him at the age of 70.

In accordance with the then existing state law, Washington stipulated in his will that elderly slaves or those too sick to work were to be supported throughout their remaining life by his estate. Orphaned children or those with impoverished or ill parents were to be apprenticed to other masters and mistresses who would teach them reading, writing and a trade until they reached the age of twenty-five. They would be liberated at that time.

Martha Washington had been married once before. Her first husband, Daniel Parke Custis was an American planter and politician who died at the age of 45 from a heart attack in 1757. The 26-year-old widow would remarry George two years later.

Custis died without leaving a will and his widow received a life interest in one-third of his extensive estate including his slaves. During her lifetime, neither George nor Martha could legally free these slaves. Upon her death, George's slaves were liberated. The slaves that Martha had inherited from the Custis estate would become divided amongst her grandchildren.

The origins of the Washington family and Mount Vernon began in 1674 when the property was first acquired. Originally it was known as the Little Hunting Creek Plantation. Beginning in 1734, the family embarked on an expansion of the estate. When George's older half-brother Lawrence Washington inherited the property, he renamed it after Vice Admiral Edward Vernon, who'd been his former commanding officer during the *War of Jenkins Ear*. In that conflict, British forces captured Portobelo in Panama from the Spanish.

When George inherited the property in 1752 upon the death of Lawrence, he retained the name. The original mansion was constructed in 1734 in the Palladian style by George's father, Augustine Washington. George would expand the house twice during the late 1750s and during the 1770s.

The plantation initially cultivated tobacco, but as the export market declined, George diversified production. By 1766, he had ceased growing tobacco entirely and experimented with sixty other crops including wheat, corn, hemp, cotton and flax. He operated a small fishing fleet, raised and bred sheep and even established a whiskey distillery, his most profitable business venture. During his two-term presidency, instead of leisurely playing golf, Washington spent 434 days in residence at Mount Vernon.

Following his presidency, Washington tended to repairs of the buildings, socializing and extensive gardening. His retirement would last only two brief years before his death.

On December 18, 1799, six days following his death, a funeral was held at Mount Vernon where his body was interred. The U.S. Congress passed a joint resolution to construct a marble monument inside the Capitol building for his body. The mausoleum was intended to be a pyramid with a base of 100 square feet. Southern elected representatives, who preferred his body to remain at Mount Vernon, organized and defeated a funding measure.

His body stayed in the family crypt, initially constructed when he first inherited the estate. By 1799, the vault was in extreme disrepair. Washington's will stipulated that a larger family tomb be constructed. During the next thirty years, *pilgrims* traveled to his grave to retrieve artifacts, often including foliage. The thefts resulted in trees and other flora surrounding the tomb being stripped bare. The most overt pilfering reportedly occurred when the Russian ambassador to the United States removed an entire branch from a tree growing next to the tomb. He presented his purloined gift to Tsar Alexander I.

In 1830, an attempt was made to steal George Washington's skull from the tomb. The thief, one of the estate's gardeners, mistakenly stole the remains from one of nephew Bushrod Washington's in-laws. The desecration of the burial site prompted renewed discussion about relocating George Washington's body from Mount Vernon to Washington D.C. Once again, southern opposition became intense and defeated legislative efforts.

The southern position was based on a growing rift with their northern colleagues that succession might become inevitable. If Washington's remains should become buried in the Capitol, any future severance with the Union would result in his Virginia-raised body being interred within a perceived *foreign shore*.

In 1831, a new family crypt would be constructed for the Washington family's remains. Six years later, George's remnants were encased within a lead inner casket and then transferred into a sarcophagus. It would be placed on the right side of the gateway to the tomb. A similar structure was provided for Martha's remains, which was placed on the left.

The legacy of the Mount Vernon estate would endure a steady decline following the couple's death. Hundreds of visitors continued to wreck havoc on the grounds. The largest part of his estate passed on to Bushrod Washington who would become an Associate Justice of the Supreme Court. He and his wife would reside at Mount Vernon.

As the mansion deteriorated, revenues from agricultural operations could not sustain the mounting expenses. Some of the remaining slaves were sold as a futile attempt to increase cashflow. In 1855, future heir John Augustine Washington III attempted to convince the federal government and the Virginia General Assembly to purchase the property. Both parties declined, as their legislative focus was oriented towards issues that would eventually lead to rupture within the United States and the Civil War.

Finally in 1858, the Mount Vernon Ladies' Association purchased the property for $200,000, taking possession in February 1860. The estate was officially opened to the public that year. Throughout the Civil War, the property served as neutral territory toured by both Union and Confederate officers and soldiers. The two female caretakers requested that the combatants leave their weapons behind or change into civilian cloths. Most complied.

A major and necessary restoration would follow in the late nineteenth century. Mount Vernon remains a privately owned property and does not receive federal government funding. The Mount Vernon Ladies' Association derives its income from charitable donations and the sales of tickets, produce and goods to paying visitors.

**A Lost Village Overshadowed By A Competing Port
Former Location of Cameron:
Jones Point Drive at South Royal Street, Alexandria**

The lost village of Cameron was situated at the conduit where the Great Hunting Creek emptied into the Potomac River. The area three hundred years ago lacked good roads, but the Potomac River tributaries provided important corridors for commerce and travel.

Great Hunting Creek linked tobacco farms to inspection stations and warehouses. Tobacco was monitored and stored before being transported to international markets. Nearby settlements became villages and hamlets sustaining the network and population.

Cameron became one of those villages that potentially might have evolved into the premier tobacco port. Oceangoing ships were able to follow Great Hunting Creek directly into the village. The prosperous trade would continue into the 1800s until a competing location, West's Point was employed as a more suitable navigational site.

Although many of Alexandria's founding families inhabited Cameron, West's Point ultimately prevailed as the dominant port. It would later become annexed into Alexandria.

Today, only a solitary marker acknowledges the former existence of Cameron. The settlement land is nestled underneath the Highway 495 overpass elevated above Jones Point. An ancient cemetery is all that remains surrounded by extensive ongoing construction.

Building
for the
Future of
Alexandria's
Waterways.
AUTHORIZED
VEHICLES
ONLY

**A Prominent Patriarch of Colonial Alexandria
Carlyle House Mansion:
121 N. Fairfax Street, Alexandria**

John Carlyle employed the essential entrepreneurial skills for success during 18th century colonial America. He was born and raised in England and apprenticed initially with the William Hicks mercantile house. He parted amicably with the firm seeking his fortune overseas.

His initial visit to Virginia was in 1739 at the age of nineteen. Two years later he would settle permanently within the territory. He married judiciously into the wealthy and established Fairfax family. His wife Sarah was the daughter of William Fairfax, a member of the Virginia governor's council.

Carlyle recognized and embraced the underdeveloped and unlimited potential of the American colonies. Savvy and ambitious, he cultivated business partnerships that would epitomize the acknowledged colonial triangle of trade. His company imported coal, rum, sugar, finished goods and even slaves and convicts for forced labor. They exported flour, grain, iron, lumber and tobacco. For amusement and recreation, he raised racehorses.

His greatest accomplishment became teaming with his Fairfax relations and George Washington's father and older stepbrother to form the Ohio Company. Their objective was to win a royal grant of land in the Ohio River Valley to sell and/or lease property to incoming settlers. The proceeds would not only repay their initial investment monies, but also create lucrative commercial opportunities for residents of the Potomac River Valley.

To realize their ambition, they required a seaport. This objective became the genesis for their petition to the Virginia General Assembly. They proposed establishing a new town built on lands owned by the Alexander and West families located at the mouth of the Great Hunting Creek in Fairfax County.

Their successful request resulted in the establishment of Alexandria. Carlyle became one of the initial eleven city trustees.

During the early 1750s, Carlyle constructed a stone Georgian mansion within the city, overseeing the construction personally. Upon completion, it was considered the most distinguished and luxurious local property. During the spring of 1755, Major General Edward Braddock, the British commander-in-chief of the thirteen colonies selected the mansion for his temporary headquarters.

During his three-week residence, Braddock met with governors from five colonies. He outlined an ambitious military campaign on multiple fronts against established French installations. He decided to personally lead an expedition against Fort Duquesne (currently Pittsburgh) at the fork of the Ohio and Allegheny Rivers.

Braddock's stay provoked intense distaste by Carlyle who described him as *too fond of his passions, women and wine.* According to correspondence with his brother, the general reportedly *abused the house and furnishings.*

George Washington would serve with Braddock's expedition as a volunteer officer. The conflict called The Battle of the Monongahela disintegrated into disaster. Braddock's troops became disoriented during the attack and the siege turned chaotic. British soldiers began firing upon American infantrymen mistaking them for French.

One American soldier fatally shot Braddock in order to cease the misdirected fire and spare the lives of his peers. Upon Braddock's battlefield death, Washington took command and orchestrated a retreat sparing further casualties. Braddock would be buried in present-day Farmington, Pennsylvania.

Throughout the French and Indian War staged between 1754 and 1763, Carlyle served as a commissary to Virginia and British forces. The role further consolidated his mercantile and leadership position.

As an Alexandria trustee, he was responsible for the community's education, public health and sanitation, streets, security and maintaining the central market. With his position as justice of the peace, he coordinated and supervised public construction projects involving courts, bridges, docks, schools and warehouses. Carlyle would reside comfortably in his mansion for twenty-five years until his death.

As a husband and parent, he endured immeasurably poor fortune. With Sarah Fairfax, he had five daughters and two sons. Only two daughters would live beyond childhood. Sarah died on January 22, 1761 following the birth of their seventh child. In October 1761, he remarried. His new wife Sybil West was the daughter of Hugh West, another Alexandria trustee. They had three sons together with two dying in infancy. Sybil died in March 1769 following a miscarriage.

As an influential local voice, Carlyle supported the colonies protests against British polices. He was credited with procuring small arms and ammunition for local volunteer militias. When the Revolutionary War erupted, his only living son, George William served in a legion commanded by Henry Lee (Robert E. Lee's father). Carlyle died in his home at the age of sixty during October 1780. He would be buried alongside his first wife and their children in the burial grounds of the Old Presbyterian Meeting House.

Less than one year later on September 8, his son would be killed at the age of fifteen during a battle at Eutaw Springs, South Carolina. Had he survived, he would have been granted a dormant barony and be known as Lord Carlyle.

During the Civil War, high-ranking Union officers and attending physicians would occupy the residence. Once again, the property was left in a deplorable state of disrepair. During the subsequent century, the house continued a steady decline. It became a museum during World War I. The Northern Virginia Regional Park Authority (NOVA) would purchase the residence in 1970. The property underwent a massive renovation before being opened to the public during the American Bicentennial celebrations of 1976.

A Critical Foreign Troop Supplement Sealing Revolutionary War Victory
Washington-Rochambeau Encampment Marker:
614 Oronoco Street, Alexandria

One of the most tangible reminders of French military assistance during the Revolutionary War are the numerous markers that designate the Washington-Rochambeau Trail.

In 1780 following significant lobbying by Benjamin Franklin in Paris, French King Louis XVI dispatched Jean-Baptiste de Rochambeau, 450 officers and 5,300 soldiers to aid the American forces in their war with Great Britain. The contingent arrived in Narragansett Bay, near Newport, Rhode Island on July 10, 1780.

In June 1781, Rochambeau marched from Rhode Island to join the Continental Army under Washington's command. He divided his unit into four regiments. An advance party would march ahead of the main contingent, another group would remain ten miles south to protect their flank and a third unit remained in Providence where it guarded the baggage and munitions stored in the Old Market House. They also reportedly supported the surgeons and attendants at the hospital in University Hall. He commanded the fourth and primary contingent.

Rochambeau's grueling 680-mile march required 14 weeks to arrive in Yorktown, Virginia. The combined American and French armies headed south in August, marching through New Jersey, Pennsylvania, Delaware and Maryland. The route enabled them to bypass British troops.

When they reached Williamsburg, Virginia in late September 1781, the French royal fleet had already won the Battle of the Chesapeake weeks before. This victory prevented the English from reinforcing or evacuating General Cornwallis' army. On September 22nd, they consolidated troops commanded by the Marquis de Lafayette in the decisive three-week siege of Yorktown. Cornwallis' surrender on October 19, 1781 effectively ended the Revolutionary War.

The critical Rochambeau troop addition has not been entirely forgotten in Alexandria. A marker signifying their encampment is located adjacent to the celebrated Potts-Fitzhugh House constructed in 1795.

Rochambeau would return to France a hero and was honored by Louis XVI by being made governor of the province of Picardy. He was one of the last generals appointed by the king. Rochambeau ironically displayed his gratitude by supporting the French Revolution that overthrew the king.

He was rewarded afterwards with the command position for the French Northern Army in 1792. He resigned shortly afterwards following decisive losses to the Austrian army. The following year, he was arrested during the *Reign of Terror*, narrowly escaping a guillotine death sentenced upon many of his contemporaries. Following the Revolution, Emperor Napoleon I pensioned him and he would die forgotten at the age of 81 in Thore, within the Loir-et-Cher department of France.

History offers a similarly ironic perspective regarding America's gratitude towards France. The timing of the Rochambeau troop supplement proved critical to victory. When King Louis XVI's reign and his family's life became imperiled a decade later during the French Revolution, American sent no one or any financial resources towards his assistance. Louis's original gift may have been dismissed as self-serving motivated by the hatred of his English antagonists.

However, his favor is generally forgotten. America would repay the debt during the liberation of France at the conclusion of World War II.

A Regional Hero Is Lavishly Feted Upon His Return
George Washington's Birthplace:
1732 Popes Creek Road, Colonial Beach
Mount Vernon Estate:
3200 Mount Vernon Highway, Mt. Vernon
Duvall's Tavern:
303 Cameron Street, Alexandria
Alexandria City Hall:
301 King Street, Alexandria

George Washington considered Alexandria his *adopted* hometown. His Mount Vernon estate was located less than ten miles to the south. It seemed appropriate on December 31, 1783 that he should be feted ceremoniously for his triumphant return home following the Revolutionary War. He had just resigned his eight-year military commission at Annapolis, Maryland. He was anxious to return permanently to familiar terrain and resume his private life.

Washington exhibited profound leadership qualities and prudent judgment orchestrating a seemingly impossible military victory over the British Empire. His English adversary, King George III expressed astonishment that Washington had willingly given up his authority. A path towards elevating himself onto an American throne seemed unimpeded if he'd been so inclined. He opted otherwise.

His close ties with Alexandria began in 1749 when his older half-brother, a founding trustee of the city, purchased two lots at auction. At seventeen, George drew up one of the earliest known maps of the city, showcasing the pair of purchased parcels.

The old town sector of Alexandria has maintained and refurbished many of the colonial-era structures of his era. Washington's presence still remains. He planned military strategy, attended church services, dined and slept in his townhouse locally.

The governing male leadership of Alexandria didn't ignore their regional hero's international celebrity.

On New Years Eve 1793, an extravagant gala honored his exploits. The lavish festivities began with banquet at William Duvall's Tavern. Following dinner, thirteen Madeira wine toasts were offered, each accompanied by a canon salute originating from Market Square across the street. The location was later converted into city hall and the square would remain a prominent component of local history.

Washington enjoyed the attention, particularly amongst the company of his close friends and colleagues. He had not yet become fully canonized into American sainthood.

Five years later, he would be elected president during elections conducted between December 1788 and January 1789. He unanimously earned all of the 69 first-round votes cast by the U.S. Electoral College. This recognition has only happened that once in American history.

He seemingly preferred to temper the cascading flow of adulation following his military career. His consistency of character and integrity became lionized. His absence of political pretension and monarchist ambition has set him apart historically from world leaders elevated to his stature. He reluctantly served two terms as president, defining the role of the executive branch. He spent over 400 days during those two terms at his Mount Vernon estate. He then resolutely declined a third term. He would die in 1799 at the age of 67, scarcely two years following his departure from office.

Washington shared a deep-rooted Virginia upbringing.

His father Augustine Washington also shared his origins in Virginia, born during November 1694. His mother was Mildred Warner and father Lawrence Washington, a member of the Virginia Houses of Burgesses. Augustine's father died when he was only four. His mother remarried and moved the family back to England. Following her death, a cousin, John Washington lobbied to become the children's guardian. He returned the family back to Virginia.

When Augustine Washington reached the age of majority, he married Jane Butler, another orphan, who had inherited 640 acres from her father. The couple had four children, but only two lived into adulthood. She died in 1729 and Augustine married Mary Ball two years later. George was the eldest of their six children, one who died in infancy. He was born approximately 60 miles south from Alexandria near the confluence of Pope's Creek and the Potomac River.

Through inheritance and investment, Augustine consolidated his holdings into an extensive estate. He became active in the Anglican Church, the local militia and political scene. He would die young at 48. George was eleven and inherited his father's 150-acre Strother property across the Rappahannock River. At the time of his death, Augustine Washington held 64 slaves assigned amongst his various plantations. George's mother managed the Strother property until he reached the age of majority. She lived there until the age of 64, when George relocated her to a residence in nearby Fredericksburg.

Augustine's complicated will and line of inheritance would ultimately grant George another property, then called *Little*

Hunting Creek. The name would evolve into the more recognizable Mount Vernon Estate and his principal residence.

His military success had secured him a permanent legacy. Duvall's Tavern was the ideal venue to celebrate a neighboring hero. The event remains immortalized by a discreet mounted plaque and a seated bronze of Washington near the front entrance. The tavern was a popular destination during his visits.

The building would subsequently become the First Bank of Alexandria, succeeded by the residence of Charles Lee, America's third Attorney General. Its prominence however remains enshrined as the celebratory venue for a local hero one New Years Eve centuries past.

CITY HALL

A Colonial Prisoner Of War Sustaining A Centuries Extended Grudge
Michael Swope's Townhouse:
210 Prince Street, Alexandria

Colonel Michael Swope became a resentful captive prisoner early during the Revolutionary War. On November 16, 1776, British forces captured him during the battle of Fort Washington. He and 3,000 other prisoners were taken hostage and in all probability mistreated throughout their interment. Detained officers became valuable trading commodities. He would remain captive until January 1781. He was reputedly exchanged for another illustrious prisoner of war, William Franklin. He was Benjamin Franklin's loyalist son who had sided with the English.

The prisoner exchange was concluded following the war. Swope never forgave his captors. After the war, he relocated from York, Pennsylvania to Alexandria. In York, he had been a prominent Justice of the Orphans Court and Coroner. His luxurious York home had once been lent to John Hancock when the Continental Congress fled Philadelphia.

Upon his Alexandria arrival between 1783-1786, he constructed his Old Town residence while operating a wharf and ship chandlery. Upon his death from a heart ailment in 1792, he deeded his business and house to his sons. He was buried initially in downtown Philadelphia before being later interned at a suburban cemetery. His sons maintained his Alexandria property within the family for an additional generation.

Despite his earthly departure, Swope has reportedly extended his spiritual presence within the residence. His loathing animosity towards British guests and visitors has become legendary. Entrants are cautioned to announce their nationalities as either *American* or *Irish*.

**A Historic Property With Pedigree Residents
Lee-Fendall House:
614 Oronoco Street, Alexandria**

Phillip Fendall, an Alexandria businessman, constructed his residence in 1785. He was a member of the Fendall family of Maryland and the Lee family of Virginia. The property supported a large household including as many as fifteen slaves. The half-acre parcel included stables, laundries, a rabbit hutch, pigeon house, warehouse and a two-story slave quarters.

By the 1850s, Alexandria had expanded as a community and the house was no longer located in rural terrain. The layout and landscape of the grounds became altered. The Industrial Revolution had removed the necessity for extensive on-site food production. Gardens were planted for strictly ornamental purposes during an 1850-1852 mansion renovation.

During the Civil War, the occupying Union army converted the property into a hospital for wounded soldiers. It was renamed the Grosvenor Branch Hospital until the conclusion of the war.

By 1903, an Alexandria liquor distributor owned the property. Prohibition necessitated him to downsize his holdings. The next prominent resident became John L. Lewis who moved into the house during 1937. Lewis was the President of the United Mine Workers of America and the founder of the Congress of Industrial Organizations. He would become one of the most controversial and influential labor leaders within the United States.

Upon his death in 1969, the house faced potential demolition. The Virginia Trust for Historic Homes purchase

the house and opened it as a museum in 1974. Major
structural restoration was completed in 2005

A Hospitality Fruit Symbol of Welcome
Old Town Alexandria Pineapple Marker
104 S. Union Street, Alexandria

Within Old Town, a customary, but obscure symbol of welcome was formerly a familiar presence. The pineapple has been an icon of hospitality dating back to the earliest sea captains of New England. Ship commanders routinely sailed to the Caribbean Islands returning to the colonies with cargos of exotic fruits, spices and rum.

The captain would spear a pineapple upon a fence post outside of his residence to announce his safe return. Displayed pineapples became an invitation for friends to visit, dine together and listen to tales from his latest voyage.

The practice spread to innkeepers who added the icon to their own welcoming signs. Many would enlist woodcarvers to fashion their bedposts in the shape of pineapples. Although less visible today, the pineapple continues to represent a symbol of hospitality in the hotel and restaurant industry.

A Renowned Alexandria Residence Where Robert E. Lee Was Raised
Potts-Fitzhugh House:
607 Oronoco Street, Alexandria

The most renowned historical tenants living inside the Potts-Fitzhugh House in Alexandria were Henry Lee III and his family. Lee was better known as *Light-Horse Harry* and an important contributor during the American Revolutionary War. He was a major general in the Continental Army, member of the Continental Congress and Governor of Virginia. His famous funeral eulogy of George Washington: *First in war, First in peace and First in the hearts of his countrymen* remains a treasured summation of his contribution towards American history.

Lee occupied the house during 1811 when Alexandria was still part of Washington D.C. His personal stay would be brief. He was severely beaten and tortured during 1812 Baltimore riots. He sailed to the West Indies to recuperate from his injuries. Returning en route to Virginia, he died on March 25, 1818 at Dungeness, on Cumberland Island, Georgia.

During his Caribbean recovery period, he left his wife Anne Hill Carter Lee to raise their nine children. His most illustrious son was Robert E. Lee, who would later earn distinction as the Commander-in-Chief of the Confederate Army during the Civil War. Robert would live in the residence until he left for the West Point Military Academy at the age of eighteen in 1824.

The initial owner of the Potts-Fitzhugh House was John Potts, Jr. who built the property in 1795. The Federal and Georgian design style was constructed with red bricks and white trim. The house was built simultaneously with its neighboring structure that became the Hallowell School. Headmaster Benjamin Hallowell tutored Lee personally as he prepared for West Point. John Potts was the Secretary of the Potomac Canal Company under George Washington who also served as the company's president. Washington dined frequently at the residence.

The second owner was William Henry Fitzhugh, a Virginia planter and politician who served in both houses of the Virginia General Assembly. During his 1824 triumphant return visit to America, French General Marquis de Lafayette stayed at the property.

The house is one of the oldest in Alexandria and operated as a museum from 1967 to 2000. Other notable residents have included Royd Sayer, head of the Bureau of Mines under President Franklin Roosevelt's administration. Ada Hitchcock MacLeish, credited as a founder of the United Nations and her husband, poet Archibald MacLeish would also reside in the notable residence.

Two Alexandria Cemeteries Acknowledging The Forgotten
St. Mary's Cemetery
1000 S. Royal Street, Alexandria
Contrabands and Freedmen Cemetery
1001 S. Washington Street, Alexandria

The ancient dead have found repose within two adjacent Alexandria burial sites. Saint Mary's Catholic Cemetery occupies an oblong plot between South Royal and South Washington Streets. The parcel is bounded to the north by St. Mary's School and on the south by the Interstate I-95 approach to the Woodrow Wilson Bridge. St. Mary's is the oldest Catholic cemetery in Virginia. Wealthy landowner William Thorton Alexander deeded the property to St. Mary's Church in 1803.

The cemetery land was originally the site for the Basilica of St. Mary constructed in 1795. It became the first Catholic parish within Virginia. Its creation was launched with a 1788 fundraising dinner on St. Patrick's Day at the residence of John Fitzgerald. George Washington pledged $1,200 that evening towards the construction.

In 1810, the congregation acquired the Chapel Alley Meeting House from a Methodist congregation located at 310 S. Royal Street. The cornerstone was laid in 1826 for a sanctuary that was dedicated the following year. The bricks from the former St. Mary's chapel would be repurposed for the construction of the Alexandria Lyceum and the land remained as a cemetery. The current Basilica of St. Mary underwent significant reconstruction in 1894 adding additional seating and a towering 135-foot belfry.

Across South Washington Street, the Alexandria Contrabands and Freedmen Cemetery served as a Civil War burial place for approximately 1,800 African Americans. They fled the bondage of slavery immigrating into Alexandria. The transition created a different set of problems.

Arriving into the Union army occupied city, their sheer numbers resulted in a refugee crisis. Some men found employment, but many became destitute, malnourished and plagued by poor health. The majority was housed in unhygienic barracks, rife with disease. In 1864 following the death of hundreds, the Superintendent of Contrabands ordered that land on the southern edge of town (across from St. Mary's Cemetery), be confiscated for use as a cemetery.

From the outset, the burial grounds provoked controversy. Black soldiers demanded that they be given the honor of burial in the Soldiers' Cemetery, currently Alexandria National Cemetery. Their request was accommodated. The final burials within the Contrabands and Freedmen Cemetery concluded in January 1869.

The cemetery fell into disrepair and vanished from local maps by 1948. In 1955, a gas station followed by an office building was constructed on the property. Historical research during the reconstruction of the Woodrow Wilson Bridge determined the presence of graves below the ground surface. In 2007, the two structures would be demolished enabling archaeological excavation.

The periphery of Freedman's Cemetery extended into the middle of the present-day South Washington Street. An embedded sidewalk plaque acknowledges the existence of these graves. Accompanying tan stones tally the number of graves discovered during the excavation process. The names have been long forgotten. In 2014, a Freedman's Cemetery Memorial bronze sculpture would be formally dedicated on the grounds honoring the anonymously departed.

THIS STONE TAKEN FROM THE CANAL OF
THE POTOMAC COMPANY OF WHICH
WASHINGTON AND FITZGERALD
WERE DIRECTORS COMMEMORATES
THE ERECTION OF THE

FIRST CATHOLIC CHURCH
IN VIRGINIA, A. D. 1795,
WHICH STOOD UNTIL 1839 ABOUT
TWENTY FEET BEHIND THIS MARKER.

IN GRATEFUL ACKNOWLEDGEMENT OF
THEIR AID IN ESTABLISHING THIS CHURCH
THE THREE TREES TO THE NORTH OF THIS
STONE HAVE BEEN DEDICATED AS FOLLOWS TO
GENERAL GEORGE WASHINGTON
AS SUBSCRIBER TO THE BUILDING
COLONEL JOHN FITZGERALD,
HIS FAVORITE AIDE DE CAMP,
AS THE COLLECTOR OF THE BUILDING FUND,
COLONEL ROBERT HOOE,
MAYOR OF ALEXANDRIA,
AS THE DONOR OF THE ACRE OF LAND.

IN COMMEMORATION OF THE BICENTENNIAL OF THE
BIRTH OF GEORGE WASHINGTON
THIS TABLET WAS DONATED BY THE HOLY NAME SOCIETY
OF SACRED HEART CHURCH (VAILSBURG), NEWARK, N. J.
ON THE 133RD ANNIVERSARY OF THE FUNERAL OF
COLONEL JOHN FITZGERALD
DECEMBER 4, 1932

CONTRABANDS AND FREEDMANS CEMETERY
1864

A Questionable Haunting Claim Of A Dubious Paranormal Source
Yates Garden House:
414 Franklin Street, Alexandria

The periphery surrounding Old Town is a destination where phantoms lurk and ghost sightings remain a familiar presence. Following over three centuries of warfare, scandal, conflict and murder, spirit-enhanced stories have become commonplace and spawned into a polished craft. The tales are accepted as credible, outlandishly incredulous and/or simply hovering in the purgatory of *maybe*.

The Yates Gardens House is located adjacent to another foreboding local sector, Jones Point. Their close proximity and gauzy reputations insure that truth should never interfere with an intriguing narrative.

The most frightening aspect of suspected haunting or paranormal histories is the cunning strategies that real estate professionals employ to downplay their significance and potential. Disclosure is not legally imperative. Ghost sightings may incite terror. It is unfair to condemn an utterly frightened victim as simply a neurotic liar.

Many individuals adamantly refuse to accept even the possibility of ghostly or unexplainable apparition encounters. Confessions are consigned to imaginative fantasy. Ironically this dismissive contingent accepts the imaginative promises of political candidates and elected officials as sincere and laden with credibility. A healthy skepticism should apply with both arenas.

Yates Gardens has a dubious and ultimately harmless history. It has been cited as a tavern and inn that George Washington habitually frequented and even celebrated

Independence Day at during 1798. The account omits whether he was alone or accompanied by his wife Martha. He died scarcely one year later joining the legions of the spirit world.

Yates Garden House has been clouded by spirit world visitations via published accounts from a former owner. He detailed the mysterious sighting of a Revolutionary War era soldier dressed in uniform. The usual signs such as suspicious footprint echoing, creaking noises and frigid air drafts accompanied his account.

Are these signs accurate or accurate? Does it really matter? Most observers have already cemented their opinion on the subject regardless of eyewitness's accounts or circumstantial evidence.

The Malpractice Killing Of George Washington
Dr. James Craik's Residence:
210 Duke Street, Alexandria

One of George Washington's closest friends might arguably be responsible for inducing his premature death. Medical quackery was at its prolific height and worst throughout his lifetime. Washington was still a vigorous man at the age of 67, only two years removed from the American presidency. On December 12, 1799, he spent the entire day on horseback supervising farm activities. The weather turned frigid and it began to snow. Upon returning to his residence, he did not change out of his wet clothing. Instead he went directly to dinner and then bed.

He woke up at 2:00 a.m. with a severe and inflammatory throat infection today diagnosed as *epiglottitis*. A team of personal physicians was summoned including Dr. James Craik, his personal physician. Epiglottis enables respiration but inhibits swallowing. Contemporary medicine would eradicate the disease with antibiotics that would kill the infection.

The physicians initially had him gargle a liquid mixture of molasses, vinegar and butter. As he was unable to swallow, their remedy proved useless. Craik suggested a more radical approach, common for the era. The doctors bled Washington until he had loss approximately 40% of his blood. Craik and another consulting doctor, Gustavus Richard Brown had earlier overruled Dr. Elisha Dick's recommendation of a tracheotomy. The procedure might have saved Washington's life, but could have spread the infection and induced sepsis.

The bloodletting treatment weakened him severely. He lacked the strength to battle the infection and regressively weakened. He passed away on the evening of December 14th and was buried four days later in the family vault at Mount Vernon.

Craik has been generally absolved from historical responsibility. His medical advice would have been commonly offered by most physicians of his era.

Craik's home in Alexandria was constructed in 1796 upon the advice of Washington. He practiced medicine in the front of the house and lived in the rear and on the upper floors. Horse stables behind the residence have since become converted into a garage extending to adjacent Lee Street. He shared an intimate friendship with Washington while serving as the Physician General of the Revolutionary Army. The two men were companions during every battle from the French and Indian War through the Revolutionary War.

The bond of trust developed between Washington and Craik became irrefutable. It sadly shortened the former's life. Craik would live an additional fifteen years locally following Washington's death, dying at the age of 87.

He had originally emigrated from the estate of Arbigland in Kirkcudbright, Scotland, the illegitimate son of William Craik, an agricultural pioneer and landowner. He would study medicine at the University of Edinburgh and then join the British Army following graduation. He served as an army surgeon in the West Indies until 1751 and then opened a private medical practice in Norfolk, Virginia. He is buried at the Old Presbyterian graveyard in Alexandria.

Lifesaving Advice Overruled By George Washington's Physicians
Dr. Elisha Dick's Rented House:
209 Prince Street, Alexandria

Dr. Elisha Cullen Dick was one of three consulting physicians during George Washington's fatal illness. Fellow doctors James Craik and Gustavus Brown overruled Dick's recommendation of a tracheotomy to treat the patient's throat infection. All three would diagnose their patient's illness as *inflammatory quinsy*.

The pair of dissenters feared the procedure might spread further infection and cause sepsis. Washington's malady, later diagnosed as epiglottitis, would ultimately kill him, but not before Craik employed bleeding on his patient that severely weakened him.

Besides medicine, Dick would distinguish himself in politics representing Fairfax County in the Virginia House of Delegates and as Mayor of Alexandria. He was a Major in the Revolutionary army and graduated from the University of Pennsylvania School of Medicine in 1782. He and his wife settled into Alexandria twelve years later when he took over the established practice of the ailing Dr. William Rumney.

They initially purchased a house at 408 Duke Street, but his poor real estate speculations prompted him to declare bankruptcy. Afterwards, he rented the house currently attributed to him. A stanch supporter of Thomas Jefferson, he escorted the newly elected President to a celebration at Gadsby's Tavern locally in March 1801.

Despite Dick's financial reverses, voters elected him to the office of justice of the peace and coroner in 1802. In the wake of Gabriel's Rebellion, a planned slave uprising in Richmond, Virginia, he cautioned against abolition societies producing *serious calamities*. His own Quaker beliefs initiated in 1812 after being raised an Anglican proved contradictory towards his political support of slavery. He reportedly freed his own slave before his death.

Dick retired from his medical practice and settled into *Cottage Farm* along the Little River Turnpike. As his health worsened, he stopped attending Quaker meetings. He resigned from the movement in July 1825 and died three months later at the age of 63.

The New Jersey Relocation of A Celebrated Historical Estate
Former Colross Estate Site:
1111 Oronoco Street, Alexandria

The remnants of Alexandria's former Colross estate mansion retain a contemporary physical presence. Instead of locally, the structure would be reconstructed within the boundaries of Princeton, New Jersey. Between 1930-1932, the two-story Georgian style mansion was transported brick-by-brick. In 1958 it would be reconstructed as a Princeton Day School administration building.

The heritage of Colross is a curious oddity. The plantation encompassing the mansion began construction during 1800 as a forced-labor cash crop farm by Alexandria merchant John Potts. He was the same individual responsible for the Potts-Fitzhugh residence constructed further eastward on the identical street.

Potts encountered financial difficulties and placed the unfinished mansion on the market in 1801. Two years later, the property sold to local merchant and city councilman Jonathan Swift. His wife was Anne Roberdeau, the daughter of American Brigadier General Daniel Roberdeau. Anne named the estate *Belle Air*, while her husband referred to it as *Grasshopper Hall*. He presided over the Alexandria city council from 1822 through 1823. He died the following year and the estate transferred to the ownership of Lee Massey Alexander. His family would own the property only briefly christening it as *Colross*.

An urn reportedly was once installed on the front lawn of the mansion. According to local tradition, it marked the precise location where famed Native American *Pocahontas* was baptized. She was historically notable for her association with the colonial settlement in Jamestown, Virginia and as a Disney animated film star.

The next ownership transfer reputedly resulted from a game of cards. The luckless Alexander lost his title following a losing hand to Thomson Francis Mason, the grandson of American Founding Father George Mason.

Mason established Colross as his primary residence, modifying and enlarging the mansion. The end result became a two-story brick, Georgian style structure that features an architectural plan similar to George Washington's Mount Vernon estate. Mason constructed a ten-foot high brick wall around the exterior.

He would be buried upon the property following his death in 1838. Two of his children, William and Ann would share misfortune on the grounds. Son William had taken shelter inside the estate's chicken coop during a violent storm. The structure toppled upon him killing him. His sister Ann drowned shortly afterwards inside an estate bathtub. Both children would be interred with their father. Subsequent residents have reported haunting by the deceased Mason children. Spooked observers have reported giggling, talking and singing by childlike apparitions dressed in pre-Civil War attire.

As Alexandria expanded, Colross evolved from a rural plantation into an urban estate encompassing an entire square block. During the Civil War, Union authorities seized the property. At least two Union deserters were executed on the premises. Another famous *bounty jumper* named Downey was shot to death after being captured by his own soldiers. Bounty jumpers were men, who enlisted to fight with an army, collected a bounty for their enlistment and then promptly deserted. Bounty jumping was a perilous but profitable occupation within the Union forces. An individual might enlist multiple times collecting bounties with each instance. A petulant ghost(s) reportedly haunted the perimeter wall for generations.

Between 1885 and 1917, lumber merchant and coal businessman William Albert Smoot purchased and lived on the property with his family. Colross steadily fell into disrepair and the mansion became dilapidated, lacking gaslights and running water exclusively in the kitchen. The mansion remained in the midst of railroad tracks. It would become merely a storage facility within Smoot's lumberyard. A 1927 tornado caused significant damage permanently making the mansion uninhabitable.

In 1929, real estate speculator John Munn purchased the property. His dream to reconstruct and restore its former prestige would need to occur within Princeton, New Jersey. His aspiration would never become realized within his lifetime. Following his death in 1956, Dr. Geoffrey Rake purchased Colross. He would only keep it for two years until his own death. In 1958, the Princeton Day School purchased Colross, repurposing it into a functioning admission and advancement office and venue for institutional events.

Alexandria's former Colross land tract would suffer future indignities. It would support an inglorious and extensive 50-truck garage, car wash, power substation and finally printer facility. In 2003, a development company intending a mid-rise condominium project purchased the property. In 2005, Alexandria's Archaeological Protection Code mandated a halt to construction in order to excavate the site for historical artifacts and ensure that all burial plots were removed and relocated.

Few artifacts were recovered. Discoveries included an underground domed brick cistern that was utilized as a water purification system. The mansion's basement floor and foundations of the smokehouse, stables, exterior wall and burial vault were unearthed. No burial remains were discovered as presumably they were removed during the early 20th century.

The 6-story Monarch development complex would be completed in 2008. Rental and purchase listings include a diverse variety of amenity options. Perpetual haunting is an accompaniment but non-negotiable feature.

Alexandria's Forced Surrender Without A Shot Fired Waterfront Park:
King Street Waterfront Park, Alexandria

The War of 1812 against Great Britain did not reach Alexandria's shores until two years following its beginning. On August 29, 1814, Alexandria awoke to discover 138 guns from a British naval squadron positioned only a few hundred yards from the shoreline. The entire city could have conceivably been leveled within minutes.

Five days earlier, British forces had overwhelmed Washington D.C. and rampantly destroyed the capitol. During the pillage, they set fire to the White House as government leaders evacuated. The seaport of Alexandria was next on their agenda. Despite the eminent threat, the city was in no position to defend itself.

The British held the town hostage while local city officials negotiated surrender. The English command promised not to destroy the town if the citizenry allowed them to abscond with all naval cargo, shipping and merchandise being exported. Several locally docked ships had already been scuttled earlier to prevent them from being captured.

Alexandria concurred to the ransom demands and the plunder commenced. The British ships occupied Alexandria for three days before being ordered to return to the main fleet in Chesapeake Bay. The looting of Alexandria proved financially valuable, but the time invested ultimately proved shortsighted. The delay resulting due to the difficult navigation of the Potomac prevented ship commander James Alexander Gordon from joining the British flotilla until September 9th.

The delay gave the American defenders of Baltimore sufficient time to reinforce their defenses. The military ultimately repulsed the British fleet and ground forces attack between September 12-15th enabling a critical stalemate. The British fleet afterwards would embark southward towards New Orleans. Their good fortune evaporated. Despite an armistice between the United States and England being signed on December 24th, the British military continued south suffering one of their worst military setbacks.

On January 8, 1815, Major General Andrew Jackson would lead American forces in the victorious *Battle of New Orleans*. Jackson's military heroics would ultimately propel him into the presidency in 1829.

Alexandria would be ridiculed nationally for their collective cowering to the British forces. The peace agreement had been signed near the present day Waterfront Park. During that era, the landing wharfs on the shoreline were not yet fully developed. The actual surrender location would have been set back further in the present Old Town. The decision by the heavily undergunned and outmanned Alexandria militia and council should not be condemned too excessively. The actions and restraint by both sides spared Old Town, enabling the commercial and residential center to remain intact and flourishing following the war treaty.

A Community's Social Axis and The Cryptic Female Stranger
Gadsby's Tavern:
134 N Royal Street, Alexandria
St. Paul's Episcopal Church Cemetery (Female Stranger Grave):
601 Hamilton Lane, Alexandria

Gadsby's Tavern is a historical building complex located across from the Alexandria City Hall. Its composition includes a 1785 tavern, 1792 hotel and an 1878 hotel addition. Since its creation, Gadsby has been intimately integrated into Alexandria's social and political legacy. John Gadsby leased and operated the facility between 1796 and 1808. He would be anointed with permanent naming rights.

Presidents Washington, Adams, Jefferson, Madison and Monroe frequented the tavern. Washington, Jefferson and the Marquis de Lafayette were featured guests during festivities staged in their honor.

John Wise constructed the assemblage in the Georgian Colonial style. The architecture features a stone belt course between the first and second floors, winged keystones with a vermiculation over the windows. Other amenities include a pronounced water table, elegant door with fluted pilasters and a broken pediment.

Wise built the noticeably larger addition during 1792. Locals regarded the elephant as a skyscraper. The structure included two large public and three private dining rooms, an elegant ballroom, 14 sleeping rooms and a celebrated ice well located adjacently.

The premises would inspire a diverse and fascinating historical provenance. A frequently repeated narrative concerns an 1816 client who travelled to the property to reside with her English husband. The woman was described as a *voluptuous blonde with large eyes and a small mouth*. The couple lived in room 8. During their residence, she developed a cruel and incurable malady.

On her deathbed, she required her husband, valet, two attending maids and the doctor to swear an oath that they would never reveal her identity. Her motives remain unclear. The 23 year-old's suffering ended when she died on October 14, 1816. Imaginative accounts claim that she expired within her husband's embrace with their lips locked.

The attending witnesses kept their promise. Her grave at St. Paul's Cemetery is headlined *To the memory of a Female Stranger*. An extended inscription follows with the second to last stanza lifted from poet Alexander Pope's *Elegy to the Memory of an Unfortunate Lady*. The gravesite is uniquely constructed resembling a table with the inscription etched on the top surface. The writing is clear and small remembrance stones are littered at the end of the inscription.

The novelty and mystery behind her tragedy has prompted significant public, magazine and newspaper attention. Speculative articles would follow over the subsequent century offering theoretic explanations for her request of anonymity. One New Orleans newspaper account maintained that her bereaved husband returned later by ship with a crew of seamen. They exhumed her body during pitch night and transported her back to their awaiting vessel, destination unknown.

The most popular speculation identified the woman as Theodosia Burr Alston, the daughter of former Vice President Aaron Burr. She officially was reported missing at sea. The corresponding dates of the two women's deaths unfortunately did not match. However, as with any potential celebrity scandal or gossip, accuracy is rarely imperative.

A Sight-Impaired Devil Bat Protects The Security of Alexandria
Alexandria Town Square Clock Tower:
Corner of N. Royal and Cameron Streets, Alexandria

A devil bat and his successive descendants have reputedly and discreetly guarded Alexandria since colonial times. In 1817, a pristine three-story city hall building was constructed along Royal Street including a wooden clock tower designed by Benjamin Henry Latrobe. He was one of the first professionally trained architects within the United States. In American design circles, he has been eulogized as the *Father of American Architecture*.

The extended tower became a distinctive component of a complex including the Masonic Lodge, courthouse, central police and fire stations. Market stalls were situated on the first floors of the western and northern wings.

A ferocious appearing and near-sighted bat chose the interior of the clock tower for his residence. The cantankerous creature discouraged human exploration into the structure's inner sanctum. Presumably, its offspring found the lodgings similarly hospitable. Bats are inherently harmless. They feed on beetles, bugs, flies, moths and cockroaches. Exposed human necks or blood have never been a staple of their diet. Their erratic appearance in flight, particularly during twilight hours, sometimes inspires panic.

On May 19, 1871, an extensive inferno gutted City Hall. Fundraising efforts through stock sales enabled the construction of an exact replica including the valued clock tower. Architect Adolf Cluss was commissioned to oversee the reconstruction based on his reputation for technical skill and attention to building safety and strength. Local architect Benjamin Price designed and supervised the reconstructed tower.

Upon the completed construction, the devil bats simply returned to their comfortable roost. One family member's alert response later was credited with preserving the continued continuity of the facilities.

During a subsequent boisterous evening, a gang of unruly and presumably intoxicated sailors was courting mischief and desecration in the process of inciting a riot downtown. A single appointed devil bat launched an erratic foray in their direction perhaps stimulated by the commotion. His ensuing appearance and persistence alarmed and then terrified the unruly intentioned vandals. The cowardly delinquents sobered up immediately and fled.

Amidst the calm tranquility of morning, the citizenry recognized the bat's bravery graciously. The gesture was interpreted as gratitude for extended complimentary tenancy.

Torrential Flames Envelop Downtown
Fire Origin Site:
Intersection of King and S. Royal Streets, Alexandria

The Great Alexandria Fire of 1827 requires perspective to evaluate the extent of the damage. The population of the city then was approximately 8,000. On the morning of January 18th, the outside temperature hovered at a frigid thirteen degrees Fahrenheit. At 9:00 a.m., a fire alarm sounded throughout the downtown. A cabinetmaker's shop was aflame near the intersection of King and S. Royal Streets across from Market Square. The flames spread rapidly onto ten houses nearby fronting an alleyway. These structures were the rear of residences fronting King and Fairfax Streets.

The flames extended without pause along Fairfax Street consuming wooden and brick structures with indiscriminate fury like kindling to a bonfire. The path was temporarily halted further up Fairfax Street, but blazing shingles ignited residences on Prince Street. Homes and commercial warehouses were destroyed. The path continued along S. Union Street.

The initial response was prompt. Fires engines stationed at Capitol Hill and the post office arrived immediately attempting to subjugate the fire. As the inferno surged with growing momentum, the collective efforts offered by soldiers and local volunteers proved futile.

Surrounding communities' support fire engines needed to travel an average of seven miles on poor roads to reach the outbreak. Their first arrivals by 11:00 a.m. aided only marginally.

Surveying the extensive damage, newspapers reported an estimated 90 houses and 6 warehouses were destroyed. The city remained scarred and ravaged with damage estimated at a catastrophic $150,000. Only one male fatality was reported. The city rebuilt from the wreckage, but the population level would stagnate over the subsequent decade.

ÆLLEYWÆY

Merchandising Human Souls As Livestock
Franklin and Armfield Building:
1315 Duke Street, Alexandria

The institution of slavery has many iconic reminders within Alexandria. The merchandising of human beings as livestock was conducted inside the Franklin and Armfield Building. Robert Young, a brigadier general in the District of Columbia Militia, constructed the original residence in the 1810s. After assuming possession, Young's financial reverses prompted him to sell the property in 1828.

Isaac Franklin and his friend and nephew-by-marriage John Armfield purchased the residence. They immediately converted it into a lucrative commercial enterprise with Armfield residing on the premises. The operation established a penal institution and holding facility for male, female and child slaves. Most of the residing adults were between the ages of 12 and 25 with reportedly 28 children under the age of ten.

The remaining structure is a Federal style design topped by a mansard roof. A protective board fence originally surrounded the complex. The property extended further east as structures were added to accommodate additional cells and trading blocks. A two-story extension at the rear of the house encompassed slave-holding facilities. The walls inside were foreboding and elevated. The interiors were stark and imposing with grated doors and windows.

Franklin and Armfield amassed a significant fortune within a brief period through their tyrannical enterprise. Their roles were clearly defined. Franklin lived in New Orleans and sold their indentured inventory via a headquarters based in Natchez, Mississippi with branch offices in New Orleans, St. Francisville and Vidalia, Louisiana. Armfield handled the sourcing of slaves. He sent agents throughout Virginia, Maryland and Delaware soliciting slaves from owners looking to sell. He arranged their logistical transportation. The three states combined supplied an excess of available slave labor.

The partners shouldered the indignity of having mortgaged more souls, separated more families and amassed more blood money than any competitor within the United States. Approximately 3,750 slaves were exported to cotton and sugar plantations in the lower southern states. Surviving correspondence from the men often bragged about their systematic sexual violation of female prisoners processed through their firm.

Isaac Franklin cashed out his half of the partnership in 1835. The following year, Armfield sold the property to another slave trader. The legacy of human misery continued until 1861 under the later auspices of Price, Birch and Company. The Union Army took possession of the building during the start of the Civil War discovering only a single elderly individual chained to the middle of the floor by his leg. During the remainder of the conflict, the complex was employed as a military prison, hospital and barracks for black soldiers and Contrabands.

Post war, the slave pens were demolished and reportedly the bricks repurposed for neighboring townhouses. Throughout the late 19th and 20th century, the surviving rooms were rented as apartments as part of a boarding house. Today, only the primary office remains. It has fittingly become reorganized into the Freedom House Museum, featuring historical exhibitions profiling the slave trade. The Northern Virginia Urban League uses the second floor.

The stench and stain of historical slavery cannot be fully eradicated or sanitized. This single symbolic establishment once espousing the basest of cruelties and inhumanity has at least achieved a resurrection in progressive purpose.

A Doric Styled Temple Espousing Adult Education
Lyceum Theatre:
201 S. Washington, Alexandria

The lyceum movement within the United States began during the 1820s by Josiah Holbrook, modeled after the British example establishing institutions for public education. The first American lyceum opened in Millbury, Massachusetts with additional lyceums spread throughout the region. New England's established transportation system enabled easy access for traveling lecturers and their audiences.

In 1838, a Quaker teacher named Benjamin Hallowell and six other prominent Alexandrians established the local Lyceum. The bricks from the razed St. Mary's Chapel were repurposed to construct the meeting hall. The structure was designed in the then popular Greek Revival style. The building was christened on the evening of December 12, 1839 with a lecture delivered by U.S. Postmaster Daniel Bryan.

The intention of the Lyceum was oriented towards improving the social, intellectual and moral fabric of society. This objective was reinforced by lectures, dramatic performances, class instruction and debates. At the height of the movement, popular celebrities such as Ralph Waldo Emerson, Henry David Thoreau and even a young Abraham Lincoln participated as speakers.

During the Civil War, the Alexandria Lyceum was employed as a hospital. Following the conflict, the local chapter was dissolved and the building purchased privately for a residence. Following the death of its last residential owner in 1938, the building was sold again and became an office building.

The elegant structure would become an eyesore by the late 1960s. Facing demolition, local preservationists were able to successfully fundraise and renovate the structure. It reopened as Virginia's first Bicentennial Center in 1974 and became a history museum and cultural center in 1985.

A Vanished Canal That Once Routed Through Alexandria
Former Location of Lock #1: 1 Canal Center Plaza, Alexandria
Former Location of Lock #3: 945 North Royal Street, Alexandria
Former Location of Lock #4: 901 North Pitt Street, Alexandria

Following extensive lobbying by local merchants, Congress chartered the Alexandria Canal in 1830. The waterway linked the city with Georgetown and required ten years to fully construct. It opened for service in 1843 enabling canal boats to cross the Potomac River without descending to the river level.

Boats would chart their trips downstream via canal on the southwest side of the Potomac until reaching the port of Alexandria. Coal, wheat, corn, flour and whiskey were transported. Rumors of runaway slaves as Underground Railroad cargo resulted in the vessels being closely inspected before departures heading in the direction of Washington D.C. The canal followed a seven-mile and fifty-five foot wide path descending 38 feet through a series of four locks terminating at the Tidal Lock (Lock #1) located on the north end of Old Town. Three of the locks were lift locks and each moved the boats up and down ten to twelve feet. The canal conduit joined a 185-mile inland navigation system that included the Chesapeake and Ohio (C & O) Canal.

Competition from the railroads eventually severed the commercial life of the canal. The Civil War halted normal operations. Following the war, Baltimore and Richmond began to take away trade via the Shenandoah Valley grain fields. The Alexandria Canal venture began and concluded as a money-loser. The canal project would be finally abandoned in 1886. Remaining mule barns, crew barracks and warehouses were converted into ice houses.

Ten years later, an electric trolley line would be constructed that traced the canal's west side. Alternative transportation upgrades condemned the aqueduct to a relic. In 1923, the former superstructure of the Aqueduct Bridge was removed. During the 1980s, city archaeologists and the developer of the Trans-Potomac Canal Center excavated the Tidal Basin and Lock. They covered the original remnants with a reconstruction.

Today, the location of Locks #3 and #4 have been replaced by residential condominium projects. Canal Center Plaza forms a picturesque termination point highlighted by an intriguing sculptural garden. Featured artworks include a multi-tiered waterfall, monumental vertical bronze arrow, 40-foot high obelisk and a grotto of sculpted ruins overlooking an amphitheater. The most amusing and iconic installation is a carved human mouth with water spraying horizontally between its pursed lips.

FORMER LOCK #3

CANAL CENTRAL PLAZA

CANAL CENTRAL PLAZA

An Elevated Public Park Sharing A Storied Local History
Windmill Hill Park:
501 S. Union Street, Alexandria

Windmill Hill Park is an easily overlooked public space near the Old Town waterfront. Much of the park's lower topography was historically beneath the surface of the Potomac River until land speculators leveled the bluffs and cliffs for commercial development.

The space derived its name based on a windmill constructed in 1843 by inventor John Remington. The subsequently landscaped parkland attracted fashionable promenades, festive celebrations, evening bonfires and a passionate public speaking forum at the conclusion of the Civil War.

During the conflict, thousands of escaped slaves and Confederate deserters (Contrabands) congregated at Windmill Hill Park to seek refuge and eventual liberty. These freedmen and contrabands lived in makeshift housing and shanties during and even following the war. They appeared so close to their promised freedom, yet many still perished from the lack of adequate shelter during the inclement months, food and water.

In 1927, aviator Charles Lindbergh was honored from the heights of Windmill Hill Park for his solo flight to Paris with a 21-gun Presidential salute. The blasts were sounded as his ship bound for Washington D.C. passed by. Windmill Hill was gifted to the city for the official use as a park in 1945. Honoring Alexandria's 200th anniversary in 1949, an amphitheater was carved into the hill to stage a historical dramatic production.

The perception of the park has altered significantly over the past century. Complaints of rowdy delinquents tainted the park's reputation in 1891 according to newspaper reports. Sixty-five years later, Alexandria's police chief lamented publicly: *We get drunks, bootleggers, fights and deaths there all the time*. The neighborhood has significantly gentrified and tamed. It is currently considered one of the safest playgrounds within the community.

A Slave Trader Earns International Distain
Bruin Slave Jail:
1707 Duke Street, Alexandria

Joseph Bruin entered the slave trading business in 1840 on the outskirts of Old Town. He became financially prominent but singularly reviled more than any of his peers. The majority of slave traders only remained in business for a few years.

He conducted operations exclusively within his still standing red brick headquarters that he purchased in 1844. He and his family lived next door in a structure since demolished. His entire property also included a fenced-in open space that was employed as an exercise yard for captives.

Bruin and partner Henry Hill recruited slave inventory from predominantly Maryland and Virginia. They merchandised their slaves via New Orleans based auction sales. They concentrated their operations on smaller consignments, typically under twenty individuals. Bruin employed steamships, brigs and schooners for his larger contingents and overland travel via inland riverways. His slaves were bound in chains throughout these merciless transfers.

Writer Harriet Beecher Stowe would brand Joseph Bruin with international notoriety. In her *A Key to Uncle Tom's Cabin* edition published in 1854, she defended her popular novel *Uncle Tom's Cabin* released two years earlier. Her critics complained that her first writing regarding slavery widely exaggerated abuses and were fabricated accounts.

The intent of *A Key* was to document the facts and proof upon which her narrative was founded. Her most pronounced example was oriented around the escape of 76 slaves aboard the ship *Pearl* sailing from Washington D.C. on April 15, 1848. The slaves were eventually captured and many simply resold to their former owners. A select group was targeted for more lucrative auction sales in New Orleans.

Bruin and Hill purchased the Edmondson slave family and transferred them to their holding facility in Alexandria. According to Stowe's account, Joseph Bruin's daughter begged her father to exclude Mary and Emily Edmondson from a group that was destined for New Orleans.

Due to their lighter complexion, Mary and Emily's future was presumably fated for prostitution. Their father Paul Edmondson traveled north in an attempt to raise funds for the purchased freedom of his two daughters. His timing and ultimate good fortune was the result from a yellow fever outbreak that was occurring in New Orleans. Bruin had previously declined lucrative financial offers for the two girls. News of the outbreak prompted him to sell them immediately to protect his investment.

Paul Edmondson would encounter Reverend Lyman Beecher, Harriet's father who raised the release sum of $2,250 overnight. The sisters were given their freedom on November 4, 1848. In Harriett Beecher's *A Key*, the Bruin's *large slave warehouse* was referenced twenty times. Stowe reproduced the transaction documents and correspondence between Paul Edmondson and Joseph Bruin. The proof further polarized public reaction towards her portrayal of slavery.

Upon the outbreak of the Civil War, Joseph Bruin fled Alexandria, but was soon captured. He would be confined inside the Old Capital Prison in Washington D.C. until the conclusion of the war. During his forced absence, his slave jail was employed as the Fairfax County courthouse until July 1865.

Generations of readers would know him as the *greedy slave trader* and his slave jail as a *monument to oppression*. The Edmondson sisters are immortalized with a cast bronze sculpture in the adjacent courtyard. Bruin's post-war fate is forgotten.

**The Legend of Oscar An Absurdist Building Sentinel
The Mill Building:
515 N. Washington Street, Alexandria**

It is an absurd tale worthy of repetition. In 1854, a 24-year-old cotton factory night watchman named Michael Kiggin had his head bashed in for unknown motives. The killer was never determined, but investigators adorned a mannequin in Kiggin's clothing. He was then positioned in the building's cupola for public viewing. This vain and imbecilic attempt to lure the killer back failed. A suspect they arrested would be acquitted of murder.

At some stage in the evolution of the mannequin's role and history, he would be named *Oscar*. An alternative and more credible narrative regarding Oscar's employment and origin exists. The Bureau of Fisheries, a former building tenant installed him as a mute marketing vehicle. They escorted Oscar around the United States at exhibitions to promote angling. A reported oilskin garment draping him then appeared to confirm this version.

The speculated history regarding Oscar's involvement with the building has become local legend. Facts remain relative to an exaggerated and often repeated account. The building has served as a military prison and spark plug factory. In 1934, Oscar was *borrowed* by dim-witted pranksters and hung in effigy from the Washington D.C. Taft Bridge. He was recovered and then shamelessly hidden in obscurity.

Purportedly, a real estate agent would recover Oscar in storage. He dressed him up in an old suit and returned him to his public perch.

Between 1992 until 2014, the Police Chiefs Association occupied the building as their headquarters. Empathetically during the late 1990s, Oscar was reportedly repaired. The workmanship was slack and lacked professionalism.

By 2015, Oscar was reported to be missing a leg. Worse, he'd been outfitted in a faded polyester suit. This fashion catastrophe resembled grandpas throughout America attending Sunday church services in their last purchased stylish formal wear…a leisure suit.

Oscar's historic commercial residence would evolve into a predictable venue. The building was rechristened *The Mill* and converted into a residential complex with adjoining vacant garden space and propane barbeque grill. There is scarcely room for an important novelty such as Oscar. He is remembered and missed solely by his prior press clippings.

One thing is certain however regarding his former role as mannequin bait. His legend has outlived and eclipsed Michael Kiggin's killer.

The Scariest Nighttime Passage Haunting Alexandria
Wilkes Street Tunnel
398 Wilkes Street, Alexandria

The Wilkes Street Tunnel was originally part of the eastern division of the Orange and Alexandria Railroad. The line was founded in 1848 to promote trade with the western sector of Virginia. The initial tracks were inaugurated on May 7, 1851 with a route following the northern extremity of Union Street to the Tunnel termination point. The tunnel itself would not be completed until 1856, significantly delayed and over budget.

The tunnel linked the railroad to wharves and warehouses along the waterfront. The trains continued operation until 1975 when declining industrial activity along the waterfront no longer financially justified service. The train tracks would be lifted and the tunnel underwent a refurbishment in 2007-2008 to create a pedestrian and bicycle passage.

The 19th century edifice is one of Alexandria's few surviving transportation remnants. Located a half-mile from the core of Old Town, the tunnel extends one hundred and seventy feet between South Royal and Lee Streets. The name was derived from English radical John Wilkes who championed the American colonies cause against King George III.

The western extremity of the tunnel features an extended ramp with brick wall sides. The vaulted walls stretch to nearly sixteen feet in height at the top of its brick arch. Beaming rays of light that peak at each extremity disappear at the center core draping it in darkness and murky gloom.

From the outset, the tunnel received public criticism for shoddy craftsmanship, accelerated decaying timber and major drainage problems. Repairs would be conducted, but criticism would persist. The frightening and sinister darkness within the core has never become adequately illuminated.

The first published casualty occurred on August 26, 1862 when an inebriated soldier tripped attempting to cross the track. His inability to rise resulted in a locomotive passing over his exposed legs. He survived. Two years, two separate individuals would be violently murdered. Neither of their perpetrators would ever be captured. Haunting reports have become commonplace establishing the tunnel as one of the most dreaded locations to avoid during the dim twilight and early morning hours.

**Floating Trade Outside The Traditional Box
Example of Remaining Potomac Ark:
McIlhenny Seaport Center
0 Thompsons Alley, Alexandria, VA**

One of the most innovative forms of brothels and gambling parlors began floating along the Potomac River during the mid 19th century. Nicknamed the *Potomac Arks*, drifting houseboats, generally twenty-four feet in length moored near the water's edge.

The arks concentrated near Alexandria because Virginia had no jurisdiction over the river while Maryland and Washington D.C. law enforcement generally ignored them. Although the houseboats were generally slow and cumbersome, periodic police raids were generally easy to evade. Madams would simply pull up the anchor and in thirty seconds float out of the pursuing vice squads jurisdiction.

The diminutive floating houses of prostitution were color-coded. The elite boats were typically painted white with blue roofs and shutters. Some were two-story. Individual entrepreneurs painted their *houses* red. Many clustered around gambling casino boats with convenient transfer shuttle service available.

At the outset of the Civil War in 1861, there were approximately 450 brothels recorded in Washington D.C. One year later, there were 5,000 sex workers in D.C. and over 2,500 in Georgetown and Alexandria. Practitioners followed the influx of soldiers and shifted to the waters edge following the conclusion of the conflict.

Few stories regarding the brothel fleet were reported in the press. There was a sharp decline in the number of arks nearing 1927. During the Great Depression and World War II, scrutiny was lessened significantly. By the 1960s, their presence had evaporated. Most of the arks had been abandoned or burned by the harbor police.

In 1993, Alexandria city workers uncovered a wooden barge sunken in the dirt while demolishing a section of the waterfront. The ark, a shack perched upon the barge was recovered, restored and donated to the Alexandria Seaport Foundation. The *Cherry Blossom,* a re-creation of a Victoria steamboat is currently docked in Old Town. It is operated by the Potomac Riverboat Company for charters accommodating up to 350 people.

FORMER BARGE ARK

POTOMAC WATER TAXI
CHERRY BLOSSOM

**The Removal of a Rooftop Confederate Flag Provokes
The Civil War's First Casualties
Former Marshall House (Later Called the Hotel
Monaco and Currently The Alexandrian):
480 King Street, Alexandria**

The initial casualty in the American Civil War for both sides was not recorded on a battlefield.

Colonel Elmer Ellsworth was considered a charismatic and dashing young infantry commander of the 11th Union New York Volunteers. His troop was nicknamed the *First Fire Zouaves* due to his recruiting many of his men from the New York City volunteer fire department. An ardent follower of military history, he admired the Zouaves, Algerian troops fighting with the French Army in North Africa.

At seventeen, he worked as a patent agent in Rockford, Illinois. He studied law simultaneously in Chicago and served as a colonel in the National Guard cadets. As an aspiring and ambitious law clerk, he was hired by Abraham Lincoln's Springfield law office in 1860. He became friends with Lincoln and accompanied the president-elect to Washington D. C. in 1861.

The war began shortly following Lincoln's inauguration. Ellsworth's zeal and leadership prompted him to accompany the initial Union troops into Alexandria on May 24, 1861. Their role was occupy the city militarily before Confederate troops arrived and prevent an invasion of Washington D.C. They encountered no organized or armed resistance upon crossing the Potomac River.

Prominently displayed atop the Marshall Hotel was an 8x14' Confederate flag that had towered over the downtown for weeks. Lincoln could view the opposition's flag via spyglass from the White House.

Ellsworth and four men rushed immediately to the site of the offending flag. He approached the hotel and headed up to the rooftop. He removed the banner. On his descent to the ground floor, Ellsworth encountered owner James Jackson. He was a staunch supporter of slavery with a reputation for violence. He pointed a shotgun at Ellsworth and blasted him fatally. One of Ellsworth's men, Corporal Francis Brownell immediately shot Jackson dead.

The two men would become the Civil War's initial casualties for both sides.

Lincoln's relationship with Ellsworth made this killing personal. His body was transported to the White House, where it lay in state. Afterwards, it would be relocated to New York City. Ellsworth's death put a public face on the erupting conflict for thousands. They viewed the cortege supporting Ellsworth's coffin and shouted for vengeance.

Jackson received similar accolades from southern sympathizers. Both men were elevated into martyrdom and became iconic rallying cries as the war progressed. Sadly, neither survived to bask in any of the subsequent acclaim.

A Repurposed and Forgotten Fortress
Former Fort Ellsworth Site: (Fort Ellsworth Condominiums)
136 Roberts Lane, Alexandria

Fort Ellsworth was constructed in 1861 to defend Washington D.C. during the Civil War. Constructed during the weeks preceding the Union Army defeat at Bull Run, the timber and earthwork fortification overlooked the southern approaches to Alexandria.

Although Alexandria remained under Union occupation during the war, southern sympathies persisted. The Union garrisons were not only necessary for the protection of the capitol, but also critical to reinforcing internal control within Alexandria.

Construction began on May 25, 1861, overseen by General Horatio Wright. General John Newton supervised the construction and managed the flow of men and materials. The Fort was constructed on Shuter's Hill to the east of Samuel Cooper's Cameron plantation house. The perimeter of the battery was 618 yards, with space allocated for 29 canons including one 100-pound Parrott gun.

Writer Nathaniel Hawthorne visited Fort Ellsworth during 1862 remarking how the ramparts had been *heaped up out of the muddy soil*. He noted the beautiful view of the Potomac calling it a *truly majestic river*. His observations seemed relevant then: *The fortifications, so numerous in all this region, and now so unsightly with their bare, precipitous sides will remain as historic monument, grass-grown and picturesque memorials of an epoch of terror and suffering.*

Hawthorne would be proven wrong regarding the

fortresses' longevity. Fort Ellsworth would completely disappear following the war. The George Washington Masonic National Memorial would be constructed upon on Shuter's Hill covering 25 acres. Another 25-acre parcel would be subdivided. The current Fort Ellsworth Condominium complex would become part of these lands. The former fortress flagpole is reportedly situated southwest of the community swimming pool.

A Timber and Earthwork Fortification Returns To The Forest
Former Fort Williams Site:
501 Fort Williams Road, Alexandria

Fort Williams was a timber and earthwork fortification constructed in Alexandria as part of the defense of Washington D.C. during the Civil War. The fort was constructed expediently following the 1861 defeat by the Confederate army at the First Battle of Bull Run. The structure overlooked the Orange and Alexandria Railroad, Little River Turnpike and western approaches to the city.

Construction was completed by the Second Connecticut Heavy Artillery Regiment featuring a perimeter of 250 yards and space for 13 canons. The most prominent soldier stationed there in 1864 was George Tryon Harding, father of future president Warren Harding.

The fort was built on property owned by Confederate General Samuel Cooper. Following the conclusion of the war, the lands were returned. Today, there is no evidence of the fortification except a single marker located 100 yards to the west of where the fort stood. The rest of the property has been absorbed into the Seminary Ridge residential neighborhood and a 7.8-acre city forested park space.

TWISTED TOUR GUIDES.com

152

Repurposing A Historic Bank Building For Medical Necessity
Market Square:
100 N. Fairfax Street, Alexandria
Former Alexandria Bank Building:
133 N. Fairfax Street, Alexandria
Former Braddock House Hotel Site:
127 N. Fairfax Street, Alexandria

Alexandria was spared as a battlefield site during Civil War within the city boundaries. It was not spared the spectacle of casualties imported from nearby conflicts. Upon the declaration of war between the Union and Confederate States, Alexandria was immediately occupied on May 24, 1861 by Union forces. The city would serve as a protective Potomac River buffer between the two warring capitols of Washington D.C. and Richmond, separated by only 100 miles.

Two months following the occupation, Alexandria became a medical collection receptacle for wounded Union soldiers from the First Battle of Bull Run staged in Manassas. The combat was conducted only 35 miles to the west and became an initial victory for the Confederate forces.

Traditionally, battlefield casualties were treated onsite within hastily constructed medical tent compounds. With Manassas being positioned close to Alexandria, Union generals concluded that the city would become a superior treatment alternative. One week following their defeat, General George McClellan would become appointed head of the Army of the Potomac.

The decision to relocate casualties proved chaotic. The

city was ill prepared for the influx of horror. A gruesome manifestation lined an entire block of Fairfax Street, near Market Square. Cadavers were piled on top of each other, many four deep awaiting burials. Stacks of human limbs accumulated and the stench were unpalatable. Blood streamed down the streets sourced from temporarily constructed hospitals. Pedestrians waded through ankle-high rivers of blood.

The reality of war had been expediently introduced to the populous. Atrocity and carnage supplanted military glory. Any expectations of a quick conflict became dismissed as idealistic and unrealistic.

Injured soldiers lined the sidewalks seeking hospital care. The dilemma would ultimately be addressed by converting many of the town's underutilized buildings into hospitals.

The former Bank of Alexandria building became one such conversion six months into the occupation.

The 10,000 square foot structure had been constructed originally in 1806 to serve as the institution's headquarters. The bank became a unifying financial center for the city's early development. It floundered and failed in 1834. Fourteen years later, local furniture maker James Green acquired the building to accompany the adjacent Carlyle House that he also owned. Town patriarch John Carlyle had formerly resided in that residence during the 1750s. The Carlyle mansion frontage is set back from North Fairfax Street.

Following his purchase, Green would convert the former bank building into a luxury hospitality property called the Mansion House Hotel. In the 1850s, Green built a four-story hotel addition that entirely blocked the view of the Carlyle residence from Fairfax Street. His hotel complex was lauded and celebrated as Alexandria's most *spacious and newly furnished* accommodation offering unobstructed views of the Potomac River. The accompanying restaurant was famed for their quality cuisine, delicacies and select wines and liquors.

Green's prosperity and three premium holdings would be sorely tested upon the outbreak of the Civil War. He was reputedly a confirmed Confederate sympathizer.

Upon Alexandria's occupation, Union officers and physicians were lodged inside a section of the Carlyle residence. Soldiers were billeted on several floors of the Mansion House Hotel. Six months later, the former hotel would become transformed into a functioning hospital, filled to capacity with over 700 patients. Day to day procedures was volatile and strained amongst the medical staff. Young women assigned as nurses met abuse and open hostility by attending physicians who opposed their employment.

Green would be returned his properties during the summer of 1865 following the Confederate surrender. The interior conditions were left deplorable by sustained disorder. Rehabilitation of the buildings required months of repairs and cleaning. Green would reopen the hotel property. Following his death in 1880, the residence, hotel addition and bank building slid into disrepair with a succession of negligent owners.

By 1970, all three buildings were crumbling. The hotel addition, afterwards renamed the Braddock House Hotel would be razed in 1973. Its demolition once again made the Carlyle residential mansion visible from

Fairfax Street. The residence would be purchased by the Northern Virginia Regional Park Authority (NOVA) and undergo six years of renovation before being opened to the public.

The plight of James Green and the Alexandria Bank building would be depicted in the television drama series *Mercy Street*, which aired on PBS from 2016-2017. The former bank building is currently undergoing extensive restoration. The intended use is for commercial offices on the ground level and residential units on the second and third floors.

JAMES GREEN'S HOTEL ADDITION SITE

BANK OF ALEXANDRIA BUILDING

An American Fortress Dating From George Washington's Farmland Era
Fort Hunt Park:
8999 Fort Hunt Road, Alexandria

One of the picturesque roads heading towards George Washington's Mount Vernon estate follows the southern course of the Potomac River. Part of Washington's former river farmlands includes the present day Fort Hunt Park. During the Civil War and Spanish American War, the lands were converted into a military installation guarding the Potomac against potential enemy excursions into Washington D.C.

The park was named after Brigadier General Henry Hunt, who served as chief of artillery for the Army of the Potomac during the Civil War. Intact concrete batteries remain from the Battery Mount Vernon, Battery Robinson, Battery Slater and Battery Porter. The latter fortress was named after Lieutenant James Porter, an officer killed in General George Armstrong Custer's Last Stand at the Little Bighorn.

Fort Hunt was constructed to complement Fort Washington stationed across the shore in Maryland. It was reinforced in 1897, just prior to the Spanish American War. It would never see action during the conflict.

Fort Hunt would continue to remain a critical center for military operations. In 1932, General Douglas MacArthur established a field hospital to service wounded military veterans known as *Bonus Marchers*. Before, they had encamped within Washington D.C. during their controversial protest. During the 1930s

Great Depression, the site was converted into a Civilian Conservation Corps camp.

Throughout World War II, the fort was established as the headquarters for top-secret military operations. Part of these operations included an interrogation center for crucial enemy prisoners of war. Soldiers at Fort Hunt interrogated prisoners, trained pilots in escape and evasion, and combed German documents for intelligence.

In June 1944, Lieutenant Commander Werner Henke was killed attempting an escape. He became the highest-ranking German officer to be shot while in American captivity during the war. He would be buried in the post cemetery at Fort Meade in Maryland.

A Large Traffic Roundabout Conceals A Former Elevated Fortress
Fort Willard Site:
6625 Fort Willard Circle, Alexandria

The remainder of Fort Willard forms a convenient car roundabout within the Belle Haven neighborhood of Alexandria. The diminutive 1.6-acre fort was constructed in 1862 amidst the feverish fortress building used to protect Washington D. C. during the Civil War. Fort Willard was the southernmost fortification located on a high point of a ridge overlooking the Potomac River lowlands. It commands a present day view of Fort Hunt Road.

The fortress was named in honor of Colonel George L. Willard who was slain in the Battle of Gettysburg on July 2, 1863. The fort was originally a small, unflanked enclosure with a bombproof structure and magazine. Fort Willard featured emplacement for fifteen canons. The entire complex featured three barracks, a guardhouse, officers quarters, cookhouse and ordinance sergeants' quarters. Two detached batteries reinforced the fort.

During the 1930s, residential development swallowed the bulk of the surrounding land. The remaining park features several artifacts lingering from the former fortress.

TWISTED TOUR GUIDES.com

NOTICE
FIREARMS
PROHIBITED.
PROHIBIDAS.

An Archaic Gun Emplacement and Former Potomac River Protector
Battery Rodgers Gun Emplacement Site: Intersection of Green and South Lee Street, Alexandria

Amidst the Union army occupation of Alexandria during the Civil War, the Battery Rodgers was established during 1863. The military emplacement was constructed along the Alexandria shoreline with a perimeter of 30 yards. Five 200-pound Parrott canons and one 15-inch Rodman were mounted overlooking a 28-foot high bluff above the Potomac River's Battery Cove. The Rodman was considered then one of the largest guns in the world.

The battery was named after Union Naval Captain George Rodgers who had been killed during an attack on Fort Wagner. The guns were positioned to guard against attacking ships passing through the southern Potomac River approaching Washington D.C. The battery complex included a hospital, barracks, mess hall, and prison. It garrisoned 6 commissioned officers and 256 men.

Following the conclusion of the war, the Battery was disbanded and guns relocated to other locations within the region. The only remaining trace is a discreet marker at the foot of Green Street. Landscaped gardens terrace the former fort's terrain.

Fixed placement guns would ultimately become obsolete in warfare upon the introduction of aerial bombardment. Unfortunately, war itself has ceased to become viewed as archaic or ultimately pointless.

HISTORICAL SITE
DEFENSES OF WASHINGTON
1861   1865
BATTERY RODGERS
HERE STOOD BATTERY RODGERS,
BUILT IN 1863 TO PREVENT
ENEMY SHIPS FROM PASSING UP
THE POTOMAC RIVER. THE
BATTERY HAD A PERIMETER OF
300 YARDS AND MOUNTED FIVE
200 POUNDER PARROTT GUNS AND
ONE 15-INCH RODMAN. IT WAS
DEACTIVATED IN 1865.
Battery Rodgers

Historic Prostitution and Flagrant Bingo Scandals Within Alexandria
Captain Hugh Harkins' Arrest Site:
301 King Street, Alexandria

During the Civil War, Alexandria hosted numerous *bawdy* institutions including the renowned Gadsby's Tavern, then known as the City Hotel. The term *bawdy* was defined as any place within or without any building or structure that was used for lewdness, trysts or prostitution.

In April 1863, Army Lieutenant Charles E. Grisson reported that over seventy-five houses of prostitution were actively operating in Alexandria. He related that Union Army officers took great delight *to clean them out without ceremony.* The women engaged in flirtatious behavior towards their overseers sometimes compromising their direct action. Grisson classified his visitations and inspections a *patriotic duty,* confessing that *he never had so much fun!*

Proliferating along the Potomac River docks, floating houses of prostitution lined the shoreline. Most were painted a distinctive red or blue. Their commerce flourished until after World War II because Virginia had no jurisdiction over the Potomac River. Hundreds of ark brothels filled nearly every cove and harbor. The *Washington Post* reported that one popular spot was opposite Mount Vernon, where at least fifteen arks were consistently moored from 1890 until the 1930s.

Amidst such rampant debauchery, one unfortunate officer would be branded with a lifetime of permanent disgrace during the middle of wartime hostilities. On July 22, 1863, President Lincoln approved an order to dismiss Union Captain Hugh Harkins for his involvement in a pickpocketing incident. The crime occurred in a *bawdy place* located on the southeastern fringe of Market Square (currently the site of the Saturday's Farmer's Market). Harkins was reportedly intoxicated during his transgression. His career would be abruptly terminated despite an apparent stellar military record.

Alexandria waged a losing battle to sanitize its reputation during the late 19th century. Physician Kate Waller Barrett headed an empathetic reform movement within the community until her death in 1925. She advocated closer police supervision, no liquor sales to ill-reputed patrons and an honest living wage for women selling their bodies. During that era, female sweatshop pay amounted to approximately $8 weekly. Upon her death, Barrett would donate sufficient funds to construct a local library. It would become the site of a notable 1939 Civil Rights protest.

When Washington D.C.'s red light district was officially shuttered in 1914, Alexandria's problem became acute. Prospective clients flooded the city and loitered around North Lee and St. Asaph Streets. During Prohibition, vice flourished, particularly originating from pool halls.

Alexandria would resume bouts of publicized corruption during the late 1970s.

In 1979, the city became the first Virginia jurisdiction to ban instant bingo, a church-supported form of the game linked to financial scandal. Local Prosecutor William Cowhig resigned his position after being acquitted of bribery trials involving bingo. One year later, the former president of the Alexandria Bar Association James L. Burkhardt was indicted by a federal grand jury on charges of funneling illicit cash payments to public officials. The monies bought police protection for an extensive metro D.C. prostitution ring. His payments were allegedly siphoned through Cowhig.

Prostitution is an impossible social problem to eradicate. Contrary to those who consider it a victimless crime, the industry is rife with victims. The Internet has facilitated direct transactions and even hotel bookings via online escort websites. Difficult-to-trace transactions and human trafficking have replaced *bawdy houses*. The demand for purchased sexual relations has never slackened with time.

A Tragic Boating Collision In Pursuit of Assassin John Wilkes Booth
Alexandria National Cemetery:
1450 Wilkes Street, Alexandria

One of the most tragic and overlooked disasters that followed the assassination of Abraham Lincoln was a marine catastrophe occurring on the Potomac River ten days following. Assassin John Wilkes Booth would remain a fugitive for nearly two weeks following Lincoln's murder.

A manhunt to apprehend him involved 10,000 federal troops. Numerous civilian resources were deployed in his pursuit. Secretary of War Edwin Stanton advertised a $100,000 reward for information leading to his arrest.

Union troops were dispatched to southern Maryland and ultimately Virginia to search for Booth based in response to federal intelligence information. On the evening of Sunday, April 23, a contingent from the Quartermaster Corps was patrolling the Potomac in search of a possible vessel ferrying Booth across the river.

The men were unaware that Booth and his accomplice David Herold had already crossed the Potomac the evening before. They were asleep that evening inside a cabin in King George County, Virginia.

The *USS Massachusetts* was a steam ship constructed in Boston in 1860. Approximately 400 former Union prisoners of war were packed on board. They were moored at the Potomac River near Alexandria that Sunday. The men were headed to be deployed for further military duty in North Carolina.

The *Black Diamond* was an iron hull steam propeller boat built in 1842. The ship's customary cargo involved transporting coal between Alexandra and Washington D.C. On board was a crew of twenty men from the Alexandria fire department.

The *Black Diamond* was assigned patrol duty on the Potomac scanning for signs of Booth. Sunday was a clear, windy and moonless evening. The ship had only one light illuminating that could barely be discerned. Nearing midnight near the mouth of the Potomac, the two ships collided on the port side of the *Black Diamond*.

The force of the impact accompanied by general panic tossed approximately 200 soldiers on board the *USS Massachusetts* into the waters. The *Black Diamond* immediately took on water and sank within three minutes. Four firemen would meet their death.

Over 100 men would be rescued from the waters, but 87 perished from the *USS Massachusetts*. Many of their bodies were never recovered. The drowned Alexandria firemen from the *Black Diamond* included Peter Carroll, Christopher Farley, Samuel Gosnell and George Huntington. They would be buried with honors at the Soldier's Cemetery in Alexandria, currently known as the Alexandria National Cemetery. A large boulder with a bronze plaque acknowledges their tragedy.

Booth would be apprehended and killed within 24 hours following their deaths. Both ship pilots would loose their maritime licenses as a result of the incident.

A Fiery Interruption For A Doomed Bride
Schafer Residence:
107 N. Fairfax Street, Alexandria

The legend of Laura Schafer's untimely demise mirrors the pathos and tragedy of Shakespeare's Romeo and Juliette. Fairfax Street is Alexandria's cursed and haunted roadway. Schafer resided midway between two Civil War era catastrophes. To the south lay the 1861-stacked Civil War soldier cadavers lain along a block of Market Square. To the north, the collective misery and echoed screams from the former Mansion House Hotel, converted into a military hospital.

The year was 1868, three years following the catastrophic war. June is historically the most popular month for matrimony. For Laura Schafer, her June 30th wedding date was eminent. She was madly enamored with her intended fiancé Charles Tennesson. His sentiments were mutual. The couple had been companions for several previous years. Their marriage would solemnize their eternal vows.

Schafer's parents had emigrated from Germany to establish a confectionary shop in Old Town. They had six children including Laura, the youngest. Tennesson's father owned a local restaurant. Charles was reportedly a soldier. The couple appeared predestined to continue a successful family legacy.

Only an unforeseen accident could prevent this inevitability.

On the evening before her wedding, Laura was carrying an oil lamp on the third floor of her family's residence. She entered her father's room to retrieve a handkerchief from his large bureau.

The lamp mysteriously cracked and hot oil began seeping. She felt the heated oil on her skin and panicked. She tossed the lantern into an adjacent fireplace. Her impulsive act became her attempt to prevent any fire from igniting. It backfired. Both her hair and nightgown caught fire. The incident might have terminated simply enough had she remained still and calmly extinguished the flames.

Instead, she attempted to flee down the staircase. She caught her heel on the edge of a stair and tumbled down violently. Efforts to smother the flames by family members were too late and futile. She sustained second and third degree burns throughout her body. She would expire the following morning in intense agony with Charles seated beside her.

He attempted to address his indescribable grief by numbing himself with alcohol. Four hours following Laura's death, he summoned a close friend Henry Green. They consumed ales together inside a nearby liquor store in morose silence. They finished their final drink with a toast offered by Tennesson: *To you and I-God Save Us*.

When Green arose to return their cups, he turned his back on Charles. During that instant, Tennesson raised a loaded pistol to his temple and fired. The bullet lodged in his skull. He would die on his planned wedding day from his injury.

The tragedy has been passed down through several generations. Eyewitnesses have claimed to verify the paranormal presence of both Laura and Charles. She is naturally wearing her wedding dress and he is often brusque with visitors demanding their immediate departure.

To authenticate the experience some have even confirmed weeping and of course, a lingering aroma of smoke.

The Thorny Continued Existence Of A Confederate Tombstone
Christ Church Cemetery:
200 N Washington Street, Alexandria

Throughout the Civil War, Alexandria was a divided city due to the Union forces military occupation. The Confederate cause was strongly supported by a notable percentage of merchants, property owners and citizenry. The majority simply suppressed their preferences and sentiments throughout the conflict. Upon the conclusion, public mourning for fallen soldiers and leadership icons became considered more acceptable.

Numerous sons from Alexandria pursed the Confederate cause. Like their Union peers, they sacrificed their lives on the battlefield. Their motivations may have been misguided, but their commitment was genuine and ultimately costly. Survivors of the conflict returned to their hometown uncertain as to the public reception they would receive.

Over one hundred fifty years later, the question concerning a polarizing divide has still not been fully resolved. The flashpoint triggering much of the debate concerns public memorials commemorating fallen soldiers, southern political figures and notable battlefields.

History should never be ignored or blatantly whitewashed. Nothing is learned from the experience otherwise. Sadly many proponents of hatred-fueled causes manipulate these war symbols to proselytize and glorify their contaminated ideologies.

Christ Church located within Old Town was constructed between 1767 and 1773. Both George Washington and

Robert E. Lee attended services there. Washington's pew and communion rail are still designated. Lee married Washington's great-granddaughter Mary Custis. He and his daughters were confirmed inside the sanctuary on July 1, 1853. A silver plaque in the chancel commemorates the spot.

The church graveyard has accommodated bereaved families since the institution's inception. The oldest legible gravestone within the cemetery is Isaac Pierce who died on March 26, 1771. There may exist older, but time has erased and defaced their inscriptions.

The most controversial burial marker on the grounds acknowledges thirty-four Confederate soldiers reinterred on December 27, 1879. Each man was originally buried at the Alexandria National Cemetery during the course of the war. Questions linger as to the appropriateness of their presence within the Old Town cemetery.

In death, soldiers may no longer espouse their respective causes. They simply become casualties whose lives were abruptly severed. Racism and the inconvenient truths accompanying the Civil War make the controversy far more potent than the simplistic notion of simply preserving history.

Racism remains a social travesty that American culture has attempted to shed with debatable success. Do gravestones and memorials acknowledge history or are they antiquated reminders of a historical page still not fully turned?

In the Western United States, all public Confederate memorials have been removed. The final two located in Helena, Montana and Seattle, Washington were detached respectively by city council degree and forcible desecration. They have not been missed. Gravestones of individual participants have generally remained unblemished within cemeteries.

For now the mass Confederate gravestone remains at Christ Church. Future public outcries and protests against its installation may one day alter its permanent location.

**A Spiritual Center For The Earliest Black Congregation
Historic Shiloh Baptist Church:
1401 Duke Street, Alexandria**

Formerly herded as animals inside the Franklin and Armfield slave pens, freed and runaway slaves immigrated to the Union controlled city of Alexandria during the Civil War. Conditions were often unwelcoming and harsh. Religious solace, ministry consolation and prayer were often the sole comforts to a life of inadequate shelter and near starvation.

The former slave prison became converted into a government mess hall and the initial meeting location for the Old Shiloh Society in March 1863. Fifty former slaves founded a worship congregation that rapidly outgrew its space. Shortly afterwards, they moved to the former slave barracks on the grounds until the structure was destroyed by fire. The Staunton School temporarily became their subsequent meeting location.

A few months following the end of the Civil War, the Shiloh Society became known as the Shiloh Baptist Church. The group dedicated a wood frame headquarters near the intersection of Prince and West Streets. The location was situated close to the L'Ouverture Hospital grounds. This Shiloh Chapel would be destroyed by fire in 1872.

Seeking a longer-term solution for an expanding congregation, church leaders purchased property to construct a permanent sanctuary. Discord within the Shiloh community created division within the membership. A faction of the congregation separated and established the Mount Jezreel Baptist Church on North Payne Street.

Construction on the new Shiloh Baptist Church began in 1891 and was dedicated on October 23, 1893. The completed structure featured a bell tower, eight stained glass windows, modern circular oak pews and a large reflector featuring glass prisms handing from the ceiling. This historic sanctuary remains a useful congregation meeting space. A more expansive worship center was constructed and dedicated in 2005 across the street.

A Racially Motivated Lynching Absent of Due Process
Former City Jail Site: 401 N. St. Asaph Street
Lynching Site: 300 King Street, Alexandria

On August 7, 1899, Lilian Clarke, the 8-year-old daughter of Edward and Julia Clarke told Alexandria police that she was walking by the house of Benjamin Thomas when he grabbed her. He purportedly dragged her inside the residence and attempted to sexually assault her. She claimed that *he was not entirely successful.*

Thomas, who was black, would be arrested immediately and charged for attempting to *criminally assault* Lilian Clark. Following the newspaper publication of the event and official charges pressed the following day, uproar circulated within the local white community. On August 8, their rage evolved rapidly into action. By that evening, the citizenry of Alexandria had begun acquiring weapons with the intention of confronting law authorities and administrating vigilante justice.

Four regular police officers and twenty sworn citizens were delegated to protect the prisoner. By 11:00 p.m., a mob of 2,000 had congregated around the jailhouse. The building was a two-level stone structure located on North St. Asaph Street. The mob's fiery momentum rationalized that due process for Thomas was unnecessary. It would never be determined or confirmed if Lilian Clarke's version of events was accurate.

Several dozen men rushed through the crowd and penetrated into the jail. They overpowered the guards and entered Thomas' cell. A rope was fastened around his neck and he was dragged through the streets. He was shot once during the procession and began bleeding. Every thread of his clothing would be scraped off as he was forcibly hauled to Market Square, struggling to free himself.

He cried, pleaded and moaned in agony. His convicting mob remained pitiless and relentless in their objective. Arriving at the corner of Fairfax and King Street, he was hung on a lamppost and immediately riddled with gunfire. The audience watched in paralyzed silence. Thomas died instantly. Some spectators rushed to his body to collect relics.

The coroner ruled his death as a gunshot wound to the heart by the hands of an unidentified mob. His mother refused to neither receive his remains at her house nor participate with his funeral.

His guilt would never be determined amidst this travesty of justice. The stain of the barbaric and macabre spectacle would taint the legacy of Alexandria.

A MAN WAS
LYNCHED
TODAY

BENJAMIN THOMAS
AUGUST 8, 1899

**Clem's Stroll With A Bloody Razor Seeking Revenge
Clem's Stalking Grounds:
500 Block of N. St. Asaph Street, Alexandria**

In the early 1900s, an Alexandria man named Clem fell passionately in love with a woman named Rose. Given the environment of the neighborhood then, Rose may have been a sex worker. She felt indifference towards Clem's pursuit, preferring a local butcher as a longer-term relationship prospect. Her overt flirting with the tradesman infuriated Clem.

A man of action and not articulation, Clem employed a sharpened razor to revenge his rejection. He assaulted Rose inside her home and slit her throat. Presuming that he might resume his unencumbered pursuit of Rose in the afterlife, he then cut his own throat.

Rose survived the attack despite notable blood loss. Clem likewise botched his own attempted suicide. His persistence at completing Rose's murder has spawned a fanciful legend. Along the promenade of the 500 block of North St. Asaph Street, Clem has been reportedly sighted armed and lurking in the darkness with his cursed bloody razor.

Alternative accounts have also cited him wandering aimlessly nearby or along the adjacent narrow alleyways with malice intent. Rose is his perceived target, however with homicidal maniacs, one may never be certain regarding exclusivity.

Clem's debatable narrative has been passed along for over a century. The tale resembles a welcome shared claret bottle among vagabonds. For some perplexing reason, confirming newspaper accounts of his original attempted homicide are nonexistent.

The Silent Sentinels and Their Passion For Equal Rights
Former Custom House and Hearing Site:
202 S St. Asaph Street, Alexandria
Occoquan Workhouse (Currently Workhouse Arts Center):
9518 Workhouse Way, Lorton, VA

The Silent Sentinels became a moral compass for an American nation that still had not recognized the equality of women. These suffragettes organized by Alice Paul silently marched and protested in front of the White House gates and Lafayette Park. The women began their determined vigil during January 1917 with the largest demonstration held on March 4, 1917 attended by over 1,000 participants.

The marchers adorned sashes with the National Woman's Party (NWP) colors of purple, gold and white. They toted large banners with sewn letters targeted towards lawmakers to consider legally enabling women the right to vote. Many of the signs pointedly accused President Woodrow Wilson of hypocrisy. These banners considered his administration more concerned with democracy overseas than within the United States. The protest movement frequently attracted harassment by bystanders and some participants were subject to arrest.

Their collective message finally struck a political nerve after Wilson had initially attempted to ignore them. In August 1917, twenty-eight suffragettes were arrested on charges of obstructing traffic. At their hearing conducted at the former Alexandria Custom House, they were sentenced to internment at the Occoquan Workhouse, located in Lorton, Virginia, southwest of Alexandria.

Conditions inside the prison were unsanitary. Some women staged hunger strikes prompting force feedings. They refused Wilson's offer of pardons, arguing an acceptance would become interpreted as an admission of guilt. The abuse and violence towards these women peaked on November 14, 1917, when the superintendent and forty of his guards viciously beat some of the prisoners. The attacks would become known as *The Night of Terror*. The NWP publicized the violent abuse igniting national press coverage. The organization continued their protests outside of the penal institution.

Despite Wilson's initial preference to avoid involvement, he recognized the severity and potential damage to his legacy. He pragmatically ordered the prisoners released on November 27. On January 9, 1918, he made his initial public declaration of support for the women's suffrage movement. In March, he declared the Silent Sentinels arrests unconstitutional.

Over the subsequent year and a half, the intensity of the protests heightened. With Wilson's support, the suffrage movement continued their objective of a Constitutional amendment guarantying their right to vote. The House of Representative and Senate proposed legislation that stalled during 1918. Wilson was often unfairly blamed for the failure. Finally, in May 1919, the House passed legislation creating the Nineteenth Amendment that the Senate endorsed in June. The Silent Sentinel daily protests ceased afterwards. A necessary 36 state legislatures agreed to ratify the amendment enabling it to become enacted.

On August 26, 1920, the 19th Amendment became law creating a substantive victory for the women's right movement. Wilson was unable to share their public victory due to a severe stroke that left him incapacitated.

Alice Paul's legacy would continue as the author of the Equal Rights Amendment (ERA). This subsequent proposed mandated equal rights for United States citizens regardless of sex. The ERA was first introduced to Congress in 1923, but lacked sufficient passage votes. The proposal would be re-introduced each session for the next fifty years. It would never achieve sufficient support to become an amendment to the Constitution.

Illinois became the last state to ratify it in May 2018, but still one additional state was required. The deadline for ratification passed and the issue expired a well-publicized death. Alice Paul died at the age of 92 in Morrestown, New Jersey during 1977. The Occoquan Workhouse has been transformed into a 55-acre cultural center and renamed the Workhouse Arts Center.

**An Unsolved Murder of an Aspiring Police Sergeant
Elton Hummer Murder Site:
224 South Alfred Street, Alexandria**

Sergeant Elton Hummer had seemingly found his career niche by employment with the Alexandria Police Department. He was the youngest of four children raised in Sterling, Virginia where he had worked on the family farm. Upon his family relocating to Alexandria, he became a police officer on August 17, 1927 at the age of 29.

One year later, he was promoted to the rank of sergeant. He played on the police baseball team and was regarded as one of the most popular officers on the force.

On August 18, 1928, he left his parents house where he resided on 806 Duke Street to begin his midnight shift. He strolled the neighborhood on foot for the next hour, inspecting his habitual beat. Around the corner from his parent's house, he heard two men arguing in an alley. One warned the other in a heightened voice that this was the *last time*. The context behind the caution was never determined.

Witnesses heard two quit successive shots followed by a third. On the pavement in front of a residence, Hummer lay dying. His gun was located near his hand, but he was barely conscious. He had been shot in the chest and groin. Upon arriving at Alexandria Hospital, he expired.

Neighbors claimed to have seen a man running west on Duke Street, holding his side as though injured. He was likely the target of the third shot as Hummer had been able to fire once. The weapon that killed Hummer was identified as an automatic .45-caliber gun.

Despite an extensive manhunt and the employment of all available resources ranging from airplane surveillance to ballistic experts, no substantive clues could identify the assailant(s). On the 80th anniversary of his death, the alley adjacent to the murder scene was renamed *Hummer Alley* in his honor.

A Masonic Pilgrimage Honoring George Washington
George Washington Masonic National Memorial:
101 Callahan Drive, Alexandria

Soaring above a detached Alexandria skyline, the George Washington Masonic National Memorial is fashioned after the ancient Lighthouse of Alexandria in Egypt. The construction began in 1922 upon the crest of Shuter's Hill, formerly the site of Civil War era Fort Ellsworth. The structure was dedicated in 1932 during the Great Depression and the interior finally completed in 1970. It is considered one of the largest private memorials constructed to honor Washington.

Washington's affiliation with Freemasonry began in November 1752 when he was twenty years old. He paid a nominal fee to join the Lodge in Fredericksburg. For the remainder of his military and political career, he was an active member within masonic circles and responsible for establishing Alexandria's Lodge Number 22 in 1788. Upon his death, numerous personal artifacts and belongings were willed to the Lodge as he had formerly served as the initial Grand Master.

Freemasonry originated during the 17th and 18th centuries. Shrouded in secrecy and clandestine rituals, initial lodges met in private rooms of public taverns or halls. Due to the elaborate paraphernalia required to facilitate gatherings, lodges began to seek out permanent facilities, dedicated solely for Masonic and affiliate use.

Masonic temple construction peaked during the 1920s within the United States. By 1930, it was estimated that 12% of the American male population were members of the fraternity.

The genesis of the Alexandria monument began with the purchase of 50-acres of land around Shuter's Hill in 1908. The intent of the purchase was to erect a memorial Masonic temple with a sizable Washington statue in the vestibule. Short on funding, organizers initially scaled down their project ambitions to solely a park. Half of the land would be subdivided and sold into housing tracts. Twenty-five acres were left allocated for a memorial. The proceeds from the subdivision sales paid for the entire cost of the land track, leaving enough funds remaining to provide for a substantial temple and monument.

New York City based architect Harvey Wiley Corbett, coincidentally a freemason, was selected as the chief architect. He planned a three-story memorial temple crowned by a three-story tower in the neoclassical style. His height plans fluctuated between 200 and the eventually determined 333 feet. Construction sputtered and staggered following the dedication ceremony. Every winter season, construction would halt to insure the memorial remained free of moisture and frost damage insuring superior fitting between stones. The granite originated from quarries in New Hampshire. Some of the blocks measured twenty feet long.

The goal established towards completion was May 12, 1932, the 200th anniversary of Washington's birth. The structure was not fully ready by then, as electrical and plumbing work had not yet reached the third floor. The glacial pace also became necessitated by the priority of not incurring debt. Work would not commence until sufficient monies were raised by masonic organizations to pay for the contracted tasks.

The scheduled May 12th dedication proceeded in torrential rain. More than 100 special trains transported an estimated 150,000 spectators into Alexandria. Hotels were fully booked and many of the guests slept in railroad sleeping cars. President Herbert Hoover, his cabinet, members of Congress and foreign ambassadors attended the dedication. A parade through the city that had anticipated 150,000 spectators drew only an estimated 20,000 due to the inclement conditions.

Over the subsequent decades, internal improvements, permanent historical exhibitions and design additions would enhance the structure. Despite being labeled *completed* in 1970, the granite facing would require an additional three years to finish. The tower remained only partially lit during that period, but would achieve full illumination by the summer of 1973. The national memorial would become the only Masonic building supported by all 52 grand lodges of the United States.

The Memorial has weathered funding challenges for upkeep with declining masonic membership, deterioration and even vandalism. Drag races have been staged illegally on the grounds, evergreen trees have been sawed off at the tops for use as Christmas trees, fences cut down for firewood, and even interior murals scissor cut out. The structure has prevailed as a distinctive meeting hall, visitor attraction and iconic curiosity from an earlier age.

The former *secret society* stigma lodged against freemasonry and their feared spiritual agenda has lessened over time. With the exception of the prominent masonic logo at the front entrance, the building can easily be mistaken for an isolated monolithic skyscraper. As a cultural attraction, the interior museum draws modest attendance, estimated at 10,000 visits annually. During many weekdays, the temple appears nearly deserted.

A Non-Violent Library Sit-In Fuels Early Civil Right Advocacy
Kate Waller Barrett Library Branch:
717 Queen Street, Alexandria

Long before the Civil Rights movement brought the injustice of racism to national attention, a determined group of Alexandria black men staged their own silent protest. The present-day Barrett Branch Library, originally named the Alexandria Library was opened in 1937 with monies donated by the family of Kate Waller Barrett, who'd died in 1925. As with the majority of county financed facilities and public services, the institution was exclusively available to white citizens.

Samuel Tucker grew up two blocks from the Barrett Branch. He graduated form Howard University and was preparing for a career in law. He passed Virginia's bar exam at twenty. Due to his age, would have to wait an additional year to be sworn in to practice law. Tucker had attempted for several years to establish equal access to that library and other community services.

During the summer of 1939, Tucker, now 26, launched a coordinated act of civil disobedience. He selected a group of men, ranging in age from 18 to 22 years, to challenge the existing statute.

On August 21, library staff and patrons observed a young well-dressed black man enter the premises and ask to register for a library card. When he was refused, he picked up a book, took a seat, and commenced to read a book. Minutes later, five additional companions repeated his action and sat at separate tables in silence reading.

The library staff telephoned the police department with

officers arriving to escort the men from the library. Tucker had arranged for a photographer to capture the procession. The six were arrested and charged with *disorderly conduct*. Tucker promptly arranged for their release.

Tucker planned to legally challenge the city in court on the grounds that all citizens were entitled to equal access to public services. The national media primarily ignored the incident, but the African American press continued to run the story across the country.

In 1940, Alexandria community leaders attempted to broker a compromise. They allocated funds and approved the construction of the Robert H. Robinson Library. They hired a black librarian to operate under the *separate but equal* premise.

Tucker found the compromise infuriating. Unable to lead the lawsuit as he had developed a serious illness, he fumed publicly over the insult. Upon his recovery, he became an influential voice and lead lawyer for the NAACP in Virginia. He would appear in cases before the Supreme Court on four occasions while establishing a prominent Richmond law firm.

He died in 1990, but a decade later, Alexandria dedicated its newest elementary school in his honor.

TWISTED TOUR GUIDES.com

A Presidential Legacy Doomed By His Predecessor
Former Gerald Ford Residence:
514 Crown View Drive, Alexandria

In 1948 when Gerald Ford was elected to the House of Representatives, he considered his commitment long-term. He married his wife Betty the same year. Following the birth of their first child in 1950, the Fords moved into a garden apartment in the Virginia suburbs. Two years later they purchased a home in the new Clover subdivision within Alexandria. They would simultaneously maintain a residence in Grand Rapids, Michigan. The resignation of then Vice-President Spiro Agnew during the autumn of 1973 would profoundly alter his legacy.

Ford was born in Omaha, Nebraska in 1913 and relocated to Grand Rapids two years later when his parents divorced. His stepfather would adopt him. He attended local schools and worked his way through the University of Michigan playing on their 1932 and 1933 championship football team. He was named the team's *Most Valuable Player* during 1934.

He opted against playing professional football, still in its infancy and financially uncertain. He enrolled in the Yale Law School. He graduated in the top third of his class during 1941 while also coaching football and boxing. During World War II, he served on an aircraft carrier in the Pacific.

Post-war, he returned to his Grand Rapids law practice and became active in community affairs. He was advised to run for Congress in 1948 against a Republican incumbent sharing isolationist views. Ford won an upset victory in the primary and easily swept the general election.

His congressional record was impressive. He handily won reelection for the next 25 years. For eight of those years, he served as the House minority leader. He was part of the controversial Warren Commission that investigated the assassination of President John Kennedy.

He emerged as the most credible replacement when Agnew resigned after pleading *no contest* to tax fraud. President Richard Nixon nominated Ford as Vice President. Both houses of Congress overwhelmingly confirmed Ford's appointment. Ford continued to reside in his Alexandria home, although the Secret Service installed a command post in the garage.

The original house was designed by Grand Rapids architect Viktors Purins. In 1955, it was only the second completed house on the block. The design featured a two-story brick and clapboard exterior with a main block and slightly projecting extension. The house featured seven rooms, two and a half bathrooms and a basement. A swimming pool was later added. Betty Ford was displeased by the developer's original landscaping. She completed much of the lawn and garden work herself.

Ford's tenure as Vice-President became abbreviated. Nixon had handily won the 1972 Presidential election, but the victory was clouded by the encroaching shadow of the Watergate Scandal. The certain threat of impeachment prompted Nixon to resign in late summer 1974. On August 9, 1974, Gerald Ford became president. The Fords remained in their Alexandria residence for ten days following Nixon's resignation enabling him time to move out of the White House.

One of Ford's initial actions was to grant Nixon a full presidential pardon. Controversy has lingered as to whether this was an agreed upon condition in originally nominating Ford as Vice President.

The pardon effectively doomed Ford's tenure as president. He was obliged to govern with the Democratic Party controlling both houses of Congress. Ford was stymied in passing legislation to address growing economic inflation and the onset of recession. In foreign affairs, he struggled, as did his predecessors with establishing peaceful coexistence in the Middle East. Dealing with the Soviet Union and negotiating restrictions on nuclear weapons became his greatest achievements. They proved insufficient for securing an additional term.

He won the Republican nomination for president in 1976, but lost to Democrat Jimmy Carter in a close election. The following year, the Fords would relocate to a new residence that they'd constructed in Rancho Mirage, California. He continued a modest public exposure role and published his memoirs in 1979. He died on December 26, 2006 in Rancho Mirage and would be buried on the grounds of the museum that honors him in Grand Rapids.

George Washington Slept Here While On Business or Play
George Washington Town House Site:
508 Cameron Street, Alexandria

Wedged into the midst of northern Old Town, a replica of George Washington's original townhouse settles in comfortably. Washington used the house as an office before the Revolution and for brief stays when he had business to conduct or social activities to attend in Alexandria.

The building is a compact three levels with each floor approximately 600 square feet. The entirety of the structure includes two bedrooms on the top level, a living and dining room on the second level, and family room in the basement. The property features a rear courtyard and stable that later was converted into a large storage shed.

The townhouse would be the sole land parcel he gave exclusively to his wife Martha in his will. She left the house as an inheritance to her nephew. The original house deteriorated significantly before its demolition in 1855.

In 1960, Virginia Governor Richard Lowe authorized a reconstruction based on drawings done by a former neighbor. During the 1990s, drummer Mick Fleetwood, patriarch of the rock band Fleetwood Mac operated *Fleetwood's*, a blues club and restaurant inside.

A Spy Plane Shot Down Over Russia Triggers An International Incident
Interrogation Site of Pilot Gary Powers:
Hunting Towers CIA Safe House (Currently Bridgeyard Apartments)
1204 S Washington Street, Alexandria

On May Day (May 1), 1960 American pilot Francis Gary Powers was shot down while flying his U-2 spycraft over Soviet Union airspace. The timing proved inopportune as American President Dwight Eisenhower and Soviet Premier Nikita Khrushchev were nearing a scheduled summit meeting to be held in Paris.

Their agenda involved discussing the contentious stalemate in a divided Germany and the possibility of an arms control and/or test ban treaty. The session between the two leaders was an attempt to relax tensions between the two nations.

Spying between the United States and the Soviet Union was an acknowledged reality. During postwar 1955, officials in both Moscow and Washington D.C. had become increasingly concerned regarding the nuclear capacity of each countries and potential threat to global stability. Eisenhower proposed an *open skies* policy in which each country would be permitted to make flights over the other to conduct mutual aerial inspections of nuclear facilities and launchpads.

Khrushchev refused the proposal. He boasted that the Soviet Union had developed numerous intercontinental ballistic missiles. Concern over clarifying bluff versus fact, the US spy plane project was developed and coordinated by the Central Intelligence Agency (CIA). Spy planes flew at heights up to 70,000 feet, perceived then to be above the capacity of Soviet radar. Satellite imagery would later make any barrier obsolete. The initial flights over Moscow and Leningrad (now St. Petersburg) originated on July 4, 1956.

For four years, the flights continued intermittently over Russia. Soviet radar was able to monitor the planes, but their aircraft and limited range missiles unable to shoot them down. Reportedly the United States did lose a plane during 1959, but there was no confirmation by either country. As the Russian military was aware of the flights and purpose, they awaited an opportunity to substantiate their suspicions. The U-2 plane was equipped with a state-of-the-art camera designed to take high-resolution photos from the stratosphere over hostile countries. The missions systematically photographed military installations and other critical sites.

The hoped-for Soviet opportunity occurred the following year when Powers departed from a military base in Pakistan en route to landing in Norway. The flight plan necessitated flying over 2,900 miles of Soviet airspace. Near the city of Sverdlovsk Oblast in the Ural Mountains, Powers' plane was shot down by a surface-to-air missile. Fourteen had been fired in his direction. He was able to eject himself from his plane, but unable to detonate the craft. He parachuted safely to the ground and was apprehended shortly after landing.

He was captured and interrogated by the Russian KGB. The aircraft crashed, but much of it remained partially intact. Images of the recovered plane were broadcast on Soviet television. This confirmed evidence proved American *deceit* and disrespect for Soviet acknowledged airspace. The violation could have been construed as an act of war, but neither country was adequately prepared for military conflict.

The CIA and United States military had been blatantly caught in the act of spying. Despite initial claims of conducting a routine experimental weather flight, the evidence against this excuse proved overwhelming. Ten days later following the crash, Eisenhower publicly acknowledged the espionage program and specifically Powers' flight. He refused to apologize, rationalizing publicly that spy planes were a necessary element in maintaining national defense. He cited the lack of an *open skies* agreement justifying their use and maintained that he planned to continue employing them.

Khrushchev demanded an American apology for past intrusions and a promise to discontinue future flights as a condition to conducting the Paris Summit. Knowing Eisenhower had no intention of consenting, he withdrew his delegation. He ceased attempting to negotiate with Eisenhower.

Khrushchev reasoned that Eisenhower's presidential term was concluding. He sensed that his negotiations would fare better against a lesser-experienced statesman in president-elect John F. Kennedy. He presumed that his aggressive negotiating tactics would intimidate Kennedy enabling preferable results for the Soviet Union's interests.

His instincts would ultimately become mistaken when Kennedy held resolute during the later Cuban missile crisis staged during October 16-29, 1962. The crisis would edge the world towards the precipice of a disastrous nuclear war against Russia. American military generals strongly advocated bombing Cuba to destroy military bases under construction. Retaliation by Russia would have been a likely response. Kennedy's calm and measured response and decision to compromise prevented a wider escalation.

Gary Powers would be tried and convicted of espionage in a Soviet court. He was sentenced to three years in prison plus seven more within a labor camp. During his interrogations, he acknowledged the allegations against him and publicly apologized for his actions. Many within the American media viewed his admission as cowardice. He attempted to limit any information that he shared with the KGB. The intact aircraft remains made such evasiveness nearly pointless.

He was held in Vladimir Central Prison, located 150 miles east of Moscow. He kept a diary and learned carpet weaving from his cellmate, a Latvian political prisoner. He developed a good rapport with other Soviet prisoners during his internment.

In February 1962, he and a detained American student were traded for Rudolf Abel, a Soviet spy convicted in the United States during 1957 and condemned to thirty years in prison. On February 10, 1962, the exchange took place on the Glienicke Bridge that linked West Berlin with Potsdam. The bridge would become famous during the Cold War as the *Bridge of Spies*. A 2015 film with the same name directed by Steven Spielberg recreated their exchange.

Abel's release would be exploited as a propaganda tool by Russian authorities asserting his espionage proficiency and elusiveness as a Master Spy. Upon his return to the Soviet Union, he was employed by the KGB to give speeches and lectures to school children on intelligence work. He reportedly became disillusioned with the Soviet system before dying of lung cancer on November 15, 1971.

The CIA was adamantly opposed to the exchange. Within their ranks, some suspected Powers of deliberately defecting to Russia. They considered Abel a significantly more valuable asset to the Soviet Union than Powers to America. Kennedy would ultimately approve the trade. Powers credited his father with initially proposing the swap idea.

During his imprisonment, Power's wife Barbara began a downward spiral fueled by alcohol, drug abuse and rampant infidelity. Her behavior contradicted the CIA portrayal of her as a devoted wife. To avert further embarrassing publicity, the CIA committed her to a psychiatric ward in Augusta, Georgia. She was eventually released to the care of her mother.

Powers returned to a hostile American intelligence community upon his release. He was criticized for not activating his aircraft's self-destruct charge that would have destroyed the camera, film and related equipment. He was severely criticized for not swallowing a CIA-issued suicide pill inserted within a silver dollar medallion hanging around his neck. He addressed these charges by claiming that he was convinced he could escape. He cited the tailspin of the aircraft during descent made activating the destruct switches impossible.

Within the Hunting Towers Apartments in Alexandria, the CIA debriefed him extensively. Afterwards, he was publicly exonerated for his behavior during captivity. In March 1962, he appeared before a Senate Armed Services Select Committee hearing. Once again, he was publicly praised for his conduct under stressful conditions. Despite a lingering cloud of suspicion that he may have betrayed important intelligence information, in 1964 CIA Director Allen Dulles lavishly lauded his behavior. Whether sincere or to reassure the public, few acknowledged Powers as heroic.

Returning to his homelife, he promptly sued his wife for divorce in August 1962. He cited her erratic behavior, domestic violence, infidelity and alcoholism as his grounds. Slightly over a year later, he remarried and would later have two children.

He worked for Lockheed as a test pilot from 1962 until 1970. He wrote a book *Operation Overflight* with co-author Curt Gentry in 1970 that resulted in his firing. He shifted careers becoming a traffic reporting airplane pilot for a Los Angeles radio station and then a helicopter news reporter for KNBC television.

On August 1, 1977, he was piloting a news helicopter covering a series of brush fires within Santa Barbara County. His helicopter was heading back towards the Burbank Airport when abruptly he ran out of fuel. A faulty fuel gage had recently been repaired but Powers misread the display. He crashed into the Sepulveda Dam recreational area several miles short of his projected landing site.

The explosion killed Powers at the age of 47 and cameraman George Spears. Although he was credited with altering his emergency landing site after viewing children playing in the area, he would be cited for pilot error in the crash. He is buried in Arlington National Cemetery.

A Supreme Court Landmark Decision Reaffirming The Right To Marry Freely
Law Offices of Bernard S. Cohen and Philip Hirschkop:
110 N. Royal Street, Alexandria
Virginia Appellate Court Building (Patrick Henry Building):
1111 East Broad Street, Richmond

Mildred Jeter and Richard Loving were raised in the small community of Central Point, Virginia. During the 1960s, Caroline County where they resided adhered to Virginia's Jim Crow segregation laws. Their town had been a mixed-race integrated community dating back from the 19th century.

Richard Loving's grandfather fought for the Confederacy during the Civil War. Richard's father worked for one of the wealthiest black men in the county for 25 years. Richard's closest companions were black, particularly those that he drag-raced with including Mildred Jeter's older brothers. In such a small town environment, integration evolved organically into the social fabric. Following high school, he became a local construction worker.

In 1924, Virginia passed the Racial Integrity Act, requiring all residents to be classified as ethically *white* or *colored*. Richard was of European American decent and classified as *white*. Mildred was a combination of African American, Portuguese and Cherokee and designated as *colored*.

The couple first met when Mildred was 11 and Richard 17. In high school, they began dating. When Mildred was 18, she became pregnant and Richard moved into the Jeter household. They married in Washington D.C. in June 1958. Their marriage was considered illegal in Virginia.

Following their ceremony, they returned to Central Point. They were arrested one evening by the county sheriff acting upon an anonymous tip. They were charged with *cohabiting as man and wife, against the peace and dignity of the Commonwealth*. At their trial on January 6, 1959, they pled guilty and were sentenced to one year in prison. The term was suspended predicated on their voluntarily leaving the state.

They relocated to Washington D.C., but suffered from social isolation and financial difficulties. In 1964, a car on one of the busy urban streets struck their youngest son. They were determined to return back to their hometown. Mildred penned a letter to Attorney General Robert Kennedy requesting the judgment against them in Virginia be lifted.

Kennedy referred her correspondence to the American Civil Liberties Union. The organization filed a motion on the Loving's behalf citing the ruling against them violated the Fourteenth Amendment of the Constitution. They began a series of lawsuits that ultimately would reach the United States Supreme Court.

The Virginia Supreme Court of Appeals initially ruled against them and affirmed the criminal convictions. The Loving's attorney, Bernard S. Cohen and the ACLU appealed their decision to the United States Supreme Court. Richard Loving's statement to the court proved impacting. He wrote: *I love my wife, and it is just unfair that I can't live with her in Virginia.*

Their Supreme Court Case, *Loving vs. Virginia*, was decided unanimously in their favor on June 12, 1967. The decision overturned their conviction, dismissing the state of

Virginia's argument that the statute applied equally and provided identical penalties for both white and black persons.

Following the decision, the Lovings returned back to Central Point. Richard built the family a house and they resided discreetly and without ceremony until each of their respective deaths. Neither considered themselves as activists. Richard would be killed at 41 when a drunk driver struck their family car in June 1975. Mildred lost her right eye. She would die of pneumonia at the age of 68 in May 2008.

The couple never viewed their actions as extraordinary. Their courage to challenge an unfair and prejudicial statute however has impacted millions of multi-racial couples that have simply wished to marry the spouse of their choice without legal interference.

VIRGINIA APPELLATE COURT BUILDING

TWISTED TOUR GUIDES.com

A Tainted Murder Site Scorched By A Concealing Fire
Donita Cutts Murder Site:
125 Wolfe Street, Alexandria

Shortly after midnight on Saturday, July 29, 1978, Donita Cutts, 38, returned home alone. She mounted the stairs to her second-floor bedroom and flicked on the lighting. She turned down her bedspread and then undressed leaving her clothing on the seat of a rocking chair. She then put on her nightgown and turned on the television set selecting a channel specializing in all-night movies. She strolled to the bathroom to wash herself.

Sometime within the next six hours, an intruder would confront her. The individual had either managed to slip into the house undetected or was already awaiting her return. Based on evidence at the crime scene, it was probable that she knew her uninvited guest.

By early morning, her body would be discovered in a four-foot-wide crawl space in her basement. She had earlier been struck on the head with an antique lamp and knocked unconscious. The intruder lighted seven separate fires within the house before exiting intending to destroy evidence.

Cutts had been bound hand and foot by an odd assemblage of masking tape, electrical cord, and clothing. She was left for dead inside a cedar closet with the cellar door barricaded. As the house lit up, she managed to free one foot. She attempted to escape as the effects of the flames and smoke intensified.

She discovered that the staircase was blocked. Feverously, she altered her escape route towards a diminutive basement window. She crawled within ten feet before losing consciousness. Her death was attributed to smoke asphyxiation.

Fire trucks arrived at 5:30 a.m. in pitch darkness presuming that no one was home. The fire fighters may have compromised murder evidence with their efforts to douse the flames. They were unprepared for approaching an awaiting murder scene. Cutts' body would not be discovered until an hour after the fire was extinguished.

Donita Cutts traced her ancestry to the American icon Dolley Madison, attended college in Switzerland and was raised on her family's 200-acre estate in The Plains, Virginia. She had purchased her house two years earlier and spent lavishly redecorating and stocking the interior with antiques.

She was a popular society figure with numerous acknowledged friends that she entertained at her home frequently. She was a broker at the Goddin Real Estate agency. Several of her friends and acquaintances suspected and reported the identity of her killer.

The suspect was interrogated by police, but never charged due to a lack of physical evidence. He was a former mental patient who lived only a few miles from her residence. He would never be publicly identified or completely eliminated as a suspect. An FBI psychological profile of Cutts' killer concluded *in all probability the killer was mentally ill.*

The investigation consumed more collective interviews, police hours, polygraph tests and travel expenses than any precedent. Leads were exhaustively pursued. Investigators found nothing missing from inside the house and her valuable jewelry remained intact inside a secret compartment beneath the main staircase. No windows had been broken, no spare keys were missing and Cutts had not been sexually assaulted. There was no evidence that she fought with her attacker.

The failure of the search and critical scrutiny prompted the principle homicide detective, Joseph Soos to resign from the police force in November 1978. He publicly expressed his outrage over the department's incompetent handling of one suspect and the lax crime scene control.

The house would remain vacant for 18 months as the fire damage was repaired. Acknowledging the notorious stigma, a buyer purchased the property in December 1979. Today the residence blends in seamlessly with the neighborhood. Donita Cutts' death is long forgotten and her killer literally got away with murder.

An Idiotic Afternoon Robbery and Pointless Murder
Murder Site: Brahm Opticians
113 North Washington Street, Alexandria

Carol Ann Dodd's store robbery and senseless shooting
death on August 28, 1980 epitomized a disturbing trend
facing Old Town merchants. Rampant drug trafficking
became the primary stimulus for a turbulent year of wasted
lives. The spillover throughout the metropolitan
Washington D. C. region in 1980 resulted in a reported 175
homicides.

Darryl Jinks, 25, entered Dodd's optical shop with
companion Gail Williams at approximately 2:00 pm. He
was anticipating an expedient and lucrative heist. Optical
enterprises rarely deal with cash. Then as now, the majority
of transactions are completed with checks and credit cards.
Online payment services today have supplanted the former.

Jinks netted less than $100. The money was destined for his
heroin addiction. Doubtlessly irritated by the poor
proceeds, he callously gunned down Dodd fatally in the
back.

The idiocy accompanying Jinks' actions made his
apprehension elemental. He was already on parole in New
Jersey while committing this and additional crimes. A few
days following the murder, police followed up on a tip
regarding the identity of the perpetrators. They arrested
Jinks inside the Fairfax County Jail. He was being detained
on another unrelated robbery charge. He would eventually
be tied to seven regional armed robberies. His companion
Gail Williams was arrested at her Alexandria home.

Three weeks before her killing, Dodd's store had been
burglarized. Afterwards, she installed a security system

inside both of her local outlets. She was a native Alexandrian who lived with her parents in the community's Del Ray section.

The trial during January 1981 was brief. Williams testified against Jinks. He pled guilty to first-degree murder. He was sentenced to life in prison. She also pled guilty to first-degree murder and received a 20-year sentence, plus five-years for robbery. Her term would be reduced ten years due to her cooperation with the prosecution.

Life imprisonment would become a relative term for Jinks. He would undergo a reported eight six-month long therapeutic drug recovery programs while in prison. He would be incarcerated within the Virginia penal system for thirty-four years. He was lauded as being an exemplary prisoner. He was granted parole on January 6, 2014, but his eventual freedom would become entangled and delayed by his previous missteps.

His 1980 crime spree had violated the terms of his then New Jersey probation. He would be transferred back and ordered to serve an additional 56 months of incarceration. He appealed the decision in 2016, but lost.

Jinks is no longer listed on either the New Jersey or Virginia inmate databases. He may or may not be still living. Carol Ann Dodd's optical shop is still operating as Brahm and Powell Guild Opticians under different ownership within Old Town.

BRAHM & POWELL GUILD OPTICIANS
Polaroid

Glacial Justice For A Violent Defilement and Shooting Constance Mellon Murder Site:
406 S. Royal Street, Alexandria

During the autumn of 1980, Constance Mellon, 36, relocated to Alexandria from New York to begin a position with Time-Life Books. She had chosen a fashionable residence in the Old Town district and was still in the process of unpacking boxes a few weeks following her move.

On October 3, 1980, her relocation and life ceased abruptly. Four days later, her lifeless body would be discovered. She had been bound, raped and shot fatally in the head. For nearly a year, the murder appeared to have neither motive nor suspect.

In August 1981, ballistic tests revealed that the weapon used to kill Pittsburgh shoe store clerk, Robert Walker was identical to the gun that shot Mellon. The perpetrator of Walker's October 2nd murder was identified by Pittsburgh police as *drifter* Frank Weston.

He had tied up Walker in the shoe store basement and shot him in the head after robbing the store. As he lay dying, Weston walked upstairs and sold a pair of shoes to a nurse who'd had just entered the store. After being apprehended and in custody, he confessed to the Mellon murder.

Expedient justice for Mellon would be delayed.

For four years, Weston would languish in an Allegheny County jail cell awaiting sentencing following a bench trial held without a jury. Weston's sole offered defense at his murder trial was that he'd been drinking at the time of the store robbery and *not in control of his actions*. Court of Common Pleas Judge Henry R. Smith Jr. found Weston guilty of first-degree murder. Smith then became the impediment for the extended delay in sentencing.

Despite a guilty verdict, Smith determined that a jury needed to be impaneled to determine whether Weston should be sentenced to life imprisonment or receive the death penalty. Smith refused to sentence Weston. The Pennsylvania Supreme Court overruled him in September 1983 and ordered him to sentence Weston.

The Pittsburgh homicide detective who arrested and recorded Weston's initial confession publicly criticized Smith blaming him for *indecisiveness*. Smith rationalized the delay based on his excessive workload. He blamed the deferment of Weston's sentencing on his original counsel who he declared *incompetent*. That lawyer had since disappeared and Smith issued a bench warrant for his arrest.

Pittsburgh prosecutors indicated that Weston would not be extradited to Virginia until his sentencing was completed. The mounting delay provoked extreme frustration, irritation and outrage amongst the Virginia judicial community and Mellon's family.

In April 1985, Judge Smith finally sentenced Weston to life in prison. Alexandria authorities immediately extradited him to stand trial for Mellon's murder. His November 22nd trial lasted only fifteen minutes. Half of the duration was consumed by a seven-minute incoherent monologue by Weston. He repeatedly asked forgiveness speaking at length about the evil and darkness that his life had descended into. His attempt at cleansing his conscience influenced none of the court attendees or altered his prearranged plea bargain agreement.

Once Weston concluded, he was sentenced to three consecutive life sentences for murder, rape and robbery. Frank Weston is currently 69-years-old and listed on both the Pennsylvania and Virginia Inmate databases. Pennsylvania has him interned at Somerset Prison and Virginia the HQ-Detainer Unit. Theoretically, he will never be released or experience the freedom that he denied Constance Mellon.

Unsolved Break-In and Vicious Stabbing in Affluent Old Town
Elliott and Lewinski Murder Site: (Virginia Civil War State House):
413 Prince Street, Alexandria

Elizabeth Elliott, 68, settled comfortably into Alexandria from her origins in North Carolina. Through her shrewd business and real estate acumen, she acquired several local historic houses. In 1984, she was sharing an Old Town residence with Karl von Lewinski, 71, formerly known as the *State House*. Throughout the Union occupation of Alexandria during the Civil War, the property was used as the Virginia State Capitol and governor's mansion. The building had been originally constructed in 1805 and employed as one of the community's first banks.

Elliott and von Lewinski had lived in an apartment at the rear of the building for nearly twenty years together. He was the son of a German diplomat and had formerly worked as a reporter in Washington D.C. for several years.

On February 10, 1984 at 9:00 p.m., the couple was found slain by her brother Robert after being contacted by a concerned building tenant. Elliott's clothed body was found on the floor of the bedroom and Lewinski's body on the living-room floor. Both had been stabbed to death repeatedly and viciously in the chest.

Police estimated that the murder occurred the evening before shortly after 8:00 p.m. There were signs of a struggle and Elliott's real estate files were ransacked. There was no overt evidence of a forced break-in, but investigators theorized that the deadly confrontation was prompted by a botched burglary.

The neighborhood is renowned for numerous historic Federal and Greek Revival style townhouses. The residential base then and now is affluent and generally professional. Such a tranquil enclave would appear on initial viewing the unlikely site for violent homicide. Criminality no longer respects decorum. Following the shock accompanying the public announcement of the murder, the case would remain cold. A suspect has still never been apprehended.

A Drug Debt Retrieval Resulting In Three Lost Lives
Murder Site Of Policeman Charles William Hall:
316 Hopkins Court, Alexandria
Memorial Plaque: Waterfront Park, Alexandria

A severed life immortalized upon a Waterfront Park podium is a nearly forgotten remembrance for police officer Charles William Hall. His death became a tragic testament to the crack cocaine epidemic that raged throughout the metro Washington D.C. region during the late 1980s and early 1990s. Obscured amidst park foliage on a stone raised pedestal, a bronze memorial plaque eulogizes Hall's sacrifice to the community and his decency as an individual and family man. The inscription fails to articulate the background details behind his death and later his partner's.

A New York City based PCP user and drug dealer named Jamie Martin Wise traveled into Alexandria on March 22, 1989 to collect a $1,100 client debt. The transaction went sour inside the confines of the Berg public housing complex. Wise barricaded himself within an apartment taking Eddie Jackson hostage. The Alexandria SWAT team was mobilized into a hostage standoff unit. Corporal Charles William Hall and partner Andrew Chelchowski were part of the arriving contingent.

Wise exited the residence with a sawed-off shotgun pointed at Jackson's head. A police sniper with a clear sighting fired a single shot at Wise striking him in the heart and ultimately killing him. The shot did not immediately incapacitate him, as he was able to open fire twice striking Hill mortally and wounding Chelchowski in the legs.

Hill would die from his injury following his admittance to the Washington Hospital Center. He was a native of Long Island, New York and a 13-year veteran with the

Alexandria Police force. He originally began his career with the New York City Police Department.

His death at the age of 40 would leave behind a wife and two sons. He would be posthumously honored with a park named after him in the Del Ray neighborhood. Chelchowski became the forgotten survivor. Four years later, he would commit suicide after battling trauma and severe depression. At that stage in local history, eighteen Alexandria police officers had lost their lives in the line of duty.

The killing became a prelude to a subsequent 13-count indictment filed against four Brooklyn, New York defendants. They were charged with conspiring to sell crack cocaine along with committing violent crimes in a drug racketeering enterprise.

Hall's fate mirrored the risk that law enforcement agents still face daily. During every professional shift, a tangible target is affixed to their bodies. Officers are acutely aware of the peril accompanying their profession.

Hall's murder epitomized the mayhem that the crack cocaine epidemic clouded upon suburban Alexandria. The year before, local high school football star Tracy Fells was arrested for possession and intent to distribute crack cocaine. The story made national headlines because Fells was the co-captain and defensive end for the T.C. Williams High School football Titans. He led the team to a state AAA football championship during 1987.

T.C. Williams High would be the identical school immortalized in the 2000 film *Remember The Titans*, starring actors Denzel Washington and Ryan Gosling. The screenplay written by Gregory Howard portrayed the 1971 football squad and their struggles with racial integration within their team composition and coaching staff.

The feel-good theme of social harmony portrayed in the film had long ago dissipated within sectors of the community. The reality framing the Titan football squad sixteen years later was far grimmer.

Fells, along with his brothers, orchestrated a violent drug ring concentrated around the local Charles Houston Recreation Center. He had been offered a football scholarship to Grambling State University following high school, but preferred the lucrative returns from his drug enterprise. He would be convicted during 1989 of cocaine distribution and sentenced to twenty years of federal imprisonment. His football career terminated within the prison system flag football leagues.

A National Trail of Tears Originating From Mount Vernon
The Purple Heart Trail
George Washington Parkway and Mount Vernon Highway, Alexandria

The Military Order of the Purple Heart originally established the Purple Heart Trail in 1992. The decoration is awarded in the name of the President to those who have been wounded or killed while serving in the American armed forces. Eligibility for a Purple Heart applies to service members who have suffered a wound: 1) As a direct or indirect result of enemy action and 2) A wound that required treatment by a medical officer at the time of the injury.

The genesis behind the trail originated from a member of a Virginia based chapter. The emphasis was to create a symbolic and honorary system of roads, highways, bridges, and other monuments offering tribute via visual reminders of those individuals who've sacrificed to preserve a free society. The format and design of the signage vary from state to state. Currently forty-five states share designated sectors plus Guam. The fitting origin point is an installed monument in Mt. Vernon near the burial site of George Washington.

ORIGIN OF
THE PURPLE HEART TRAIL
MOUNT VERNON
VIRGINIA
OF THE U.S.A.
DEDICATED THIS 7TH DAY OF AUGUST 1996
BY THE
MILITARY ORDER OF THE PURPLE HEART
AND THE LADIES OF THEIR AUXILIARY

A Publicly Recognized Serial Killer and Failed Political Candidate
Murder Sites:
Ruthanne Lodato
2419 Ridge Road Drive, Alexandria
Dr. Ron Kirby
204 Elm Street, Alexandria
Nancy Dunning
214 West Mount Ida Avenue, Alexandria

Charles Severance rationalized murder via abstract motives and/or simply mental illness. When he was offered the opportunity to speak before his courtroom sentencing, he rambled passages from the *Book of Common Prayer*, *Henry VIII*, *Elizabeth* and the 37th article of religion. He concluded his detached soliloquy by announcing *It is lawful to wear weapons*.

For his three victim's families, friends and acquaintances that he tragically impacted, his ramblings resembled the scattered incoherence of a lunatic. His imposed nightmare to others could not be condoned by society nor explained by the perpetrator.

Severance's defense attorney, Bryan Porter likewise lacked an ability to articulate motive or explanation. He traced the senseless killings to *anger, hatred and a proclivity towards violence*. His unenviable task was to defend indefensible acts. Severance had requested to have him removed as his counsel. Before reciting his demand, he had entered the courtroom in a wheelchair. He leaned into a microphone and began mumbling *sadism, sadism*.

Over the course of a decade, Severance would murder three complete strangers. Prosecutors cited motive as his bitterness over a child-custody decision compounded by his hatred towards Alexandria's elite. Each of the dead was murdered in senseless daylight attacks at their homes.

Before his killing spree, Severance attempted to penetrate into mainstream Alexandria society and even national politics. He was soundly repelled.

In 1996, Severance ran for Alexandria's mayoral position in a special election. As a fringe candidate, he earned over 8% of the popular vote. He followed that candidacy the same year with a run for Congress in Virginia's 8th congressional district. He ran on the Independent Party platform garnering significantly less than 1% of the vote. His two sound defeats still prompted him to run for mayor once again in 2000. This time, he earned barely 2% of the vote. His political prospects were finished and any novelty he once attracted had become soundly discarded.

His campaign appearances and speeches were consistently erratic. He dressed entirely in black wearing a cloak and sunglasses. He periodically displayed flashes of impulsive violence. During his congressional run, he picked up an American flag and pointed the spiked end at incumbent Jim Moran before dashing out of the building. During his second mayor campaign, he punched one of the organizers.

His initial murder occurred on December 5, 2003 when he shot to death real estate agent Nancy Dunning. She answered her front door following his knock. Ten years elapsed before he killed Dr. Ron Kirby at his home on November 11, 2013. His final murder in February 2014 targeted music teacher Ruthanne Lodato. Severance was living in Park Fairfax, on the outskirts of the neighborhood where his three victims resided.

Following his detainment, police investigators discovered disturbing Severance writings. In one, he had penned: *Knock. Talk. Enter. Kill. Exit. Murder.* Each shooting was done with an identical brand of .22 caliber firearm loaded with low caliber bullets. The guns were never recovered. The pistol used to kill Dunning was probably destroyed by a court order in 2006 after he was found guilty of carrying a concealed weapon.

His subsequent trial and guilty verdict resulted in three terms of life imprisonment. He is currently incarcerated at the Greensville Correctional Center following an earlier stint at Wallens Ridge State Prison.

DR. RON KIRBY

NANCY DUNNING

**A Contract Killing Concluding A Clouded Past
Betty Ayele Murder Site:
Intersection of Commonwealth and Mount Vernon
Avenues, Alexandria**

Bethlehem *Betty* Ayele had a focused strategy for success. She had miraculously reached the age of 34. This benchmark followed years of trafficking cocaine and establishing an extended connection with drug dealers. In 2000, she was arrested in Maryland with $19,000 and 9 kilos of cocaine in her possession. She was charged with conspiring to distribute cocaine and convicted in 2004. She was given only probation.

Her long-term plan involved testifying against six members of the Washington D.C. based gang known as *Murder Inc.* She exchanged a potential death sentence accompanying her role for leniency with her sentencing. She publicly avowed to distance herself from her past and expressed aspirations of operating a legitimate business.

She and her sisters opened the Ohio Restaurant located at the intersection of 14th and H Street in Washington D.C. The area then was a reputed vortex for drug activity. The taint of association trailed Ayele. Rumors spread that trafficking was part of her operations aiding in paying the spiraling expenses of the restaurant. The Ethiopian cuisine and soul food served had received promising reviews.

Murder Inc. did not obtain its moniker incidentally. They operated the most notorious enterprises plaguing the Capitol involving a ruthless gang of drug dealers and witness silencers. Their operation would ultimately become dismantled by federal and regional law enforcement agencies and their leaders imprisoned. Betty Ayele became unfinished retribution.

On October 25, 2006, she was driving through Alexandria's Del Ray neighborhood via Commonwealth Avenue nearing 10:15 p.m. She had no idea that her successive string of good fortune had elapsed. When she braked at the traffic light at the intersection of Mount Vernon Avenue, a gunman awaited her. He approached her vehicle and shot her at close range. Her car then traveled across the intersection before striking a utility pole on the northeast corner.

She would be ambulanced to Inova Alexandria Hospital and pronounced dead upon arrival. The targeted shooting was neither surprising nor difficult to comprehend. The shooter would never be identified or arrested. Her Ohio restaurant would be shuttered shortly following her murder. The nearly dilapidated location would be purchased in 2008 and later become gentrified and integrated into a maze of freshly constructed mid-rise office buildings.

A Buried Maritime Past Prompts Cargo Questioning
Hotel Indigo Excavation Site:
220 S. Union Street, Alexandria
Robinson Landing Excavation Site:
2 Duke Street, Alexandria

The construction site of the future Hotel Indigo offered intriguing evidence into Alexandria's formative history. Anticipated archaeological remains were excavated. The most prominent included a seventy-foot ship hull along with the remnants of a 1755 public warehouse owned by town patriarch John Carlyle. A research team excavated the site extensively during 2015-2017.

The findings reconfirmed the evolution of the town's natural shoreline reconfiguration. In 1749 when Alexandria was originally founded, the southwestern half of the Hotel Indigo land was perched atop a bluff overlooking a cove of the Potomac River.

During that era of unregulated development, waterfront property owners had an enticing incentive for knocking down seaside bluffs and leveling the terrain. They were allowed to legally retain title for any fresh land that they created in front of their own parcels. Owners then constructed commercial wharves reaching out to the channel. This process was known as *banking out*. The pristine natural topography would be completely filled in by the conclusion of the 18th century leaving a landfill extended shoreline.

Old ship hulls were periodically buried amidst the fill enabling and reinforcing the wharf framework. During the late 18th and early 19th centuries, industries such as iron foundries, grocers, coopers, carpenters, blacksmiths and merchants established operations on the wharfs.

Throughout the Civil War, the Union Army secured the future Hotel Indigo grounds and constructed a hay shed, grain and commissary storehouse. In the 1890s, the entire property was purchased and converted into a fertilizer company.

Historical artifacts become entrenched strata. Following decades and centuries, fresh development requiring digging raises history to the surface. The Hotel Indigo excavation was followed by another prompting additional findings.

During 2017-2018, archaeologists concentrated their efforts on a Robinson Terminal South construction site. They unearthed the remains of three 18th century shipping hulls accompanied by the foundations of a similar era warehouse and 19th century pioneer mill.

The largest shipping vessel was measured at 102 feet in length. The two additional were a mid-size 62-foot and 49-foot landing vessel. Researchers from the Conservation Research Laboratory at Texas A & M University coordinated efforts with the Alexandria archaeology staff. They documented, laser scanned and reconstructed the three ships employing computer models and 3D printing.

The Robinson Terminal site would ultimately evolve into the expansive *Robinson Landing* development featuring commercial and residential mid-rise structures.

The recovered four ships have since been documented as cargo merchant vessels. Their discovery has stimulated further questioning regarding their employed cargos. During the Colonial era, there existed widely acknowledged triangular shipping routes. The routes involved trade between the American colonies, Europe and the Caribbean. Slave transfers were commonly part of the hypotenuse across the Atlantic Ocean.

Raw goods such as tobacco and wheat were commonly exported from Alexandria. Sugar was imported from the Caribbean and finished goods from Europe. Were any of these discovered hulls from slave transfer ships?

Until the identity of each ship and their registered logistics are officially confirmed, it is impossible to document their specific cargo. Over time and continued investigative research, these questions will likely become resolved.

ROBINSON CENTER SITE

A Congressional Baseball Practice Tainted By Gunfire
Eugene Simpson Stadium Park Field:
426 E. Monroe Avenue, Alexandria

In March 2017, James Thomas Hodgkinson began an unraveling process. His Bellevue, Illinois neighbor telephoned police to complain that the 66-year-old was indiscriminately firing a rifle at trees within their neighborhood. The responding officers checked Hodgkinson's gun permit, cautioned him, but did not arrest him. Over the previous two decades, sheriff deputies had been called an estimated half dozen times to his residence. In 2006, he had been accused of beating his foster daughter. She refused to testify and the case was dismissed.

Hodgkinson may have dodged domestic accountability, but he couldn't sustain the adhesive that glued his existence and perspective intact. He had formally operated a local home inspection business, but had allowed his license to expire.

He left Bellevue, began living in his van and relocated to Alexandria in early May 2017. He frequently parked near the YMCA where he used their shower facilities for hygiene. The YMCA was located across the street from the local Eugene Simpson Stadium baseball field.

His marriage of 30 years was disintegrating. He was low on finances and vainly seeking employment. His increasingly desperate circumstances reflect a growing demographic segment of the chronically unemployable. There is no political party or competent social services capable of espousing or eradicating their plight. They recede into the topography financially destitute, unnoticed and flailing in untethered desperation. They once patiently followed society's rules and expectations. One day they concluded that their once comfortable existence was a vanishing mirage.

Hodgkinson remained politically active during his personal turmoil. He participated in the 2016 Bernie Sanders presidential campaign. He frequently submitted editorials to his local newspaper, posted his opinions on social media and maintained periodic contact with Republican Congressman Mike Bost's district office, which represented Bellevue.

He became enraged and increasingly disillusioned upon the presidential election of Donald Trump. He aggressively spiked his vernacular with accusations of Trump's treasonous and traitorous behavior. He refused to acknowledge him as President. He fiercely advocated the legal removal of Trump and Vice-President Mike Pence. He developed an intense loathing towards the Republican Party based on his perception of their *racist and sexist politics*.

Despite his visible public outrage, he simply remained an estranged, ignored and isolated figure, distant from any law enforcement radar. His public demeanor alarmed none of his associates or affiliated associations.

The perception towards James Thomas Hodgkinson changed radically on the early morning of June 14, 2017. Each year elected senators, congressmen and staff members set aside their ideological differences and participate in the Congressional Baseball Game For Charity. The event has been staged since 1909. Both partisan teams practiced at the Eugene Stadium Park in Alexandria.

Twenty-four Republican team members organized a 6:30 a.m. practice session that Wednesday morning. Hodgkinson approached a few team members including Congressman

Ron DeSantis before the start to inquire what team would be utilizing the facility. He had formulated a strategy to introduce himself into public consciousness. He was likely unaware that three U.S. Capitol Police officers were stationed at the practice. They were assigned to protect Congressman Steve Scalise, the House of Representatives Majority Leader. Each was positioned behind the first-base dugout.

Hodgkinson returned to the ballfield at 7:09 a.m. armed with an SKS rifle and 9 mm Smith & Wesson. He began firing the rifle immediately. He wounded six individuals. Scalise became his most prominent target or simply one of his unfortunate hits. The police presence prevented a certain massacre. Two of the officers, David Bailey and Crystal Griner rushed onto the playing field to protect the players and any civilian spectators. They directed their fire towards a fleeing Hodgkinson resulting in his stationing inside the third base dugout. Griner was shot in the ankle and Bailey sustained a minor injury unrelated to the gunfire.

The fusillade between Hodgkinson and the three officers would last ten minutes with an estimated 50-100 rounds exchanged. While being pinned down by gunfire, he was unable to target additional unarmed victims. He would be severely wounded and then transported to George Washington University Hospital where he died from his injuries.

Scalise was shot in the hip near second base and attempted to drag himself off the field. He was aided by some of his peers. He would be airlifted to MedStar Washington Hospital Center where he underwent immediate non-life threatening surgery. Tyson Foods lobbyist Matt Mika was the most critically wounded victim, being shot multiple times in the chest and arms. He was transferred by ambulance to George Washington University Hospital for emergency surgery. Both men would recover.

The charity game would take place as scheduled the following day at the Washington Nationals Park. The annual attendance normally attracted 10,000 spectators. Following the notoriety of the shooting, nearly 25,000 attended raising $1 million for charity. Injured officer David Bailey threw out the first pitch on crutches to a standing ovation. The Democratic team won 11-2, but ceded the trophy to the Republicans until Scalise completed his recovery.

The FBI would classify James Thomas Hodgkinson as a *domestic terrorist* and his actions as *extremist violence*. Following an abbreviated research of his past and potential motivations by media outlets, he returned to the ranks of the marginalized and forgotten. A cowardly assassin historically fails to cultivate a supportive following. His heinous action merely epitomized the consequences of a socially and politically polarized society.

YMCA PARKING LOT

FIRST BASE DUGOUT

HOME OF THE TITANS
EUGENE SIMPSON STADIUM
"Our youth is our future"
REP. STEVE SCALISE'S WOUNDING SPOT

THIRD BASE DUGOUT

TWISTED TOUR GUIDES.com

A Symbol of Defiance and Defeat Removed Amidst Changing Times
Former Appomattox Monument Location:
699 Prince Street, Alexandria
Relocated Statue Base (Bethel Cemetery):
1430 Wilkes Street, Alexandria

The Battle of Appomattox was waged between Union and Confederate armies on the morning of April 9, 1865. By afternoon, it became one of the final and defining conflicts of the Civil War. The battle was the last engagement for Confederate General-in-Chief Robert E. Lee and his army of Northern Virginia.

Fittingly, Lee surrendered to his principle antagonist Union Commander Ulysses S. Grant. The ceremonial ceasefire signing was conducted in the parlor of a house owned by Wilmer McLean that same April 9th afternoon. The decision averted certain substantial casualties. Three days later, Confederate Major General John B. Gordon led a formal surrender procession that featured the stacking of weaponry in front of Union Brigadier General Joshua Chamberlain. The act officially marked the disbandment of the Northern Virginia force.

The 28,000 Confederate soldiers and officers spared were allowed to freely return home with their horses. Soldiers were obliged to shed their armaments. Officers were allowed to maintain their pistols and swords. It was a somber conclusion to warfare that had radically divided a nation.

Virginia was impacted the most by the surrender. The Confederate capitol was based in Richmond. The Union army had occupied Alexandria throughout the war.

The defeat signified a definitive military humiliation for Lee. His forces had been obliged to abandon Richmond following the nine-and-a half month *Siege of Petersburg*. He had vainly hoped to regroup his military ranks by heading west. His tactical retreat was terminated at the central Virginia village of Appomattox.

Significantly outmanned and outgunned, he launched a failed attack attempting to breech the Union lines. For Grant, his victory was particularly gratifying. Detailed throughout his later autobiography, he frequently lamented the excessive credit that Lee had accumulated for his military tactics. He didn't join the chorus of admirers, citing Lee's numerous mistakes. Grant chafed under the criticism that he had personally endured for his own tactics. Appomattox defined each man's respective role in the Civil War's outcome as either *winner* or *loser*.

The Alexandria based Appomattox memorial sculpture became a perpetual traffic impediment.

Elevated atop a centered pedestal in the middle of the intersection of Prince Street and South Washington Street, a solitary bronze Confederate soldier towered over traffic affixed to a marble and concrete base. The solder was holding his hat as an apparent act of defiant submission. His arms were crossed and back faced to the north. Proponents of sculptor John Adams Elder's creation contested the positioning of the potentially viewed snub. They argued that the soldier was simply viewing the Appomattox battlefield in the distant southerly direction.

An expansive crowd attended the dedication ceremony on May 24, 1889. The United Confederate Veterans (UCV) commissioned the monument. They anticipated future controversy and lobbied for the statue to become protected by Virginia state law.

On the early morning of August 20, 1988, a van driver crashed into the installation toppling the sculpture. The impact revealed a time capsule installed at the base of the statue. A resident of the nearby YMCA expediently stole the capsule and contents. Police apprehended him and returned the still intact contents to the owners, the United Daughters of the Confederacy (UDC). Rather than remove the sculpture, the city council voted unanimously to reinstall it. On December 14, 2019, another vehicle crashed into the edifice resulting in both the sculpture shifting and evident cracking to the pedestal.

There were numerous legislative attempts to remove or relocate the monument following the second collision. All concerted efforts failed despite even the city council voting in September 2016 to relocate the work upon the lawn of the nearby Lyceum Theatre. The debate expanded statewide with preservationist organizations stressing the historical significance and financial value of the work.

Times and attitudes however have changed.

On June 2, 2020, the debate was abruptly silenced. Alexandria Mayor Justin Wilson ordered the statue removed. The symbolic decision followed the seventh straight evening of peaceful and violent protests following the police murder of George Floyd in Minneapolis. The statue was relocated to a private destination by the UDC, which they have refused to reveal publicly. The inscribed pedestal was removed the following month and would be later relocated to the local Bethel Cemetery. The former intersection location was repaved to completely remove any indication of the monument's former presence.

ERECTED
TO THE MEMORY OF THE
CONFEDERATE DEAD
OF ALEXANDRIA VA.
BY THEIR
SURVIVING COMRADES.
MAY 24TH 1889

FAIRFAX

The Civil War Battle of the Fairfax Courthouse
Fairfax County Historic Courthouse:
4110 Chain Bridge Road, Fairfax

Construction of the original Fairfax County Courthouse began in 1799 with the building's completion the year following. The structure gained historical prominence as the first land engagement of the Civil War. The battle involved a Union scouting party clashing with members of the local Fairfax militia.

The Union Army had expediently occupied Alexandria during April 1861 upon the commencement of the war. Their military was hoping to rapidly mount an offensive towards the future Confederate Capitol of Richmond. A swift assault by the Union forces offered the prospect of an expedient conclusion to the national rebellion.

On June 1, 1861, Union Lieutenant Charles Tompkins was ordered to infiltrate enemy territory to estimate the existing military presence within the region controlled by the Confederacy. At the Fairfax Court House, his contingent surprised a rifle company under the command of Captain John Marr.

Marr rallied his surprised troops in response before becoming mortally wounded. A civilian Virginia ex-governor, William Smith, assumed his command. Under Smith's leadership, the militia forced the Union troops into retreat. The scouting party's objective remained unfulfilled. Tompkins was criticized by his superiors for exceeding his orders. Most historians agree that the blame became the consequence of imprecise instructions.

The firefight began around 3:00 a.m. when visibility was minimal. The Fairfax Confederate contingent consisted of approximately 210 men. During the ensuing chaos and disarray, many of Marr's cavalrymen fled in confusion. Some were shot accidentally by their own troops amidst flight. Multiple sources indicated that Marr challenged his riders by shouting: *What cavalry is that?*

His challenge became his final words before being shot dead. No one directly witnessed his death or the reason for his ensuing silence. His body was found in a clover field later the following morning. The entirety of the conflict resulted in two deaths and several wounded. Five Fairfax soldiers were taken prisoner. Lieutenant Tompkins had two horses shot out from under him. One landed on him injuring his foot.

Despite the criticism leveled against him for his impetuous charge through Fairfax, Tomkins received the Medal of Honor for his actions in 1893. A monument to the fallen Captain Marr was erected on June 1, 1904 near the front of the courthouse. It remains today.

Several weeks later, on July 17, Union forces would fully occupy the Fairfax Court House as they gathered their troop assemblage towards Manassas Junction. On July 18, they would lose the *First Battle of Bull Run*. The extent of the casualties became the first noticeable proof the war would not be briefly conducted. The Fairfax Court House and the neighboring vicinity would be the site of numerous skirmishes and raids throughout the conflict.

The Final Execution Of A Serial Rapist Following Due Process
Historic Fairfax County Jail:
4000 Chain Bridge Road, Fairfax
Lynching Site of Joseph McCoy:
Southwest corner of Cameron and Lee Streets,
Alexandria

Ida von Bethmann Riedel, 63, was a native of Germany who spoke little English. She had immigrated to the United States in 1895 travelling alone on the *SS. Weimar* from Bremen. She arrived in Baltimore following fifteen days at sea. Her travel intention was to join her son Emil and his wife Clara in Alexandria.

Emil was a writer and theatre journalist and correspondent for the *New York State Newspaper*. His wife was the daughter of Congressman Charles Atherton of Ohio and reputed to be *a linguist of considerable ability* working in the War Department in Washington D.C.

Emil and Clara initially followed an affluent path of wanderlust. After residing in Malta, Rome and Hamburg, the couple settled in Newark, Ohio, residing with Clara's parents for the birth of their second child. Emil's interest in language, travel and writing furthered their travels to Yuma, Arizona, California and Mexico City. They returned to the United States and in 1894, purchased a 391-acre plantation in the Mount Vernon region called *Rose Hill*.

On February 1, 1895, a fire from a defective chimney flue completely destroyed their residence. Emil had the property reconstructed along with the addition of a small home for his mother to reside inside the estate grounds.

At 2:00 a.m. on Wednesday, April 14, 1897, a light

knocking on her front door awakened Ida Riedel. She got out of bed, opened a window and viewed the figure of a man bathed in bright moonlight. She recognized him as James Lewis, 23, a former black field hand employed by her son and surrounding farms. She presumed that he was looking for Emil. She pointed in the direction of her son's house, but was unable to speak directly with him due to her limited English vocabulary.

Lewis departed in her pointed direction, so she returned to her bed. Soon afterwards, she heard someone attempting to gain entry to her house via a downstairs window. She raced out of bed and managed to escape through a window to the ground below. She intended to seek assistance, but an awkward landing from her descent left her barely able to stand.

Lewis pulled her to the ground, raised her nightgown and penetrated her sexually. He then fled the premises. Ida Riedel managed to stagger to her son's house. Emil reported the sexual assault to Alexandria police.

The Alexandria police spent the next four days combing the region seeking Lewis. They visited his favorite haunts and spoke with his wife of only four months. He would be finally be located and arrested in Charlottesville, where he had previously informed his wife that he was seeking employment. A dispute arose over the legal jurisdiction of the arresting officers with local authorities.

Lewis protested his innocence upon his apprehension and begged not to taken to the Fairfax Court House for arraignment. He knew like any suspected black perpetrator that the threat of lynching was a potential and predictable outcome. His fears were legitimate, but the legal authorities were able to protect him during the transference process.

Ida Riedel positively identified him inside the County jail lined up with a dozen other black incarcerated prisoners.

What seemingly appeared a certain conviction became otherwise. Public unrest over another sexual violation case had enflamed the city of Alexandria.

An Alexandria rape suspect, Joseph McCoy was arrested locally for repeatedly penetrating the ten-year-old daughter of his white employer. The young girl was suffering from venereal disease as a consequence. McCoy's apprehension nearly incited an immediate lynching with a crowd of nearly 700 men encircling the jail. They nearly battered down the jailhouse door and the officers inside were only able to disburse the mob by firing their weapons in the air.

The reprieve proved only temporary. During the early morning hours, the vigilante mob returned with a twenty-foot wooden beam. The law enforcement officers were quickly overpowered and disarmed. They were unwilling to shoot their neighbors and likely out of ammunition from the earlier encounter.

The mob demolished the jailhouse door and violently dragged McCoy out of his cell. He was severely beaten enroute to his hastily constructed gallows on the southwest corner of Cameron and Lee Streets. His execution was excessively gory. He was strung up from a lamppost and shot multiple times. As he expired in agony, he was torched in his groin region. One assailant split his head open with an axe. He was left hanging and not removed until the next morning. A subsequent jury ruled *his death by strangulation at the hands of persons unknown.*

James Lewis was spared such an ordeal and would be successively tried on three separate occasions. The Fairfax

County sheriffs department and protective posse kept him under their protection, often escorting him through hidden country roads.

Conviction appeared certain when Ida Reidel related the facts of her assault and identified her attacker in court. Another sexual assault attempt by Lewis was submitted as evidence by another couple, Wilson and Rosie Jennings. They accused Lewis of attempting to assault her earlier the same day as his attack on Reidel. The aged Jennings, then 93, had heard his wife's scream and successfully battered Lewis with a club. A neighboring farmhand claimed that Lewis was frightened off by his approach and headed in the direction of the Reidel farm.

The first trial ended in a hung jury with eleven advocating guilt and the lone dissenter, preferring a 20-year prison sentence instead of the death penalty. A second jury concluded with a similar result. Eleven favored execution and one holdout stubbornly advocated only a 6-year prison sentence.

Guilt never seemed to be the impediment towards a decision. Only two individual's opposition to capitol punishment briefly spared Lewis' life. His case could not invoke the double jeopardy clause of the 5th amendment of the Constitution. Retrial is a permitted option for a hung jury. A third trial followed resulting in the prosecution's desired objective. The observing and swelling mob became menacingly impatient. Virginia Governor O'Ferrall ordered the state militia to travel to Fairfax as a preemptive measure.

The third jury, perhaps influenced by an impending crisis convicted Lewis and sentenced him to death. Once the verdict was read publicly, deafening cheers and shouts were heard inside and outside the courtroom. The judge cleared the courtroom and ordered the prisoner back to jail. The following day at his official sentencing, Lewis reaffirmed his innocence and claimed that he was being unjustly persecuted. The outcome surprised no one present except the condemned. The fact that he had undergone a trial and due process was significant.

Lewis languished in jail throughout the month of May 1897. Numerous clergymen, concerned regarding the fate of his soul, frequently visited him. His wife only spent a single twenty-minute session with him and his mother refused to see him based on her rationale that *she could do nothing for him*. Lewis continued to profess his innocence, hoping for intervention or new trial ordered by Governor O'Ferrall. He erroneously based his confidence on the assumption that O'Ferrall must be interested in him because *he has authorized troops to protect him from being lynched*.

Lewis appeals for a new attorney prompted interest, but all efforts to gain a fresh trial were denied by the Virginia Court of Appeals in Richmond. During the final week of May, Lewis' gallows was ordered to begin construction. The materials had recently been used to hang two other individuals in Manassas. Interest towards witnessing the spectacle was high, but local Sheriff Gordon determined to limit the number to avoid the event becoming a spectacle. The scaffold gallows and a boarded fence surrounding it were constructed in a small area located between the jail and courthouse.

Lewis could hear the construction process clearly and recognized its completion would become his own. On the morning of Thursday, June 3rd, the day before his appointed execution, Lewis indicated a desire to confess. Twelve men were invited by Reverend Robert Nourse of Falls Church to witness. Lewis, intimidated by the gathering, decided that he'd changed his mind. Nourse returned with only three men shortly afterwards upon Lewis' request.

Following prayer, Lewis made a full confession of his guilt before the small assemblage. He also indicated that he had raped three other women, the first occurring in 1887, when he was only thirteen. He elaborated that he had denied his guilt to protect his wife, not to escape punishment.

His admission apparently cleansed Lewis spirit. He admitted to feeling certainty of forgiveness and eternal salvation. He ate his dinner heartedly and was observed to remain in lively spirits that evening. He was awakened at 4:00 a.m. and escorted following breakfast to the scaffold. A reported 50-70 individuals gathered around the enclosed execution site. Lewis was serenaded by prayer and when asked for any final words, repeated his confession of guilt and request for Divine pardon.

Sheriff Gordon had grown emotionally attached towards Lewis during the period they'd become acquainted. He could not summon the initiative to spring the trapdoor. A member of the second jury energetically volunteered. At 5:03 a.m. Lewis dropped abruptly six feet down. What followed would make even a staunch proponent of capitol punishment cringe. Lewis' body rebounded up slightly three times. His neck was not severed from the descent. He lingered involuntary twitching and convulsing. He would die from strangulation twenty minutes later. The grotesque spectacle resembled more like murder than justice.

The body was cut down at 5:30 a.m. and he was placed in a wooden coffin. An autopsy was performed that removed his brain. The certifying doctor labeled it *normal*. His body would remain unclaimed, so he was buried in a pauper's grave at the Fairfax County Poor House in Clifton. His execution would become the last public hanging in Fairfax County.

The Accumulation of Hostilities Between Motorcycle Gang Rivals
Frederick *Dutch* Burhans and William Sitko Murder Site:
3915 Lyndhurst Drive, Fairfax, VA

The Pagans Motorcycle Club was assembled in 1959 in Prince Georges County, Maryland. Lou Dobkins organized the gang based on his ambition to become the East Coast incarnation of the Hells Angels. Many members embraced white supremacy and neo-Nazi themed insignias. Their club jackets bore back patches depicting Surtr, the king of the Fire Giants in Norse mythology.

By the 1970s, the gang would be linked to violent activities including torture, rape and murder. Most members were the products of blue-collar and fractured households. Many were employed in manual labor work or in construction trade professions. They wore denim and leather and swaggered with public defiance. Their weapons of preference were knives, .22 caliber pistols, but most commonly fistfights.

Within Arlington, a rival motorcycle gang formed called the Avengers. Their sporting leather jackets were emblazoned with a Maltese cross and skull. The two gangs reveled in their outsider status deriding their perceived wealthier and conformist peers. Both groups shared a fascination and adoration towards fast cars and Triumph motorcycles.

Over time, antagonism between the two gangs intensified. Perceived slights, blood oaths and brandished firearms upped the ante. The death of Pagan member Samuel Frederick resulted in murder threats targeted towards Wayne Hager, a leader of the Avengers. Frederick was involved in a biker bar skirmish with a member of the Avengers. Afterwards, Frederick crashed full speed into the rear of a truck riding his motorcycle while returning home. The Pagans swore vengeance.

An armed confrontation climaxed at the Lee-Harrison Shopping Center in Arlington. On Tuesday afternoon, June 14, 1966, the Falls Church Police Department was notified that 200 Pagan members were descending upon a local Safeway where Hager was employed as a meat cutter. Their intention was reportedly to massacre Avenger members from the shopping center rooftop. By 8 p.m., Avengers began arriving armed with automatic weapons, assault rifles, hunting rifles, clubs, and baseball bats studded with nails.

As darkness approached, the first shots were fired nearing 11 p.m. The timing was planned just as police officers on location began changing shifts. A fusillade erupted between the two gangs where 100 shots were reportedly exchanged. Eighteen gang members were taken into custody, most of them Avengers. They were charged with disorderly conduct, possession of a concealed weapon and inciting a riot. Eleven were found guilty, fined between $100-$250 and given suspended jail sentences.

The motorcyclists proved to be errant marksmen. No one was killed in the melee and only a state trooper injured when a ricocheting bullet grazed his leg. The gangs would negotiate a truce and disarmament agreement afterwards. Both agreed that they would neither carry weapons nor wear their colors in the other's gang's territory.

The two gangs would suffer significant attrition over the ensuing decades. The majority of deaths involved motorcycle accidents. During the 1970s, the Pagans established a Virginia chapter. Frederick *Dutch* Burhans became their president by mid-decade.

On New Years Day, 1980, he would be added to the casualty rooster at the age of 35. He and associate William Sitko, 28, visited David Keiser, 29, at his apartment in Fairfax. Both arrived armed, but neither would leave. Their quarrel involved the accusation that Keiser had destroyed Sitko's marriage. Seven shots were fired. Burhans and Sitko died from head wounds. Keiser suffered leg and chest wounds. No charges would be filed against him.

**The Christmas Tree Lady's Mysterious Farewell
Joyce Meyer-Sommers Suicide Site:
Pleasant Valley Memorial Cemetery Children's Section
8420 Little River Turnpike, Annandale**

Joyce Marilyn Meyer-Sommers was born in 1927 and raised on a Davenport, Iowa farm with four siblings. She attended Iowa State University before moving to Los Angeles to live with an aunt and work at *Seventeen Magazine*. During the 1950s, she taught second grade at a local Catholic elementary school. Part of the motivation for her relocation was her strained relations with her family, particularly her mother.

During the 1960s, she began psychiatric treatments and attempted briefly to reconcile. She pursued happiness in Seattle with her marriage to James Sommers and later relocated to Tucson, Arizona living in a trailer park. She divorced Sommers in 1977 and last saw her siblings in the early 1980s. The final connecting bridge crumbled when she asked them to build her a home, which they refused.

Her subsequent decades of wandering included her possibly joining a cult and living in Massachusetts, Washington D. C. and Northern Virginia. During this period, she wrote a book entitled *The Target Child*. Her trail became untraceable to family members who even engaged a private investigator to locate her.

On December 18, 1996, shortly after opening hours at 9 a.m., workers at the Pleasant Valley Memorial Cemetery discovered the body of a woman near the children's section of the cemetery. A bag was secured over her head with tape. She was dressed in a red shirt, blue pants and jacket.

An 8" Christmas tree was wedged into a backpack found next to her. She had been listening to a cassette tape using a tape player and headphones before she expired. She had penned two notes, one indicating not to wake her until *her eternal sleep*. The other indicated that she'd committed suicide with Valium plus alcohol. She stated that she wished no autopsy. Two $50 bills were found on her. She instructed that one was designated for the cemetery and the other for the coroner. Her death was determined to be caused by suffocation. There were no documents indicating her identity.

She was dubbed the *Christmas Tree Lady* by authorities and estimated to be age 50-70 years old. In 2000, a color rendition of her face was released to the public. Her identity remained undetermined for the next two decades. In January 2022, her DNA testing was funded by donations. In May, one of her brothers was tracked as a possible connection. Viewing her drawing, he was uncertain. One of their sisters however definitively identified her. Her DNA matched.

There remain questions as to why Joyce Sommers selected the children's section as her suicide site while keeping her identity anonymous. Her sister speculated that it might be symbolic representing her perception of parental abuse. She also maintained that her sister never bore children despite a large scar across her stomach possibly indicating a Caesarean section.

TWISTED TOUR GUIDES.com

PLEASANT VALLEY
BABYLAND
MEMORIAL PARK

**The Spy Fished Out From The Cold
Robert Hanssen Money Drop Location:
Wolftrap Creek Crossing Bridge, Near 1900 Block of
Creek Crossing Road NE, Vienna**

During January 1975, Robert Philip Hanssen swore his oath to become an FBI special agent. Approximately ten years later, he analyzed the prospects and risk for financial gain. He betrayed his American loyalty and mortgaged his soul to Russian intelligence. He nearly retired undetected, but upon collapse of the Soviet Union and aroused suspicion from working peers, his actions prompted closer scrutiny.

His experience and training as a counterintelligence agent enabled him to evade suspicion. The early 1994 arrest of Aldrich Ames initially convinced internal investigators that they'd caught the principle culprit providing information to the KGB and successor agency, the SVR. When both agencies realized that they had not successfully ceased the outflow of precarious information, they re-focused their attention towards another veteran CIA case officer. The investigation continued for over two years before their realization that he was not the source of the leaks.

The damaging information transferred to Russia agents compromised numerous human sources, counterintelligence techniques, investigations and documents of extreme importance and security value.

Hanssen remained off the radar of suspects until 2000, when the investigating bureaus were able to secure original Russian documentation regarding an American spy. The evidence pointed towards Hanssen. He was nearing retirement, so a sting operation was expediently instituted. At the time, Hanssen was serving as a detailee to the Office of Foreign Missions at the Department of State.

Launching his entrapment rouse, he was assigned to a temporary position at FBI Headquarters. Another FBI agent was chosen to replace him. During his supposed training process, he had unlimited opportunity to observe Hanssen's work habits.

The agent was tasked with observing Hanssen's information technology setup inside his office and monitor who he was meeting and speaking with. These observations supplemented the monitoring attached to Hanssen's bogus *temporary position*. Hanssen was promised a two-year extension with his foreign service and a promotion to the Senior Executive Service. The outcome would further enhance his actual retirement. He accepted the position unaware of the trap being laid.

In January 2001, Hanssen moved into his small FBI office secretly outfitted with surveillance cameras and microphones. His appointed assistant kept investigators apprised of Hanssen's movements. Over 300 FBI personnel were assigned to monitor Hanssen and track his every movement, both at work and at his residence.

Hanssen was completely unaware of these activities. He continued supplying Russian secret service with documents. On February 18, 2001, he had scheduled a drop site of classified information for his Russian handlers under a pedestrian bridge crossing Vienna, Virginia's Wolftrap Creek.

The site was selected by Hanssen, as was his preferred custom. He parked on a nearby residential street and strolled down a wooded path to the footbridge with the classified materials wrapped inside a plastic bag. A payment of $50,000 in $100 dollar bills awaited him at a

Russian designated location. Hanssen would never claim his reward. After leaving the documents under the bridge, FBI agents apprehended him as he returned to his car.

At his trial, his unconventional lifestyle was revealed. He shared a penchant for strip clubs and consummated a relationship with Washington D.C. stripper Priscilla Sue Galey. According to Galey, the relationship did not include sex. He provided her with money, jewels and a Mercedes-Benz and she traveled with him periodically. His rationale for abstinence was based according to her on his attempt to convert her to Catholicism. Hanssen reportedly attended early morning mass daily at the Oakcrest Catholic Church.

He would plead guilty to 15 counts of espionage on July 6, 2001 to avoid the death penalty. On May 10, 2002, he was sentenced to life in prison without parole. Hanssen was later profiled in numerous books, novels and the subject of a 2002 made-for-television movie called *Master Spy: The Robert Hanssen Story*. He was allowed to view the movie while incarcerated, but became so enraged by his portrayal, he only watched a small portion.

As his notoriety faded into obscurity, he remained in prison until being found unresponsive inside his jail cell on June 5, 2023. He died of natural causes at the age of 79 years old.

**A Fairfax Mayor Who Squandered His Public
Credibility
Crown Plaza Hotel Sting Operation Site (Currently
Courtyard By Marriott):
1960 Chain Bridge Road, McLean**

Scott Silverthorne had a secure position as mayor of
Fairfax and a family pedigree to likely insure a stable
future. His father had previously been a two-term mayor
and by most accounts Scott was a respected and beloved
leader. He had been involved in city politics for over two
decades and was considered by many as the *face of the
community*. He won his first election in 2012 with 86% of
the vote. He won re-election in 2014 by nearly a 50%
margin. His margin of victory during the 2016 election
became significantly smaller as his mounting financial
problems became first exposed to public examination.

He harbored two secrets. One was considered publicly
acceptable for most individuals and already acknowledged
by many of his constituents. He had come out discreetly as
gay during the 1990s following a brief, but failed marriage.
His gay lifestyle however included group orgies that
remained clandestine. He would later stipulate than none of
them occurred with the boundaries of Fairfax.

His more excessive secret would decimate his legacy. He
suffered from a self-admitted twelve-year
methamphetamine addiction. Until mid-2016, he had skated
precariously close to exposure. His final misstep was
foreseeable. His life and finances had plunged into free fall.
His professional salary coupled with his modest mayoral
stipend could not cover his lifestyle expenses.

His outside employment income continued to lessen
significantly upon leaving a secure and affluent position as

a credit card lobbyist. He suffered both foreclosure and bankruptcy proceedings.

Events consummated on July 28, 2016 would ultimately unravel his life. He had cultivated a secretive online presence seeking sexual partners and drugs. Trawling a gay hookup website BarebackRT.com, he responded and began a correspondence with another man. Their brief exchange resulted in scheduling both a meth purchase and group sexual encounter inside a nearby hotel room in McLean.

Unknown to him, his Internet correspondent was part of a sting operation established by investigators from the Fairfax County Police Department. Whether he was specifically targeted or arbitrarily selected remains unknown. Silverthorne willingly and carelessly followed a reckless path to his demise. Short of cash, he even resorted to borrowing the drug purchase funds from a friend. Ignoring cautionary warning signs, he was arrested in the Crown Plaza Hotel parking lot follow an exchange of cash for purchasing meth.

The publicity and circumstances follow public disclosure of his arrest resulted in immediate consequences. The unraveling of life became frightening.

His drug addiction consumed his existence. His usage and partying drained his finances and his online solicitations isolated him into dangerous scenarios. Friends were reportedly threatened and robbed during group sexual encounters. Four of his associates died from drug-related complications. He flailed futilely amidst a failed effort to cleanse himself of addiction starting in 2005. He confessed to resuming his drug habit following his father's death in 2009.

With his lifestyle and excesses publicly revealed, he was ridiculed and humiliated internationally in the press. He resigned as mayor and attempted vainly to address the corresponding avalanche of negative media requests.

His arrest potentially and probably saved his life. He was obliged to admit and face the consequences from his addiction. At his initial arraignment, he had anticipated facing serious legal penalties. Charges filed against him potentially carried a maximum 40-year prison sentence and a $500,000 fine.

The arraignment courtroom was packed with friends, family, city officials, politicians and a sprinkling of the idle curious. Most anticipated that Silverthorne would remain free until his actual sentencing hearing. He had not negotiated a plea deal and pled guilty to the charges. His judge surprisingly ruled for his immediate incarceration. There was no evidence to consider Silverthorne a flight risk.

Initially he was incarcerated in a protective custody cell. For a social and outgoing personality, the conditions seemed unbearable. They included solitary confinement, an absence of physical contact, natural daylight, reading and writing materials. He was only allowed to shower twice weekly.

Following his lawyer's complaint over the conditions, Silverthorne was transferred to a cramped cell with two cellmates, but given common inmate access. His confinement extended three months until his sentencing trial. When he arrived to the hearing, it was observed that he had gained twenty pounds from the prison starch based diet. He was not however alone or absent of support despite his absence from public exposure.

Silverthorne's support group extended throughout the leadership ranks of Northern Virginia. Many had voluntarily sent correspondence to the court espousing his character, commitment and contributions to Fairfax. In the courtroom, he publicly acknowledged responsibility for his actions and addiction. He requested leniency for his sentencing, but had no guarantee that his former status mattered. The presiding judge requested Silverthorne to face the audience composed primarily of his supporters as she announced his sentence.

He would be sentenced to his jail time already completed and to complete an additional 200 hours of community service. He was released immediately following the announcement.

The favorable decision was greeted positively, but not universally. The acknowledged worst fate an offender may face is poverty or the lack of connections. Silverthorne had profoundly embarrassed Fairfax, but exclusively due to his personal demons. The debate remains whether justice was served or his avoiding additional prison time was fair, in comparison with other lesser-connected and incarcerated drug offenders.

Justice is presumably blind towards social standing, but that conjecture is frequently debatable with legal sentencing regarding race, wealth and social status.

Silverthorne's contrition and remorse deeply affected many influential individuals. His attempt to reconstruct his life is admirable. He reportedly began working following his release at a hardware store in Bethesda, Maryland. He has kept out of the public limelight. Rumors of a future screenplay portrayal on his life have circulated, but not yet morphed into fruition.

Redemption is a difficult character trait to measure. No matter how many Narcotics Anonymous sessions he attends or public apologies he repeats, Silverthorne is chained until the conclusion of his life with the acknowledgement of being *that* ex-mayor of Fairfax.

FREDRICKSBURG

An Episcopal Church Bearing Witness To Three Centuries of Local Trauma
St. George's Episcopal Church:
905 Princess Anne Street, Fredericksburg

The House of Burgesses in Colonial Virginia established the Rappahannock Church (later St. George's Episcopal) in 1720. Eight years later, an act of Assembly founded the City of Fredericksburg. Two lots were set aside for the church and accompanying graveyard. The chapel began construction in 1732. Services began two years later amidst the building process. Members of the Washington family attended services beginning in 1738 with Charles Washington (George's brother) serving as a vestryman. William Paul, the brother of later Naval hero John Paul Jones served in the same capacity.

Paul would die in 1774 and be buried in a grave close to Faulker Hall located inside the front church gate to the left. Martha Washington's father, Colonel Dandridge was buried during 1756 in a tomb located nearby the church building near the bottom of the cemetery.

Upon the American declared independence, the church-state relationship was dissolved in 1776. St. George's joined the newly created Protestant Episcopal Church organization of the United States. In 1813, Reverend Edward McGuire became the rector for the small congregation of twelve. He would remain in that position for the next 45 years until his death. A fresh new brick building replaced the former wooden structure in 1815. The present building was erected in 1849.

The church could not evade collateral damage resulting from the 1862 *Battle of Fredericksburg*. The structure was struck by shell fire at least 25 times and a 4-piece communion set was stolen. One piece would be retrieved almost immediately afterwards. The New York City police department in 1866 and 1869 would return two additional pieces. The final piece would resurface in Massachusetts during 1931 following a $50 sale to a local church.

Throughout the year of 1863, General Robert E. Lee's troops staged religious revival meetings. As the Confederate cause flagged and the Union army controlled the city, the church would become repurposed into a temporary hospital for 10,000 soldiers wounded during the *Battle of the Wilderness*.

Following the end of the war, the institutional history concentrated primarily on the more mundane and functional, but less dramatic upgrading of the interior stained glass windows, chancel pipe organ and other exterior maintenance.

JOHN JONES GRAVE

The Esteemed Mother of The Father of Our Country
Mary Washington House:
1200 Charles Street, Fredericksburg
Mary Washington Monument:
1500 Washington Avenue, Fredericksburg

Mary Ball Washington, the mother of George, was an invaluable resource for him during his lifetime. She presided over the family plantation of 276 acres at Ferry Farm until her eldest son came of age. She lived to see George command the Continental Army to independence and become inaugurated as the initial American president in 1789.

After learning that he'd been elected president in April 1789, George traveled to her home in Fredericksburg to visit her. He knew that she was suffering from terminal cancer. She knew that her own death was eminent. George offered to decline the presidency to take care of her during her remaining months. She refused his offer and urged him to fulfill his higher destiny. On August 25th, she succumbed to the disease.

Mary Washington had spent the final seventeen years of her life residing in a large white frame house that George purchased for her in 1772. It was located near her daughter Betty Washington Lewis's home, Kenmore Plantation and a town house owned by her younger son Charles Washington. In 1780, Charles moved to Charles Town, West Virginia and the portion of the house facing Main Street was converted into a tavern.

George made frequent visits to his mother along with his contemporaries including John Marshall, George Mason, Thomas Jefferson, the Lee family and Marquis de

Lafayette. Following her death, the property would be converted into a museum as it remains today.

She was held with such high regard that her son ordered a memorial stone within months following her death. That stone became so ravaged by souvenir hunters that a movement began in 1826 to erect a more sustainable and elaborate monument. In 1833, President Andrew Jackson laid the initial cornerstone. Completion and fundraising languished until 1894 when President Grover Cleveland unveiled the completed obelisk marker. Thousands attended the unveiling ceremony. Additional surrounding landscaping would be added in 1937.

In 1908, the Fredericksburg Teaching College was founded. Thirty years later, the university would change its name to Mary Washington College in her honor. The present day university continues to offer a public liberal arts curriculum.

MARY
THE MOTHER OF
WASHINGTON

A Debt Of Honor Tainting An Aristocratic Family's Reputation
Former Benson's Tavern Site:
205 William Street, Fredericksburg

During October 1791, George Carter became inebriated and exhausted from playing three consecutive days and nights of *Twenty-One* at Fredericksburg's Benson's Tavern. Carter was the son of the patriarch from nearby Sabine Hall. He was a notorious gambler, patsy and loser. By the conclusion of his three-day debacle, he could barely lift his head or his cards. His accumulated losses amounted to an astronomical £1,893. His opponent John Cooper became in possession of a demand for payment and had no intention of forgiving the debt.

Gambling accompanied the settlement of Virginia and the initial permanent European residents. Whether employing cards or dice, participants risked imprisonment, whipping and disgrace. As with most extreme addictions, the consequences mattered minimally to aristocratic young men.

George Carter was born in 1762 and lived with his family at his grandfather Landon Carter's estate. The property was known as Sabine Hall. The mansion had been completed by his grandfather in 1740 and considered one of Virginia's *great houses* of *distinction*. Landon Carter during his lifetime owned more than 300,000 acres of land and 750 slaves. He was considered the richest and most powerful man in Virginia. He was profiled as an authoritarian parent and curmudgeon. He abhorred gambling.

Landon's son Robert resented his father's tyrannical control. The pair quarreled frequently. Robert's libertine behavior revolved around excessive daytime sleep, gambling excess and horse racing. He exhibited minor interest in inspecting or managing the family estates. His vices established a poor example for his two sons, George and Landon.

George's behavior mirrored his fathers. He was less defiant against his grandfather wishes, but regarded as *dull and weak*. His grandfather lectured and pitied him, but could not wean him from his ruinous card playing passions.

Benson's Tavern was located within the center of downtown Fredericksburg. It was considered an ordinary establishment similar to a dozen identical locally. Tavern master John Benson leased the property in 1788 from Revolutionary War officer George Weeden. When George Washington traveled to Fredericksburg, he habitually lodged at the property. He considered Weeden a valuable contributor to the war effort, but observed regarding his character *rather addicted to ease and pleasure, and no enemy it is said to the bottle*.

Benson's Tavern included private rooms for dining, meetings and card playing. A billiard table was installed in a separate room. During the post-Revolutionary period, gambling was illegal in Virginia, but generally overlooked by authorities. Benson was portrayed as a respectable figure serving as local postmaster. Thomas Jefferson was one of his notable friends.

John Cooper's triumph at cards against George Carter was likely fraudulent, although never proven. Carter drank excessively urged on by Cooper. A deceitful liaison between Cooper and another table participant John Willis resulted in speculation that he had diverted some of his winnings towards his *silent* partner. Willis sat next to Carter during most of the proceedings. Carter's lack of skill and ill fortune cemented his downfall.

Patriarch Robert Carter found himself in the unenviable position of settling his son's debt. He had found himself in identical positions earlier during his own gambling career. He understood the necessity of preserving his family's honor by promptly arranging payment to his new creditor. Reportedly he lacked the immediate resources.

Since gambling was illegal in Virginia, George Carter's debt was unenforceable through the legal system. Cooper began pressing for payment. Robert Carter consulted local lawyer John Minor for advice. Carter negotiated a settlement with Cooper two weeks later. Cooper would be paid £100 annually, without interest until the debt was repaid. Cooper consented.

Shortly afterwards, writer Mason Locke Weems composed a widely distributed fictional story portraying a young and naïve Tom Tittles of Culpeper County. Tittle had suffered a similar fate as George Carver with cards in coincidentally Fredericksburg. Losing his dignity, reputation and not being able to draw from deeper family finances, Tittles hung himself. Weems was the identical author of the manufactured tale concerning young George Washington chopping down a cherry tree.

The Carter gambling catastrophe was followed by a succession of calamities affecting all of the involved parties.

Robert Carter died in 1797 followed shortly afterwards by his son George in 1802. George remained deeply in debt and his widow and three children were severed adrift under perilous financial conditions upon his death. She would marry John Browne Cutting soon afterwards. He was profiled as a respectable but eccentric figure that titled himself as *Doctor*. There was no record of his ever earning a medical degree.

In London, he had established himself as an advocating agent for American sailors who were being exploited by British and European vessels. He advanced his prospective clients small sums of money and then sought inflated reimbursements from the U. S. Treasury. His ethically questionable enterprise was cynically portrayed as *18th century ambulance chasing*.

The marriage of John Brown Cutting with George Carter's widow proved highly unfortunate for creditor John Cooper. Cutting would challenge the validity of the debt in court. He prevailed eventually in 1816. The Virginia Supreme Court of Appeals ruled that the gambling obligation was void. Benson's Tavern would be consumed during a fire on October 19, 1807 that destroyed three blocks of Fredericksburg. John Benson reportedly died in 1815.

The Most Excessive Carnage From A Civil War Engagement
Fredericksburg Military Park Battlefield Memorial: 1013 Lafayette Boulevard, Fredericksburg

During December 11-15, 1862, the largest military engagement converged on the city of Fredericksburg. The drama evolved into the deadliest battle of the Civil War involving over 200,000 combatants.

Union General Ambrose Burnside with an army of 123,000 soldiers squared off against the undermanned Robert E. Lee, leading 78,000 troops. At stake was the potential capture of the Confederate capitol of Richmond and a resolution to the war. After Ambrose's predecessor George B. McClellan failed to aggressively pursue Lee's army following the Battle of Antietam, Abraham Lincoln demanded swifter response to lead the Army of the Potomac.

Ambrose positioned his army 35 miles to Falmouth on the north bank of the Rappahannock River in only two days. Opposite Falmouth was the prize of Fredericksburg occupied by only a few hundred Confederates. An expedient capture would enable direct access to Richmond.

Despite Ambrose's initial stealth, he was obliged to wait ten days for the necessary portable pontoon bridges to arrive to enable an invasion. The delay due to Washington D. C. bureaucratic and logistical obstacles enabled Lee and his generals, James Longstreet and Stonewall Jackson to consolidate and entrench their forces. They awaited the Union army approach.

A Union engineering regiment began to assemble the bridges under fire from the awaiting Confederate forces. The process was lengthy and delayed. The Union army shelled the city from across the river and met armed resistance from sniper upon finally reaching Fredericksburg with half of their regiments. This form of urban combat would become a first in the annals of warfare.

Despite initial success, the Union forces were suffering horrific casualties. Wave after wave of Union soldiers advanced over open ground and were raked by devastating rifle and artillery. The flight during December 13 and 14 created a monumental bloodbath. On the final evening, it became clear that Lee's army has prevailed despite losing an estimated 6,000 men. This loss became a statistic that the South could ill afford. His reputation for military genius and maneuvering was elevated by the victory.

On December 15, Burnside retreated from Fredericksburg and crossed back across the Rappahannock. He evacuated from the region to avoid being trapped. His casualties were twice that of Lee's. The disaster ended the military campaign of 1862 with an acidic taste. Returning to Washington D.C., Lincoln removed Burnside from command and replaced him with Major General Joseph Hooker.

Hooker would not become Lincoln's solution. The victory at Fredericksburg boosted Southern morale. Lee would triumph again in May 1863 at Chancellorsville. The victory became the apex for the Confederacy. The war would continue to grind their forces down before Union General Ulysses S. Grant would efficiently trounce Lee's army on the battlefield two and a half years later.

Burnside and Hooker would become remembered for far different reasons than either ever imagined. Burnside's enormous whiskers become the prototype for *sideburns*. Hooker led army's penchant for prostitutes would denote these unfortunate women with a publicly derogative term.

An Empathic and Controversial Creator of Verse
Leading By Example
Chatham Manor:
120 Chatham Lane, Fredericksburg

Walt Whitman became known as an unconventional writer, best recognized for his poetic edition, *Leaves of Grass*, published in 1855. The work's release followed several years of journalistic employ that included a stint under editor Samuel Clements (Mark Twain). Whitman's poetry was heavily criticized due his employment of free verse and erotic imagery that was considered obscenity. His work did not conform into the existing British model of poetry, which was a tradition of rhyme, meter and structure.

Upon the eruption of the Civil War, his brother enlisted in the Union Army. George Whitman earned the rank of lieutenant in the 51st New York Infantry. On December 10, 1862, his name appeared amongst the wounded during the Battle of Fredericksburg. Walt traveled south from New York in search of his brother.

He successfully located him and several days later visited nearby Chatham Manor, site of a makeshift hospital. He compiled his candid observations on conditions that he would publish years later. The visit altered the direction of his life. He had witnessed Armageddon. His vivid accounts of amputated limbs, dead bodies, overcrowded and frightful conditions prompted him to reassess his own priorities. He could never return to New York and revert to a purposeless existence.

Upon returning to Washington D.C., he volunteered at the various hospitals to serve as a nurse. His Quaker religion had long before confirmed his belief in pacifism. He concluded that simply opposing the atrocities of war, as a spectator was an insufficient role.

According to Whitman, his nursing duties *saved* his soul. He found purpose, meaning and substance in befriending the weak and wounded, bearing gifts, playing games and writing letters home to wounded soldier's families. Many of these correspondences were farewells.

In 1875, he published his wartime journals, *Memoranda During The War*. He continued writing up until his death in 1892. The empathetic sincerity behind his verse was reinforced by the commitment he'd opted to invest in through his medical duties.

The Chatham Manor grounds still remain. Soldiers are still being wounded and dying upon global battlefields. Walt Whitman turned his back upon conformity and the pursuit of literary recognition. He would still ultimately become acknowledged as one of America's most heralded poets. His works today endure as relevant as during his turbulent era and are far better comprehended.

TWISTED TOUR GUIDES.com

**An Embezzlement Scandal That Tainted
Fredericksburg's Knox Family
Thomas Knox House (Currently The Kenmore Inn):
1200 Princess Anne Street, Fredericksburg**

One of the largest heists during the Civil War was an embezzlement orchestrated by Thomas Soutter Knox. He was the second oldest of six sons of Thomas and Virginia Soutter Knox of Fredericksburg. Upon the outbreak of the war, he enlisted in the 30th Virginia infantry eventually earning the rank of captain. He later found employment as the Commissary at Camp Jackson in Richmond.

As the tide against the Confederate movement began to reverse, Knox colluded with a Treasury Department pay clerk George Butler over an ambitious plan. The pair embezzled $700,000 from the Confederate Treasury. They exchanged the rapidly devaluating currency for gold, Federal greenbacks, jewelry and any other stable investment items. At the time, 23 Confederate dollars equaled one dollar in gold. Their estimated haul was approximately $30,000.

Butler's motives were easily understood. He had recently been suspended from his Treasury position and allowed back briefly to settle his accounts. He'd accumulated significant debts carousing and had recent been ordered to report to the army at Camp Lee. Knox was considered the more prudent minded of the pair. The only known evidence hinting at his motive came via an expressed personal dissatisfaction following a mishap that left him with diminished memory.

On Saturday, September 10, 1864, the pair traveled north from Richmond. Their theft had not yet become discovered.

Butler wore dark goggles pretending to be Knox's blind brother. Their destination was presumed to be Fredericksburg under the pretense of returning home. Knox mascaraed as his brother's escort, obtaining the necessary passes from the Provost Marshall in Richmond. Their travel was uninterrupted and upon reaching Fredericksburg, they simply continued north towards the Union lines.

The discovery of the theft and accompanying scandal shattered the Knox's family reputation. Butler and Knox had both abandoned their wives and children with their intrigue. A subsequent report in 1900 indicated that Knox had since divorced his wife and remarried. He would re-settle in Brooklyn, New York working as a bookkeeper and served as an enumerator for the U.S. Census Bureau. He died in 1904.

Family patriarch Thomas Fitzhugh Knox became particularly devastated by the scandal. He was a leading Fredericksburg citizen, entrepreneur and firm supporter of the Confederacy. He had sent six sons into the Confederate Army and was taken hostage by the Union Army twice in 1862 and 1864.

By the 1880s, the property became home to a reputable boarding school and renamed Kenmore Hall. The institution maintained an affiliation with the Boston Museum of Fine Arts as a summer art school. Kenmore would return to becoming a private residence and during the 1930s, a summer guesthouse. Composer Leonard Bernstein spent summers in the guest cottage and dined with companions such as Aaron Copland in the main house. In January 2018, the property was renovated extensively and opened as a hospitality inn.

**A Former Slave Escaping To Tell A Shackled Narrative
Farmers Bank Building:
900 Princess Anne Street, Fredericksburg**

John Washington never achieved the international fame of Frederick Douglass, but his 1873 literary account *Memorys of the Past* is considered one of the most complete perspectives told by an enslaved individual. Washington was born into slavery and worked inside the Ware family household. Captain William Lewis Herndon, regarded as one of the U.S. Navy's greatest peacetime heroes, had initially resided inside the property.

The Federal Style structure was considered one of the finest architectural examples within Virginia. The front portion of the main floor was employed for retail banking and later renamed the Farmers and National Bank Building. The rooms in the rear and on the second floor were used to house the bank's cashiers and their families until 1920.

During John Washington's residence, he reputedly lived on the second floor in a small room later converted into a bathroom. He served as a personal servant and continued in that role even after his mother was hired out to a school principal in Staunton, Virginia.

In 1860, he labored in a Fredericksburg tobacco factory. The following year, he worked as a waiter in Richmond before returning to his hometown. The *Battle of Fredericksburg* offered him an opportunity for liberation. When Union troops occupied the city in April 1862, he was tending bar in the local Shakespeare Hotel. He seized the opportunity to escape and work at the headquarters of Union General Rufus King.

When the Union troops abandoned the city in August, he left with them to Washington D.C. His wife and infant son eventually joined him along with his mother and her husband. He worked as a painter and became active in a local Baptist Church. He died in the Massachusetts home of one of his sons in 1918.

**The Acknowledgement of Free Religious Protection
Thomas Jefferson's Monument to Religious Freedom
Washington Avenue Mall at Pitt Street, Fredericksburg**

Thomas Jefferson was considered a freethinker throughout his fully lived existence. There is scant surprise that he rejected many of the conventional Christian doctrines of his era including virgin birth, original sin and the resurrection of Jesus.

Jefferson was intensely interested in religious studies, theology, and morality. He considered himself a Deist that recognized God, but valued reason over revelation. More importantly, he believed that an individual had the right to choose his or her own religious beliefs without the intervention of a government. On January 13, 1777 before he became governor, he met with a committee to draft the Virginia Statute for Religious Freedom. The law declared that *no man shall suffer on account of his religious opinions or beliefs*. The text would later become incorporated into the United States Constitution as the First Amendment of the Bill of Rights.

On October 16, 1932, the 200th anniversary of George Washington's birth, Fredericksburg unveiled a monument acknowledging Jefferson's text regarding Religious Freedom. Representatives from sixteen of the leading denominations in the United States participated in the commemoration. In 1977, the edifice was relocated to its present location. Jefferson considered his Virginia statute one of the three major accomplishments of his life. The other two were the Declaration of Independence and establishment of the University of Virginia.

His words guaranteeing religious liberty have never been more poignant. Contemporary religious fanaticism, censorship and political fascism threaten the very core of our freedoms. Jefferson completely understood.

A Serial Killer's Shocking Violence During A More Innocent Era
Carroll Jackson's Body Discovery Site: (Currently Central Park Shopping Center):
1340 Central Park Boulevard, Fredericksburg

Serial killer Melvin David Rees became known as the *Sex Beast* in an era when multiple murders and serial killers were an anomaly. Little is known about Rees upbringing. During the early 1950s, he attended the University of Maryland concentrating his studies and interests towards music. He was an accomplished saxophonist, pianist and clarinet player. He dropped out of college but performed at jazz venues throughout the Washington D. C. music circuit.

He first encountered legal troubles when he was arrested in 1955 for assaulting a 36 year-old woman who he had tried to forcibly shove into his car. His victim refused to press charges resulting in the incident being dismissed by legal authorities.

Two years later, he encountered Margaret Harold and her boyfriend, an army sergeant on weekend leave, parked on a secluded road. They were heading towards Annapolis. Rees stopped his vehicle, approached their car window and pulled out a gun. He demanded cigarettes and money, but was rebuffed. Furious, he shot Harold in the face. Her horrified companion fled the scene and sought assistance from a local farmhouse. He telephoned police.

During his absence, a police patrol car arrived at the scene. They discovered that the killer had removed the deceased Harold's clothing and sexually violated her. Rees vanished, but investigators discovered a nearby abandoned cinder block-constructed house. The residence had been broken into via a downstairs basement window. Inside the basement, violent pornographic images and autopsy photos of female corpses were taped to the walls. A yearbook picture of 1955 University of Maryland graduate Wanda Tipton was discovered. She was located and questioned, but denied any knowledge of the individual (Rees) described by Harold's boyfriend. The case went cold from lack of clues and evidence.

On January 11, 1959, Carroll Jackson, his wife Mildred, and their two young daughters disappeared after visiting relatives in the Apple Grove area, located between Charlottesville and Fredericksburg. Their car was left abandoned by the roadside with no indications of a struggle. A massive search effort was coordinated to locate the missing family.

Two months later, a pair of men gathering brush discovered the decomposing body of Carroll in a ditch lying atop his 18-month daughter Janet. His hands had been tied behind his back and he had been shot in the rear of the head. The location was amidst the present-day Central Park Shopping Center in Fredericksburg. During that era before the construction of Interstate 95, the rural community had only a population of approximately 13,000. Two weeks afterwards, Mildred and daughter Susan were discovered dead inside a Fredericksburg forest. There appeared evidence of torture and sexual assault.

The horror and outrage from the disclosures prompted important clues to surface. A local couple reported a similar experience when a man forced them off the road. The driver was able to put his transmission into reverse and escape avoiding a potential confrontation and abduction.

The discovery of Mildred and Susan prompted investigators to examine the previous evidence left from the murder of Margaret Harold two years before. Inside the same house located nearby Harold's murder site was a valuable clue. A red button missing from Mildred's dress was identified. Investigators speculated that the killer had transported her and her daughter there before sadistically murdering them both. After comparing numerous similarities between the murders, investigators linked the crimes to the same source.

Amidst the investigation, a self-proclaimed psychic named Peter Hurkos emerged. He visited the Jackson's gravesite in Falls Church and purportedly handled some of their personal possessions. Unaware of the ongoing police investigation results, he linked the two crimes, described in detail the murders and positions in which the victim's bodies were discovered. He led police to the house of one of their primary suspects, a trash collector. The suspect would confess to the murders. Hurkos reportedly predicted that the killer would eventually be indicted for nine total murders.

Hurkos revelations piqued the interest of investigators, but did not ultimately catch the killer. An anonymous letter, later attributed to Glenn Moser of Norfolk, was mailed to Fredericksburg authorities. Moser recommended that police question Rees. Moser suspected that Rees was involved with all five murders. He based his suspicions on their previous conversations and admissions by Rees. The pair had worked together as salesmen in the Annapolis area during the time of Harold's murder.

Police followed up the lead and found Rees' trail both evasive and complicated. They determined that Wanda Tipton had lied to them during their questioning regarding the Harold murder. She did know Rees. They had dated during college, but she broke off their relationship when he claimed that he was married. His admission proved correct.

In June 1960, Rees would be apprehended and put on trial for the five murders. He was convicted and during interrogations, confessed to killing two more individuals. Police additionally suspected him of another two murders. He would not be put on trial for any of these four killings. The *Washington Post* had lampooned psychic Peter Hurkos for his earlier perceived inaccuracies. While some of his comments might be dismissed, his body count may have been accurate. Worse, Rees may have been responsible for even more deaths.

Rees would be sentenced to life in prison for Harold's murder in Maryland and given the death penalty for the Jackson Family murder in Virginia. His sentence was commuted to life in prison during 1972. He would die incarcerated during 1995.

Rees would never publicly confirm a motive behind the killings. Glenn Moser revealed that during a conversation with Rees, he had confessed that *he considered murder to be another part of the human experience that he eagerly wanted to take part in.* He added, *You can't say it's wrong to kill, only individual standards make it right or wrong.* He never admitted guilt to Moser.

Other serial killers would chillingly replicate Rees amoral attitude in the future. The mania to kill without remorse or motive has been documented frequently over the successive six decades. The novelty and revulsion that once shocked the public during 1959 would evolve into popular television programming in our contemporary age.

CENTRAL PARK
LOWE'S
Walmart
target
KOHL'S +SEPHORA
BEST BUY
Ashley
HOMESTORE
HOBBY LOBBY
Total Wine
& MORE
FUN LAND
sleep number
PETSMART
BARNES&NOBLE
Office DEPOT
VIRGINIA
Chick-fil-A
noodles
& COMPANY
Bassett
ETHAN ALLEN
DSW
crumbl cookies
Panera BREAD
RED CRAB
LIFEPOINT CHURCH
GERMANNA
COMMUNITY COLLEGE
verizon
xfinity
the JOINT chiropractic
5.11

**A Police Department Renowned For A Dunking Stool
and Burglary Ring
Fredericksburg Police Headquarters:
2200 Cowan Blvd, Fredericksburg**

During the early 1700s, law enforcement in Fredericksburg consisted of a lone night watchman. The town legislative council elected John Legg as the *Sergeant of the Town* in March 1782. His position entailed enforcing city ordinances and administering and overseeing punishment for crimes.

Legg employed a *dunking stool* that amounted to a chair strapped to an extended pole attached to a fulcrum. Perpetrators were strapped to the device and dunked repeatedly into the Rappahannock River. The punishment was not only uncomfortable, but also periodically fatal.

Law enforcement and administered criminal punishment has evolved significantly over the last three hundred years. Accompanying police ethics have periodically stumbled.

During the winter of 1987, Fredericksburg residents were stunned to discover that five members of their police force, one a 25-year veteran, were involved in a burglary ring that had targeted local businesses for the previous six years. A similar scandal tainted neighboring Spotsylvania County, where three sheriff's deputies were fired during December 1986 for stealing toys and other merchandise from a shopping mall shortly before Christmas.

The population of Fredericksburg then was approximately 19,000, a growth spurt of 30% from the 1980 census. Many of the indicted officers were raised locally and familiar faces. Most of the city's growth was attributed to the opening of Interstate 95 creating a commercial, commuter and cultural suburban hub. The police department scandal affected 15% of the patrol force. City officials were quick to publicly distance the burglary ring as an isolated incident. They marginalized the scandal *as only a blip on the radar* or a *temporary setback* to sustained growth.

Nearly forty years have passed since the burglary revelation. The population has increased to nearly 30,000 residents. The current police force includes more than 100 full- and part-time employees organized into three divisions: Patrol, Detective and Support Services. The thoroughly contemporary operation is housed in a headquarters opened in 2007 and integrated with technology and state-of-the art computerization. The dunking stool has become relegated to charity fundraising events.

**The Profound Darkness of John Muhammad's Soul
Beltway Sniper Virginia Victim's Sites:
Dean Harold Meyers: Sunoco Station, 7203 Sudley
Road, Manassas, VA
Kenneth Bridges: Exxon Station, 5409 Patriot Highway,
Fredericksburg, VA
Linda Franklin: Home Depot, 6210 Seven Corners
Center, Fall Church, VA
Jeffrey Hopper: Former Ponderosa Steakhouse
(Currently Panda Express), 809 England Street,
Ashland VA
Brookside Gardens:
1800 Glenallan Avenue, Wheaton, MD**

The demons that prompted John Allen Williams to murder strangers by sniper fire were complex and incomprehensible to understand. His hatred seemed personified by a sense of empowerment over determining life and death.

What influences created these demons?

Williams, better known as *John Allen Muhammad* changed his surname in October 2001 shortly following the 9/11 attack on New York City's World Trade Center complex and the Pentagon.

The unraveling of his personality began more than a decade earlier. He was born in Baton Rouge, Louisiana on New Years Eve, 1960. The family moved to New Orleans when his mother was diagnosed with breast cancer. She died when he was three. His father abandoned him and his maternal grandfather and an aunt raised him.

He enlisted during August 1978 in the Louisiana Army National Guard at Baton Rouge as a combat engineer. He transferred to the conventional army in 1985 and trained as a mechanic, truck driver and specialist metalworker. He qualified as an expert marksman.

His tours of duty included Fort Lewis, Fort Ord and in 1991 he served in the Gulf War in Kuwait. He earned numerous honors for his service and was honorably discharged as a sergeant in April 1994.

While on active duty in 1987, he joined the Nation of Islam. He helped provide security after his discharge in 1995 for the *Million Man March* on the Capitol.

His personal life deteriorated. He had married twice and fathered three children. His second wife sought and was granted a restraining order for alleged abuse. In 1999, the troubled Muhammad kidnapped his children and transported them to Antigua. He was reportedly engaging in credit car and immigration document fraud. It was during this abduction that he would encounter Lee Boyd Malvo, who later partnered up with him on his infamous string of murders.

Malvo would testify that Muhammad had indoctrinated him into believing that his ultimate goal was to establish a camp in Canada where homeless children would be trained as terrorists. In Muhammad's deluded logic, he initiated his goal with a nationwide scourge of terror. He envisioned a ransom to stop the killings as the source of funding for his terrorist camp. At his later murder trial, his defense attorney stated his *true* ultimate goal was to kill his ex-wife Mildred in order to regain custody of his three children. Like most of his sparsely publicized rhetoric, little of it made sense.

John Muhammad and Lee Boyd Malvo's legacy of violence would begin on February 16, 2002 at a hillside residence in

East Tacoma, Washington. The first killing was a bungled revenge murder. It became the sole homicide that seemed accompanied by a plausible motive.

John Muhammad had instructed Malvo to kill the best friend of his ex-wife. She had assisted his former spouse's escape from their abusive relationship. The murder was intended as repayment for her aid.

Malvo's relationship with Muhammad has been scrutinized extensively. Malvo claimed that his older accomplice exerted a Machiavellian influence over him that was punctuated by a pattern of sexual abuse. He followed instructions without questioning or conscience.

Malvo botched the instruction by shooting the first person that answered his knock. Keenya Cook, 21, was the niece of the intended victim, living at the residence in the midst of sorting out her own life. She was in the process of undressing her baby daughter for a bath while preparing food on the kitchen stove. She had just broken up with her child's father and had moved in with her aunt and cousin. She managed a woman's clothing store.

The hurried gunshot to her head was fatal and Malvo fled the scene. Investigators and family were baffled by a seemingly absence of motive. It wasn't until Muhammad and Malvo's later East Coast murders that the killing was linked directly to the pair. Malvo confessed, while Muhammad remained defiantly silent.

From February until October 2002, the pair traveled cross-country between Washington State to their end destination in Washington D.C. via southern states. They engaged in a robbery and shooting rage killing six more individuals and wounding seven. Their victims were identified in Los

Angeles, Tucson, Denton, Atlanta, Montgomery and Baton Rouge. Neither perpetrator would ultimately stand trial for these murders.

Muhammad and Malvo arrived into the D.C. metropolitan area at the beginning of October. Muhammad was driving a blue 1990 Chevrolet Caprice. A firing port was created above their New Jersey license plate enabling them to shoot and remain concealed. The contraption enabled easy escape following their attacks.

On October 2nd, Muhammad fired a shot through a Michael's craft store in Aspen Hill, Maryland. The bullet narrowly missed a cashier and was presumed by police to be random. James Martin was shot to death one hour later in the parking lot of a Shoppers Food Warehouse store. The following morning, four people would be killed within a two-hour span in the Aspen Hill district and nearby Montgomery County, Maryland. A fifth was added that evening in the Takoma neighborhood of D.C.

On October 4th, a woman was wounded in the chest in the parking lot of the Spotsylvania Mall in Spotsylvania, VA. By now, the shootings were being linked and journalists were converging to cover the events. School officials reassured the public they were exerting every cautionary measure possible. Security was tightened and all outdoor activities were canceled. The D.C. metropolitan region was paralyzed in terror.

Muhammad began spacing out his shootings two to three days apart. He was monitoring news coverage of his killing spree and attempting to exhort authorities to provide him with funds to cease the murders.

Conscious of the public announcement regarding school safety, Muhammad shot 13-year-old Iran Brown critically as his aunt was dropping him off at the Benjamin Tasker Middle School in Bowie, MD. He survived despite serious internal injuries. At the crime scene, investigators discovered a shell casing and the Tarot Death Card with written inscriptions.

On October 9, the spree continued further south into Virginia with the shooting death of Dean Meyers at a Sunoco gas station. Two days later, Kenneth Bridges was killed at an Exxon Station near Fredericksburg, On October 14, Linda Franklin was killed inside a covered Home Depot parking lot at the Seven Corner Shopping Center.

The desired panic sought by the perpetrators had enflamed into its desired effect. Service stations had begun to install tarps to conceal their clientele. Numerous media dispatches identified the sniper's vehicle as a white van, slowing the accuracy of the investigation.

On October 17, either Muhammad or Malvo became overly cocky. One of them telephoned the Montgomery County Police Department to indicate that he was responsible for the murder of two women during a liquor store robbery a month earlier in Montgomery, Alabama.

What the caller didn't realize was that only one woman had died and that fingerprint and ballistic evidence were available from the case. Over 400 FBI agents from around the country were working the capturing the newly monikered *Beltway Sniper*. A fingerprint from the gun in Montgomery was traced to Lee Boyd Malvo from an earlier warrant in Washington State. He was immediately paired with John Muhammad and the Bushmaster .223 rifle registered to him. The trail quickly led on October 22nd to the license plate tracking of their blue Chevy Caprice.

The information would be distributed to the news media for global circulation. The net was closing rapidly on Muhammad and Malvo. They hadn't completed their rampage nor were aware that their freedom was nearly over. How long they had chosen to continue was never revealed.

On October 19, Jeffrey Hopper was shot in a parking lot near the Ponderosa Steakhouse in Ashland, Virginia. Three days later, bus driver Conrad Johnson was gunned down while standing on steps at a bus stop in Aspen Hill, Maryland. He would become their final victim.

The closure of the carnage came discreetly on the morning of October 24. The blue Chevy Caprice was spotted at a rest stop parking lot off of I-70 in Maryland. Within an hour, law enforcement had set up a perimeter blockage to prevent any escape. During the morning, a team of Maryland State Police, Montgomery County SWAT officers and Hostage Team special agents arrested the sleeping pair without a struggle.

The first trial of Muhammad was conducted in Virginia during October 2003. He was charged with murder, terrorism and the illegal use of a firearm. His extortion attempt was also revealed. On November 17th, he was convicted and sentenced to death. He would be returned to Maryland to face charges. He would be convicted on six counts of murder and given six life sentences.

As Virginia still conducted capitol punishment, his death sentence precluded any punishment that his other murder convictions might result in. Muhammad sullenly protested his innocence throughout the proceedings. He requested prosecutors to terminate any appeals to spare him his death sentence.

On November 10, 2009, John Muhammad would be executed at the age of 48 at the Greensville Correctional Center in Jarrat, Virginia. His calloused premeditation and complete disregard for human life forged him into an unsympathetic figure. He declined to make a final statement prior to his death by lethal injection. His body was cremated and the ashes given to his son in Louisiana.

Malvo's defense team attempted to parlay his juvenile status as an argument against conviction. During Muhammad's Virginia trial, Malvo stated that he had been the triggerman for every shooting. His tactic was employed to spare the death penalty for Muhammad. The precision aim of the shootings and his own lack of arms experience made his confession implausible. During the Maryland trial, he admitted that he had lied. His detailed testimony filled in numerous gaps of the pair's activities and travels. He freely confirmed the murders that they were suspected of.

Malvo would be sentenced to life imprisonment without the possibility of parole. He is currently interned at the Red Onion State Prison in Pound, Virginia. The facility is designated as a Supermax security prison housing 848 inmates and considered one of the toughest national institutions with stringent controls.

Films and media portrayals have documented the D.C. Sniper's exploits. These exposés have attempted to piece coherence into the pair's monstrous actions. Malvo has periodically attempted to shed light into the unimaginable darkness behind their thinking. He has since married, but there remains only a slight probability that he will ever experience freedom again.

An engraved memorial stone with each of the Maryland, D.C. and Virginia victims is located as an oasis setting inside the Brookside Gardens facility in Wheaton, Maryland. The 50-acre property is landscaped with terraced tropical gardens, winding streams, walking trails and shady gazebos. It is a serene alternative to the horror that once characterized the petrified region. It symbolizes the antithesis of a shrouded soul that John Allen Williams could never evade.

SURVIVORS:

Follow up accounts of the wounded victims often remain dated and incomplete. After the murder trial, news outlets ceased their coverage with the exception of periodic anniversary updates. The majority of the victims have chosen to resume their lives in as normal a manner as possible. They are scarred for life. The physical, mental and psychological damage never entirely heals.

John Gaeta was changing a flat tire on August 1, 2002 at a shopping mall in Hammond, Louisiana when Lee Malvo walked up to him and fired a gun five feet away. His truck tire had been slashed while Gaeta was shopping in Sears to buy a new pair of shoes. Malvo aimed at Gaeta's head, but the bullet entered the side of his neck exiting his back sparing him his life. Gaeta pretended to be dead and Malvo stole his wallet containing $40.

Gaeta went directly to a hospital where doctors informed him that he had fortunately dodged damage to his spine and arteries. He was released after an hour. He was left with no permanent physical scars from the wound. Malvo would later write him a letter of apology.

Paul LaRuffa was a Clinton, Maryland pizzeria owner who was shot at six times. He had just closed his restaurant and placed his laptop and day's receipts in the back seat of his car. It was nearing midnight on September 5, 2002. He felt his life slipping away as he struggled to breath following collapsed lungs in the restaurant parking lot. A reassuring 911 dispatcher promised him that he wouldn't die. Nine hours later following surgery, he would persevere. One bullet had passed through his arm into his chest, one went into his diaphragm and two others passed through his side and neck just missing his spine.

Lee Malvo had run up to his car and shot him repeatedly through the driver's side window. He then opened the back door and grabbed the laptop and receipts bag containing $3,500. LaRuffa would miraculously recover following an extended rehabilitation. He would sell his restaurant and retire, reportedly *living near the water* in St. Mary's County. He began working with the Campaign For Fair Sentencing of Youth to assist young offenders upon their released from prison. Although Malvo's attorneys have lobbied for leniency due to his age when the crimes were committed, he has never apologized to LaRuffa for his actions.

On September 14, 2002, Rupinder *Benny* Oberoi, 22, an employee of the Hillandale Beer and Wine Liquor store in Silver Spring, MD was shot in the back while in the process of closing the store with the owner nearing 10 p.m. The bullet entered his chest and cut through his diaphragm. He was a student at Anne Arundel Community College working the night shift. Following his recovery, he would relocate to a town outside of New York City where he purchased a small store.

The next evening, Muhammad Rashid was alone when he was shot while closing Three Roads Liquors in Brandywine, MD. The first two bullets hit the door and the third entered his abdomen from four feet away. Malvo approached him as he lay expiring, cold-bloodedly checked his pockets and then took his wallet. His recovery was slowed by serious infections and an extreme lack of energy and ability to sleep. He would identify Malvo as the shooter in court.

Muhammad and Malvo traveled south before arriving to the Beltway killing Million Woldemariam, 41, outside a liquor store in Atlanta. On the same day, Kellie Adams, 24, was critically wounded with a shot through the neck during a liquor store holdup in Montgomery, Alabama. Her co-worker, Claudine Parker would be shot to death in the chest during the robbery. Adams would endure thirty surgeries and complications that left her dependent on a tracheotomy tube for three years.

When she was finally was able to resume working, she was employed briefly by the Alabama Alcoholic Beverage Control's central office. She and her husband moved to Benton, Kentucky. She would have additional surgeries and her marriage collapsed due to the fatigue and stress of her husband being her caretaker. She would be diagnosed with post-traumatic stress disorder.

She would earn an online degree in veterinary science and work in a nearby humane society until her next surgery, requiring eight weeks of recovery. She would relocate to the small town of Lumpkin, Georgia. The nightmares and accompanying terrors have kept her hyper vigilant towards unusual sounds and surrounding people.

On October 4, Caroline Seawall was wounded in the chest during the afternoon while in the parking lot of a *Michael's* store at Spotsylvania Mall in Virginia. She was loading purchases into her minivan. The sniper's shot passed through her back and shredded her liver before exiting her body. Reports following her recovery have not been publicized and she has reportedly moved to South Carolina.

Iran Brown was a seventh grade student at Benjamin Tasker Middle School when a single hollow-point bullet hit him in the upper body. His aunt who was a nurse had just dropped him off at school. She put her car in reverse, placed her nephew into her vehicle and drove immediately to the nearest medical clinic. Her instinctive reaction saved his life. The shell damaged his internal organs. He would be hospitalized for several weeks. He continues to suffer from internal nerve damage injury. The shooting was timed at the height of the sniper scare. The killers targeted society's most vulnerable victims to further enflame media coverage.

Brown originally grew up in Georgia and would relocate there years later. He testified against John Muhammad during his October 2003 trial in Virginia Beach. He stressed his appreciation for the gift of survival and has expressed interest in a newspaper interview of meeting Lee Malvo one day. The interest would be his attempt to gauge Malvo's remorse and understand his perspective behind the killings.

The final wounded victim, 37-year-old Jeffrey Hopper was shot on October 19, 2002 in the stomach at the rear parking lot of the Ponderosa Steakhouse in Ashland, Virginia. He and his wife were vacationing from Florida. They had purposely avoided filling up their old Cadillac near the Beltway service stations due to the heightened danger. Feeling more secure in their chosen location, they dined inside the restaurant. Hopper was shot as they returned to their car.

His wife called out to passersby's who telephoned for an ambulance. Their prompt response enabled Hopper to survive his injuries. The bullet damaged his kidney, pancreas, liver, diaphragm and a rib. The surgeons had to disconnect his stomach from his intestines to make repairs. He spent 29 days in the hospital primarily in intensive care.

His shooting would provide the first tangible piece of physical evidence that would lead to the killer's eventual capture. A pink extortion note was found in the nearby woods tacked to a tree that had the killer's fingerprints on it.

LINDA FRANKLIN

JEFFREY HOPPER

WOODS WHERE PINK EXTORTION NOTE FOUND

BROOKSIDE GARDENS

WE REMEMBER
JAMES D. MARTIN
SILVER SPRING, MD
JAMES L. "SONNY" BUCHANAN
ROCKVILLE, MD
PREM KUMAR WALEKAR
OLNEY, MD
SARAH RAMOS
SILVER SPRING, MD
LORI A. LEWIS RIVERA
SILVER SPRING, MD
PASCAL E. CHARLOT
WASHINGTON, DC
DEAN H. MEYERS
GAITHERSBURG, MD
KENNETH H. BRIDGES
PHILADELPHIA, PA
LINDA FRANKLIN
ARLINGTON, VA
CONRAD E. JOHNSON
ASPEN HILL, MD

The Insanity Behind A Deliberate and Disturbing Murder
Grace Mann's Murder Site:
1900 Washington Avenue, Fredericksburg

The sanity of Steven Briel became the determining facture as to whether he understood his actions prompting the death of roommate Grace Mann. She was a twenty-year old student at the University of Mary Washington sharing a house with Briel and two other roommates. She was majoring in history and American studies while Briel was a political science major.

Without any preconception of danger on April 17, 2015, Mann returned home. Upon brushing past Briel inside their house, he violently and abruptly grabbed her. During their ensuing struggle, he strangled her to death.

Their two other roommates Holly Aleksonis and Kathryn Erwin would return home to discover a disheveled and profusely sweating Briel. He confessed about his altercation with Mann, indicating her abusiveness with him and being bitten violently. He claimed that he was forced to retaliate by slapping and then strangling her.

Erwin ordered him to go upstairs to his room. She spotted Mann, whose skin had already turned blue. Briel had stuffed bags down her throat and placed a plastic bag over her head to insure her suffocation. Erwin frantically attempted CPR compression on Mann. Her efforts elicited no response as Mann had already expired.

Briel was arrested and during his subsequent trial, dueling psychiatrists offered conflicting observations. The forensic psychiatrist for the defense testified that Briel did not understand the nature, character and consequences of his actions…textbook insanity. She provided an imaginative scenario where Briel believed that Mann had been tasked with killing him by pumping poisonous gas into his bedroom. His attack was prompted by his fear that Mann was moving in to kill him.

Briel's mother collaborated that her son had previously expressed concern *that his female roommates were going to kill him and make it look like a suicide*. She feared that he might kill himself predicated on a rambling and troubling worded email. His parents had urged that he give his roommates notice and move out. She claimed on the morning of the homicide, her son had confirmed plans to move out and planned to take the train home.

Back on planet Earth, the prosecution's own forensic psychiatrist was convinced that Briel was both sane at the time of the attack and had displayed no previous signs of schizophrenia. The most damaging evidence against his insanity strategy was a recorded jailhouse phone call from Briel to his parents two weeks following Mann's death. The conversation was light, jovial and the subject matter about books and jail food. Listeners did not detect the voice of a tormented or fearful individual.

The jury deliberated only three hours before convicting Briel of first-degree murder, recommending a sentence of life imprisonment plus an additional 11 years. He is currently interned at the River North Correctional Center in Independence, Virginia. Briel's premonition regarding being murdered by his university roommates was absurd and unfounded. Given his present residence, those fears may be indeed rational.

JOEL
GRIFFIN

TWISTED TOUR GUIDES.com

**Insuring For A Squandered Future
Former Bailey Funeral Home Site:
1207 White Street, Fredericksburg**

Owner Ambrose Bailey offered an enticing scam to prospective clients of his respected funeral home. Bailey Funeral Services was a fixture within Fredericksburg for a half-century, established initially and run by patriarch Weldon Leon Bailey. Ambrose had assumed the ownership and operations upon his father's retirement. He had established his own local legacy and was a former member of the city council.

Approximately 60 clients had purchased pre-need funeral services purportedly dating back to the 1980s. The monies were legally supposed to be held in trust. Instead, it was reportedly spent on personal and business expenses.

An investigation commenced when a 72-year-old neighbor and client read a news account that Ambrose Bailey was being charged by the Virginia Department of Health for forging doctor signatures on death certificates. She contacted the police department to determine if her pre-paid funeral monies were still safe. Investigators responded by obtaining a search warrant for the funeral home that also served as Bailey's residence.

The search revealed a box of documents containing over 60 files relating to pre-arranged funeral services. No tracking of the monies or documentation establishing escrow accounts were discovered. Ambrose Bailey was expedient in publicly denying any culpability. His father Weldon maintained in the press that while operating the funeral home, he had never sold pre-need funerals.

At his trial during May 2015, Ambrose Bailey was ordered to serve two years in prison for taking money from pre-funeral accounts and forging death certificates. His sentence would never be carried out. On May 24, he passed away from natural causes at his home after suffering from long-term kidney illness. On September 22, 2015, his father Weldon would die at his residence at the age of 88. The purloined monies would never be recovered.

RICHMOND

An Orator's Famous Demand For Liberty...For Some Old St. John's Church:
2401 E. Broad Street, Richmond

In March 1775, tensions between Great Britain and the American colonies had climbed to a feverish crescendo. The protest movement by the colonies galvanized when the Second Virginia Convention was assembled within Richmond's Henrico Parish Church. George Washington, Thomas Jefferson, Peyton Randolph and other prominent Virginians were convention delegates. The collective dissidents sought unity amidst their own prevalent discord. On March 23, Patrick Henry addressed the body with a concluding sentence that would immortalize his life and inspire direct action by the body.

Give me liberty...or give me death!

His words still resonate globally when nationalities attempt to secure their right to freedom. Viewed identically today through the raging conflagration of Ukrainian battlefields, men and women are still willing and determined to sacrifice their lives against evil and oppression.

The American Revolutionary War was a potential death sentence for each signer of the Declaration of Independence, had the cause been lost. The risks were enormous.

Patrick Henry grew up in an Anglican (father) and Presbyterian (mother) household during his formative years in rural Virginia. Observing itinerant preachers shaped his introduction into classical oratory. He assimilated that reaching an audience through their hearts, rather than simply persuading by reason elevated the finest. He harbored resentment then towards the prevalent Virginia's policy regarding slavery and religious intolerance. His philosophical contentions would fall short personally regarding enacting social change despite having the elected authority to do so.

In 1754, he married Sarah Shelton in Rural Plains, Virginia. His wedding gift of six slaves and 300 acres was directed towards establishing an operational agricultural planation. Henry worked alongside his slaves to clear the fresh fields for planting. The lands had formally become fatigued from over cultivation and during the latter half of the 1750s were plagued by drought. After the property manor house burned down, he abandoned the enterprise and moved into the Hanover Tavern owned by his wife's father.

He served as a host and barkeeper and entertained guests by playing the fiddle. He encountered a younger Thomas Jefferson passing through en route to his studies at the College of William and Mary. The pair became well acquainted despite their age difference.

While at Hanover Tavern, Henry briefly studied law. He passed the bar exam in April 1770 before a board of prominent attorneys in the Colonial capitol of Williamsburg. He established a legal practice amongst the courts of Hanover and nearby counties.

One of Henry's earliest legal triumphs occurred with the *Parson's Cause* case where he was engaged as counsel by the Reverend James Maury's parish vestry. The case revolved around a tax reimbursement disagreement. Maury's defense headed by Henry was the only party to emerge victorious. Henry's father, Colonel John Henry was the presiding judge.

Henry gained a following in backwoods Virginia due to his

oratory skills defending the rights and liberties of common residents. He achieved recognition for his speech in opposition to the 1765 Stamp Act. His continuing legal conflicts with the British crown led him to conclude that separation from English rule was inevitable.

His speech at the March 23, 1775 Second Virginia Convention concluded his amendment to raise an armed militia independent of royal authority. Such an action was interpreted as a call to arms against England. His *Give me liberty…or give me death!* oath concluded his impassioned speech before the convention. As he finished, he simulated plunging an ivory letter opener towards his chest. The dramatic flourish was an imitation of the Roman patriot Cato the Younger.

Henry's speech inflamed his audience and the convention narrowly adopted his amendments. The text of his brief speech would first appear in print inside a biography of Henry in 1817, published 18 years following his death. Scholars would debate the accuracy of the text immediately following publication.

Patrick Henry shared conflictive views regarding freedom, particularly concerning the rights of slaves. As he acquired fresh lands, his slaveholdings grew. By the time of his death, he accumulated and owned 67 slaves. He publicly advocated abolition, but cited slavery's economic necessity towards sustaining Virginia agricultural production. The state ceased importing slaves by 1778, but the practice of distributing excess human inventories into southern states did not conclude until the Civil War.

Henry would enlist in the Revolutionary War as a colonel of the 1st Virginia Regiment. George Washington felt he was better suited as a senator than soldier. He saw no armed action and left the army by the winter of 1776. He missed the Fourth Virginia Convention in December 1775 due to his military commission.

On June 29, 1776, he was narrowly elected by the Continental convention as Virginia's first post-independence governor. He was taken ill almost immediately and recuperated at Scotchtown, Virginia. He became active behind the scenes in the war effort. He arranged for livestock and other foods to be sent to Washington's troops during their residence at Valley Forge during the brutal the winter of 1777-78. He served three years as governor before being replaced by Thomas Jefferson.

Following the conclusion of his first term, he served in the Virginia House of Delegates. He feared the concentration of a strong federal government. He actively opposed the United States Constitution at that time lacking an accompanying Bill of Rights. Henry would become elected Virginia's sixth governor in 1784. He completed a two-year term and was then replaced by Edmund Randolph. He returned to his law practice during his final years attempting to extricate himself from debt. He declined several political offices under subsequent federal governments including envoy to France.

He repaired his strained relationship with George Washington, who urged him to run once again for public office. He agreed and was elected as a delegate from Charlotte County in 1799. He died at the age of 63 inside his home before the legislature convened. His will left his estate and slaves to be divided between his wife and six sons. He did not authorize liberating any of his slaves. His posthumous tributes were overflowing and memorialized throughout the United States and Europe. His writings were few creating a handicap for historians evaluating his historical legacy. No one questioned his superb oratory skills and effectiveness as a public speaker.

The site of his most famous speech, Henrico Parish Church shares its own distinctive history. Founded in 1611, Henrico would become colonial Virginia's first college. The site was where colonists held Pocahontas captive, the daughter of Chief Powhatan. During her year of captivity, the first rector of the church, Reverend Alexander Whitaker taught her English and instructed her about Christianity. She was baptized as *Rebecca* and married John Rolfe, the pioneer of tobacco growth, who established Varina Farms, a plantation across the James River.

The remaining Anglican Church building was completed in 1741. During the Revolutionary War in January 1781, British General Benedict Arnold quartered his troops on the property during the occupation of Richmond. Arnold would become known as the most infamous historical American traitor. He initially served with the American forces before switching over to the British side. The chapel, accompanying structures and cemetery would be renamed to St. John's during the early 19th century.

George Wythe, the first law professor in the United States and a signor of the Declaration of Independence is buried on the grounds. Elizabeth Arnold Poe, mother of writer Edgar Allen Poe is also interred. A memorial marker acknowledges her, although her precise burial location remains unknown.

The Chief Justice Who Shaped The Philosophy of the Supreme Court
John Marshall Residence:
818 East Marshall Street, Richmond

John Marshall became one of the most influential individuals shaping the United States during its early formation. He was born in a log cabin in Germantown, Virginia in 1765 and would join the Continental Army during the Revolutionary War. He was involved in several battles and towards the end of the conflict, he was admitted into the state bar before winning election to the Virginia House of Delegates.

Marshall became an important cog in the mechanism of American government. He supported the U.S. Constitution playing an important role in Virginia's ratification. President John Adams recognized his abilities and sent him to France as an envoy to negotiate with French Prime Minister Talleyrand. The negotiations, later known as the XYZ Affair were an attempt to halt French attacks on American shipping bound for England.

Marshall traveled to France in 1797 as part of an American delegation, but found the French unreceptive unless the United States agreed to pay bribes. This policy was common practice during that era. The delegation refused the French demands and returned back without a treaty. An unofficial state of war continued between the two countries concentrated within the Caribbean shipping lanes. Once Talleyrand's tactics were exposed to the French ruling council, he backed off from his demands and the armed conflicts ceased.

Returning home, Marshall was elected to Congress emerging as a leader of the Federalist Party. President John

Adams chose him briefly as Secretary of State during a cabinet shake-up. In 1801, he was appointed to the United States Supreme Court where he would earn his primary historical distinction. He would hold the unique honor of serving on all three branches of the American government.

The Federalist Party was voted out of office upon the presidential election of Thomas Jefferson. Marshall quickly emerged as a key figure on the court, due to his personal influence with other justices. He was credited with moving the court away from seriatim opinions, replaced by a single majority opinion. The objective behind the decision was to express a clear ruling.

Within two years, many of the major decisions issued by the Marshall Court confirmed the federal government and Constitution supremacy over individual state rulings. Most observers credit Marshall with implementing the separation of powers principle cementing the judiciary branch as both independent and co-equal to the executive and legislative branches. He would serve as Chief Justice until his death from natural causes at the age of 79. President Andrew Jackson appointed Roger Taney to replace him

Marshall resided throughout his political and judicial career in his Richmond residence following its construction in 1790. The Federal-style brick building is located in the fashionable Court End featuring an expansive dining room and parlor on the first level and three bedrooms on the second. Outbuildings including a law office, kitchen, laundry and horse stables surrounded the original core.

One of Marshall's neighbors was attorney John Wickham, who defended Aaron Burr on treason charges, in a case presided over by Marshall. Burr had killed former Secretary of State Alexander Hamilton in a July 11, 1804 duel in New Jersey. Afterwards he became entangled in a land dispute in Louisiana. A private expedition that he organized resulted in a near-armed conflict with Spanish forces. The action was perceived by Jefferson as a violation of the Neutrality Act of 1794 and a treasonable offense.

Burr, who had been Jefferson's Vice President during his first administration was arrested in Mississippi Territory and returned to Richmond for trial before the United States Circuit Court. The charges were difficult to clarify and Burr was arraigned four times for treason before a grand jury finally indicted him. During his 1807 trial, Jefferson employed maximum influence towards a conviction. The prosecutor attempted to prove that Burr planned to raise an army and invade Mexico. His purported aim was to elevate himself into Mexico's monarch. Marshall was unmoved by the argument and the absence of evidence. Burr would be found *not guilty*.

**A Consuming Fire Destroying the Richmond Elite Richmond Theatre Fire Site (Currently Monumental Church):
1224 East Broad Street, Richmond**

On the day following Christmas in 1811, six hundred spectators filled the Richmond Theatre located near the State Capitol building. The patrons included recently elected Governor George William Smith. The audience had packed the venue to watch two full-length plays by the South Carolina-based Placide and Green Company troupe.

At the conclusion of the first act of the second play, a lit chandelier was raised by mistake igniting the backdrops and roof on fire. Those seated inside two levels of raised box seats were obliged to exit down a narrow winding staircase that collapsed from the stress. Panicked spectators leapt out of second and third-story windows. More than seventy people would perish including the governor. A significant percentage of Richmond's wealthy elites would be listed as fatalities

The disaster during that era became the deadliest urban calamity in American history. The dead were interred on the site. Over their crypt as a memorial, the city would construct Monumental Church, designed by renowned architect Robert Mills.

A Washington D.C. Equivalent Executive Mansion in Richmond
White House of the Confederacy:
1201 E Clay Street, Richmond

Marooned amidst the contemporary Virginia Commonwealth University (VCU) Medical Center, the White House of the Confederacy was the executive residence of President Jefferson during the Civil War between August 1861 and April 1865. The initial Executive Mansion was located four months previously in Montgomery, Alabama.

John Brockenbrough, President of the Bank of Virginia, constructed the Richmond residence in 1818. The mansion was located two blocks north of the State Capitol Building. The neighborhood then included U.S. Chief Justice John Marshall, famed attorney John Wickham and U.S. Senator Benjamin Watkins Leigh. During the antebellum period, Lewis Dabney Crenshaw purchased the house and added a third floor. He sold the home to the City of Richmond, which then rented it to the Confederate government for its executive mansion.

Jefferson Davis moved into the residence with his wife and young daughter Margaret and son Jefferson, Jr. Two additional children would be born during their residence. His third child Joseph would die during the spring of 1864 following a 15-foot fall from an east portico railing. The children's neighborhood playmates included George Smith Patton, whose father commanded the 22nd Virginia Infantry. His own son, George Jr. would famously command the U.S. Third Army during World War II.

The mansion would be left abandoned during the evacuation of Richmond during April 1865. Soldiers were able to seize the White House intact while the rest of Richmond's historic core burned. Abraham Lincoln toured the first level of the residence during his brief visit in Richmond. He considered viewing the second and third private levels of the house improper etiquette. He met with several local officials on the bottom level.

During Reconstruction, the residence served as the military headquarters for Virginia's District Number One and as residence for the commanding officer of the Department of Virginia. In October 1870, the city of Richmond reclaimed the house and used it as the Richmond Central School.

By 1890, the city officials planned to demolish the structure and upgrade the grounds into a more contemporary school. The Confederate Memorial Literary Society was established to raise funds in order to preserve the building. They purchased the title from the city and established the Confederate Museum in 1896.

From 1976 until 1988, the museum underwent a full-scale restoration returning the first and second floor interiors to their former Civil War appearance. The historic house would reopen for public tours in 1988 and is currently included as a visitor experience at the American Civil War Museum.

**Downtown Canal Walk Tracing Historic Richmond
Richmond Canal Walk:
1200 East Byrd Street To 1700 Dock Street, Richmond
Richmond Former Hydroelectric Plant and Mural
Venue:**

Corner E. Byrd Street and S. 7th Street, Richmond

The downtown Richmond Canal Walk stretches nearly two-miles. The route follows the contours of the James River passing the Kanawha and Haxall Canals. There are numerous access points located between 5th Street and 17th Street. The route has become a desirable Richmond attraction accommodating pedestrians, joggers, bicyclists and even boating enthusiasts during enticing weather months.

The canal trail offers an intriguing insight into urban Richmond history. In 1784, George Washington appeared before the Virginia Assembly to support legislation creating a waterway to bypass the fall line of the James River. The intent was to link the James River with the Kanawha River in western Virginia, ultimately continuing further into the Ohio River. The canal system enabled streamlined trade routes allowing boats to transfer tobacco and wheat from western Virginia to the Richmond marketplace. The vessels could then return home with finished goods. By 1840, canal construction was completed between Richmond to Lynchburg and a decade later terminated in Buchanan. The entire length spanned 197 miles.

During the late 20th century, the Richmond waterfront segment was integrated into an ambitious urban core development. On June 4, 1999, the grand opening ceremony was christened for the Canal Walk and canal boat excursions. A pipe measuring 1.3 miles long and up to eight feet in diameter was installed in the bed of the Haxall and Kanawha canals from west of the Robert E. Lee Bridge eastward to 16th Street. The pipeline collects wastewaters that are then processed through the city sewer system. When the sewers become overloaded, the water is routed to a 50-million gallon Shockoe retention basin until it can be treated at the wastewater treatment plant.

Over 20 historic medallions are embedded in the Canal Walkway acknowledging historic sites and attractions. Among them include Haxall Headgates, Belle Isle, Tredegar Iron Works, a former Confederate Army munitions plant, Brown's Island, Manchester and Free Bridges, CSX railroad trestle bridge, an Electric Trolley system, Tobacco Row, Burnt District and Shockoe Slip.

Near the junction of East Byrd Street and South 7th Street, a former hydroelectric plant has become repurposed into an open-air painted wall mural gallery. The venue features more than a dozen large murals, part of the city's collection exceeding over 150+ murals and street art installations. The Canal Walk is lined with restaurants, boutiques, residential complexes, sculptures and even benches for repose. Kayaks, canoes and rental bicycles are alternative transportation modes. The American Civil War Museum is located near the Tredegar Street extremity.

TWISTED TOUR GUIDES.com

The Permanent Resting Place for Presidents and Civil War Icons
Hollywood Cemetery:
Cherry and Albemarle Streets, Richmond

Established in 1847, the Hollywood Cemetery is Richmond's largest parcel of land stretched upon the banks of the James River. The cemetery spans 135 acres of valleys, hillsides and stately trees. The natural terrain and accumulated foliage resembles a lush parkland of serenity and repose. The terrain is solely blemished by an exorbitant sea of burial markers and gravestones within this community of the fallen.

Richmond's fabled *city of the dead* is concentrated upon Oregon Hill that was once part of William Byrd III's substantive estate. It would later become owned by the Harvie family and known as *Harvie's Woods*. Cemetery founders William Haxall and Joshua Fry became so enamored by the grandeur of Boston's Mount Auburn Cemetery, they resolved to create a similar environment within their hometown. The name *Hollywood* was derived from the abundant holly tree groves located throughout the property. The landscape was originally intended to resemble a garden themed cemetery. The mass casualties resulting from the Civil War intensified the concentration of burials.

There are few images more paralyzing and sobering than viewing a panorama of graves.

Two American Presidents, James Monroe and John Tyler are interred on the grounds. Yet it is the roster of Confederate Generals and President Jefferson Davis that attracts the majority of tourists.

Twenty-eight generals including George Pickett and J.E.B. Stuart are buried on the property, more than any other cemetery nationally. Jefferson Davis' monument towers over the Confederate designated sector mounted on a pedestal. His gaze mutely surveys the surroundings. A trace of past defacement scars the beard on the right side of his face.

Davis began his political journey with his election to the House of Representatives in 1846. He served only a single year before enlisting as a colonel in a volunteer regiment during the Mexican-American War. He was appointed to the United States Senate that same year, before resigning to run unsuccessfully for governor of Mississippi. In 1853, President Franklin Pierce appointed him Secretary of War. At the conclusion of Pierce's term, Davis returned to the Senate. He resigned in 1861 when Mississippi seceded from the United States.

During the Civil War, he guided the Confederacy's policies and became their commander-in-chief. Upon their surrender and his flight from Richmond, he remained in exile for two weeks accompanied by an intimate entourage. His troupe fled towards Wilkes County, Georgia with no defined agenda. The U.S. War Department assumed erroneously that he had been responsible for Abraham Lincoln's assassination. A hefty $100,000 reward was offered for his capture and his pursuers were close behind.

On May 4, he held a final meeting with his existing cabinet members and disbursed the remaining Confederate treasury to Captain Micajah Clark. He reunited with his wife Virginia, and their children. Five days later, he was captured in the farming community of Irwindale, Georgia. His party was awakened by gunfire from their pursuers. They resisted firing back and were soon surrounded.

Amidst the confusion, Davis dashed towards a nearby creek for cover. He had grabbed his wife's overcoat and lifted it upon his shoulders before he was detained. His capture was parodied by a song called *Jeff in Petticoats* that suggested he had attempted to escape in women's clothing. His humiliation was just beginning.

He would be transferred to Fort Monroe, Virginia and imprisoned. He was interned for more than two years before being released without a trial. He was often uniformly blamed for the Confederacy's defeat and ensuing misfortune.

The perception towards Davis amongst extremists would eventually alter. Over the subsequent decades, he would achieve an unmerited heroic redemption amongst proponents of the *Lost Cause of the Confederacy* mythology. Ignoring indisputable and the indefensible motive that slavery was the cause behind the conflict, followers attempted to claim that the Civil War was merely a dispute over state's rights. This discredited argument is still repeated today within political discourse.

Davis' post war absence of remorse coupled by his overtly racist rhetoric and policies has served his heritage poorly. He remains a contentious symbol of history and irreconcilable pride. The majority of public memorials honoring him throughout the southern states have been removed, either forcibly or by legislative decree. He has historically cultivated no middle ground for tolerance or negotiation towards his legacy.

From Aristocratic Household to Physical Rehabilitation Center
William H. Grant House:
1008 E. Clay Street, Richmond

The William H. Grant House was one of the largest houses built in Richmond before the Civil War during 1857. The sturdily residence features ornate cast iron window caps and Italianate detailing set upon an imposing red brick façade. The heavy cornice is composed of wood. The property is connected to the Benjamin Watkins Leigh House that was built between 1812 and 1816.

In 1892, the mansion would be acquired by the Sheltering Arms Hospital, who occupied it until 1965. The Sheltering Arms Institute has evolved into a state-of-the-science inpatient physical rehabilitation facility and network of outpatient centers. Clinicians, scientists, innovators and technologies research physical medicine and rehabilitation designed towards stroke rehabilitation, spinal cord damage and traumatic brain injury. The structure would be acquired by Virginia Commonwealth University Medical Center and currently houses office space for the Department of Dermatology and Risk Management Unit.

A Master Union Army Spy Who Wore Petticoats
Adams-Van Lew House Site (Currently Bellevue School)
2301 East Grace Street, Richmond

Elizabeth Van Lew was a prominent member of Richmond society when the Civil War ignited in 1861. She lived with her widowed mother in a lavish three-story mansion. She had been educated in the North and firmly opposed both slavery and succession.

She kept her private thoughts in a diary and pretended to be a loyal Confederate. Her wealthy neighbors celebrated early Rebel victories. She discreetly focused her energies on helping the Union army. Over the four years of the conflict, she would provide food and medicine to prisoners of war and assist in planning their escapes.

Her initial direct intervention occurred following the Battle of Manassas during July 1861. The Confederate military had no vacant space to detain prisoners of war. They herded them into a tobacco warehouse called the infamous Libby Prison. The harsh conditions resulted in the men suffering from disease, hunger and despair.

Van Lew volunteered to become a nurse, but was initially reject by Lt. David Todd, the half-brother of Mary Todd Lincoln, the wife of the President. Van Lew employed flattery and persistence to persuade General John Winder to allow her and her mother to bring food, books and medicine to prisoners.

The *Richmond Enquirer* and her neighborhood peers harshly criticized their efforts. Focused on her objectives, she ignored the abuse. She passed on information to prisoners via a custard dish with a secret compartment and through messages hidden inside her provided books. She bribed guards to provide prisoners with extra food and clothing. She had many transferred to hospitals where she could interview them in private. She aided prisoner's plans of escape and concealed some inside her residence for brief periods.

In December 1863, she assisted two prisoners escape Libby Prison via her underground network. Union General Benjamin Butler was so impressed by her stealth that he sent one man back to Richmond with orders to recruit her as a spy. She concurred with his request and began writing dispatches in a colorless liquid that turned black when combined with milk.

Van Lew would provide valuable information concentrating her efforts from contacts within the Belle Isle and Libby Prisons. By 1864, her spy network had expanded to a dozen informants. General Ulysses S. Grant acknowledged her efforts following his army's capture of Richmond and Petersburg in April 1865. She would be given marginal payment for her efforts, but she had already spent the majority of her personal fortune.

Once she was acknowledged publicly as a spy, Richmond society reviled her. Grant never forgot her assistance and appointed her as Richmond's postmaster upon his ascendency to the presidency in 1869. She held the position for eight years until Grant's successor, Rutherford B. Hayes, removed her from the position. She was left nearly financially destitute and contacted the family of Paul Revere, one of the Union officers that she'd assisted during the war. He was the grandson of the famous Revolutionary figure of the same name. His family along with other wealthy Bostonian families that she'd aided regularly provided her with funds.

A primary reason for her success was that Confederate officers presumed women did not possess the mental capacity or physical endurance to partake in espionage. This limited mindset applied to all other attributed *unladylike* activities. Over the course of the war, both sides eventually recruited hundreds of women to act as covert agents. The penalty for their capture was death.

Elizabeth Van Lew survived on a meager income until her death in 1900. She remained an outcast within Richmond. Her private diary detailing her Civil War adventures and thoughts would be discovered posthumously. Her mansion dated back to 1802 when Richmond Mayor Dr. John Adams constructed the building near Old St. John's Church. The structure would be razed in 1911 and the Bellevue School erected in its place the year following.

A Cursed Prison Evolves Into A Recreational Paradise
Belle Isle:
Middle of James River in Downtown Richmond

Belle Isle straddles the James River and was formerly known as Broad Rock Island. It was initially explored by Captain John Smith in 1607 and employed during the 18th century as a fishery. In 1814, the Old Dominion Iron and Nail Company operated a factory. A village including a school, church and general store inhabited the island throughout the 1860s.

During the Civil War between 1862 and 1865, the island was employed as a detention center for Union soldiers. An estimated 30,000 POW's were housed under the cruelest of conditions. An estimated 1,000 men died while under captivity. Many were left in semi-states of nudity prompting exposure related diseases and frostbite. Prison conditions were harsh and food scarce. Many prisoners suffered from scurvy, starvation and chronic diarrhea. They became emaciated and filthy in the extreme, covered in vermin. The conditions shocked President Lincoln following an eyewitness account and report in May 1864 by Lucius Chittenden, Assistant Secretary of the Treasury.

Following the war in 1904, the Virginia Electric Power Company built and operated a hydroelectric power plant there until 1963. The cursed former prison was converted into a natural wildlife habitat and recreational center. Today, hiking, birdwatching, picnicking and kayaking dominate the activities. Sections of the island remote from human presence are designated as the *East Coast Greenway*.

Insightful But Unpopular Clarity Expressed By A Globally Savvy Local Architect
Samuel Putney Houses:
1010 and 1012 East Marshall Street, Richmond

The Samuel Putney Houses are a set of two historic residences located near the former Confederate White House. Both are three-story, three-bay styled Italianate townhouses featuring extensive architectural subtlety and decoration. Delicate and ornamental iron works from the local Phoenix Iron Works (no longer in existence) are integrated into the exterior. The two houses were built for Sam Ayers in 1859, but named after later residents Samuel and Stephen Putney, father and nephew. The Putney's operated the renowned local shoe manufacturing operation Battle Axe Shoes. They resided there from 1862-1894.

Samuel Putney arrived from Massachusetts into Richmond in 1817 to sell shoes. His nephew, Stephen Putney, joined the family business that sustained the name following the Civil War. The company prospered despite the conflict and manufactured shoes for Confederate troops. During the post war 1880s, Battle Axe Shoes established an industrial plant at the intersection of Ninth and Perry Streets in the Manchester district.

By the first decade of the 20th century, the company had outgrown the facility and purchased a section of the former state fairgrounds. They constructed a manufacturing facility there at 2220 West Brand Street. The city of Richmond then was the fifth largest distributor of shoes within the United States. Putney Shoes remained at that location until 1946 when the building was sold to retailer Miller and Rhoads, employed for the store's mail order center.

The Putneys originally commissioned Richmond native architect Walter Blair for the design. His architecture practice was based in New York City. Blair attended Richmond College for two years before transferring to the University of Virginia, where he earned bachelors and master's degrees. The following year, Blair became accepted into the University of Pennsylvania School of Architecture. His award winning entry in an international competition sponsored by the Ecole des Beaux Arts in Paris earned him admittance there where he graduated in 1902.

Blair was related to Putney executive vice president Lewis Harvie Blair. His global perspective separated him from his local professional peers. Although a Confederate veteran, Blair staunchly supported the racial integration of blacks and whites in business and education.

He wrote essays, pamphlets and letters articulating *that dividing the races was neither cost effective nor good for business prosperity or citizenship*. His clarity of vision amidst the darkest ignorance behind Jim-Crow laws eventually became acknowledged as a welcomed rebuttal to Southern prejudicial presumptions. The immediate response towards his controversial and conflicted observations frequently isolated him locally.

The Putney family residences are currently located amidst the Virginia Commonwealth University (VCU) Health System's Court End campus.

TWISTED TOUR GUIDES.com

A Lone Survivor From A Catastrophic Pre-Invasion Inferno
Old Custom House (Central Portion of Former US Court of Appeals Building)
1100 East Main Street, Richmond

On Sunday morning April 2, 1865, the Confederate military lines near Petersburg severed following a nine-month siege by the Union army. The retreat of the rebel forces left the capitol of Richmond vulnerable and defenseless. The city was located only 25 miles north of Petersburg.

The Union army had made a previous attempt to invade Richmond during 1862 only to be thwarted by General Robert E. Lee's counterattack. This time with Union General Ulysses S. Grant in command and Lee's forces retreating, there would be no savior to protect the city.

Confederate President Jefferson Davis, his Cabinet and armed defenders abandoned the capitol and fled south on the last open railroad line, the *Richmond and Danville*. Retreating soldiers set fire to bridges and supply warehouses upon their departure. Amongst the numerous explosions was an Alms-House that was destroyed killing several of the residing paupers. Fires spread throughout the historic downtown leveling the commercial sector. The inferno reached the edge of Capital Square unrestrained. The travesty became known as the *Evacuation Fire*.

On April 4, the mayor and other citizens surrendered the city to the advancing military forces. Union Generals Godfrey and Ord oversaw the occupation. President Abraham Lincoln toured the fallen city by foot and carriage with his young son Tad. He visited the former Confederacy White House and Virginia State Capitol Building between April 4-7. Two days later, the war ended and one week later, John Wilkes Booth would kill Lincoln.

The Old Custom House was one of only two buildings within the historic core to survive. The edifice was originally completed in 1858 and housed both the treasury and offices of Jefferson Davis. Local architect Ammi B. Young designed the gray granite structure that would later be designated for Davis' treason trial in 1867.

Young's distinctive Palazzo design was maintained forming a backdrop for Capitol Square. The original Custom House building formed the center core of the modified structure. The postal service abandoned the building in 1991. The remaining structure accommodated the U.S. District Court and U.S. Court of Appeals for the 4th Circuit until the construction of a new federal courthouse was completed in 2008.

**Worshiping On The Alter Of a Lost Cause
Stewart-Lee House:
707 East Franklin Street, Richmond**

The Stewart-Lee House located near the State Capitol in Richmond was constructed in 1844 for Norman Stewart. The three-story, three bay, Greek Revival style brick townhouse features four interior end chimneys and is surrounded by a simple cornice.

Confederate General Robert E. Lee's wife, Mary Anna Custis Lee and daughter occupied the house following the confiscation of their Arlington mansion. Mary Anna was the great granddaughter of George Washington. Following his surrender at the Battle of Appomattox, Lee joined them on April 15, 1865. His stay would be curtailed after only three months due to *the result of constant callers.*

Lee was the son of Revolutionary War officer Henry *Light Horse* Lee III and a top graduate of the United States Military Academy. His military career began exemplary amidst the Mexican-American War. During the initial year of the Civil War, he served in minor combat operations and as a senior military advisor to Confederate President Jefferson Davis

Lee assumed command of the Army of Northern Virginia in June 1862 during the Peninsula Campaign in southeastern Virginia. His elevation followed the wounding of General Joseph E. Johnston. Lee's military fame gained traction when his force successfully drove the Union Army of the Potomac forces away from Richmond between June 25-July 1, 1862. The Union forces were under the command of General George McClellan.

Lee followed up his triumph with a victory in the Second

Battle of Bull Run that August. His forces attacked Maryland during the inconclusive Battle of Antietam before retreating back to Virginia. He won significant victories at Fredericksburg and Chancellorsville before attempting a second invasion of the North during the summer of 1863. Lee's acknowledged triumphs would cement his military legacy. His gains established the highest level of achievement for the Confederate military.

His forces would be defeated at the Battle of Gettysburg and then suffer decisive setbacks once General Ulysses S. Grant took command of the Union armies. Lee's aggressive and risky tactics resulted in excessive casualties for the doomed Confederacy due to their shortage of manpower. Despite later criticism, Lee developed a reputation as a skilled tactician by many historians. Grant was not one of his admirers. On February 6, 1865, Lee was appointed General in Chief of the Armies of the Confederate States. Two months later, he would surrender to Grant at Appomattox and the Civil War concluded.

Following the surrender, Lee urged former Confederates to cease their fighting. After President Abraham Lincoln's assassination, he supported the Reconstruction policies of successor Andrew Johnson.

Lee was neither arrested nor punished for his wartime participation. He lost the right to vote and was never returned his former mansion seized by the Union military. The property became the Arlington National Cemetery. Ten years following the war, his family would finally receive financial reparations.

Upon his retirement from battle, Lee shared conflictive views regarding the rebellion and slavery. He claimed that he opposed slavery philosophically, but supported its legality. He backed a free public school system for blacks, but opposed their right to vote. His rationale was fueled by his opinion that Southern blacks lacked the ability to vote intelligently.

Lee's military involvement towards the Confederate cause sometimes appeared lukewarm. He initially expressed indifference politically, but followed his home state of Virginia into the secessionist movement. He stated his desire for the United States was to remain intact. He curiously confessed that he would have accepted a senior Union command position at the beginning of the conflict. None had been offered.

Lee reflected that he had hoped to retire to a farm of his own following the war and live in obscurity. His perception as a celebrity Christ-like icon for ex-Confederates made that status impossible. Following his departure from the Stewart-Lee residence, he accepted an offer to serve as the president of Washington College based in Lexington, Virginia.

The institution's trustees parlayed his name for large-scale fundraising appeals. Lee is credited with transferring the university into a leading Southern college. He was well regarded by faculty and students and expanded the college's subject offerings by adding programs in commerce, journalism and law.

He established a policy of actively recruiting students from the North. He stressed tolerance, reportedly expelling white students cited for violent attacks on local black men. He publicly urged obedience towards authorities and respect for law and order. He privately chastised former ex-Confederates including Jefferson Davis and General Jubal Early for their frequent tirades and angry responses towards perceived Northern insults. He steered his public activities towards avoiding controversy.

In 1869, his former adversary, now President Ulysses S. Grant invited Lee to the White House as a symbol of reconciliation between former warring armies. He accepted the invitation. Lee opposed the construction of public memorials honoring the Confederate rebellion on the grounds they would prevent the healing of wounds inflicted during the war. He himself was memorialized significantly.

During the late 20th century, his own life would become further scrutinized, re-examined and sometimes criticized.

On September 28, 1870, Lee suffered a stroke at the age of 63 and died two weeks later from the effects of pneumonia. Initially no suitable coffin could be located for his body. Three caskets had been ordered for him, but a torrential rainstorm with flooding had blockaded access to Richmond.

All three caskets washed down the Maury River. One was swept ashore undamaged. The interior dimension proved slightly short, so that Lee was buried without shoes. He would be interred with his wife who died three year later beneath the chapel at Washington University. The institution would be later renamed Washington and Lee University.

In Richmond, a towering equestrian statue of Lee was erected on Monument Avenue along with four other prominent Confederates. Over 100,000 people attended the dedication on May 29, 1890. His statue was designed by French sculptor Jean Antonin Mercie and would be the largest of the five monuments. Four would be removed in 2020 with Lee's becoming the final decommissioned on September 8, 2021 at the direction of the state government.

Lee's reputation historically has evaded the scathing condemnation of other Confederate leaders. His perceived detachment from the cause and calls for post war reconciliation and solidarity spared him vicious attacks. He cultivated an admiring following from the North after the war. His stanch admirers have praised his character, devotion to duty and military success against a stronger and superior armed foe. One of his most enthusiastic epitaphs was delivered in 1874 praising him as *a foe without hate, a friend without treachery, a soldier without cruelty, a victor without oppression, and a victim without murmuring.*

Hero worship becomes a dangerous proposition when classifying mortals. It is questionable whether Lee would have allowed his iconic status to become propaganda for future generations espousing white supremacy and hatred.

Lee became a symbolic embodiment of the romanticized Southern *Lost Cause* mythology. Such falsehoods were as inaccurate then as today. He may have lived a steadfast life molded by character, yet his admission into sainthood or immortality is not based on credible grounds.

TWISTED TOUR GUIDES.com

**Repose and Recovery Atop Church Hill
Monte Maria Academy:
2100-2200 East Grace Street, Richmond**

Richmond's *Church Hill* is the highest vantage point in the city. It occupies two of the original squares laid out in 1737 by William Byrd II and William Mayo. Byrd chose the city's name because it reminded him of Richmond Hill, located outside of London. The view of the James River resembled to him the Thames River that splits the center of London.

In 1866, the Sisters of the Visitation of Monte Maria established a settlement one block away from the hillside vantage point. The community became a gathering location attracting residents of affiliated neighboring monasteries. When a sister member passed away, she was buried in the rear of the garden with three white roses clasped in her hands. When their headquarters moved to Rockville, Virginia, the order relocated the old graves to the new property.

For the first sixty years of their Church Hill residence, the Sisters operated a girls' school. Students were allocated a garden space for cultivation of their preferred plants and flowers. The present garden includes a walled combine including fishponds, fountains, birdbaths, and flowers. A cottage constructed on the grounds was built to accommodate Father A. J. Van Ingelgem, who became the Sisters' first chaplain. Since his passing, the cottage has housed members of Church Hill's residential community.

A walkway around the fountain designates the boundaries of the initial house constructed on the property. Richard Adams, Richmond's largest landowner during 1785, built the structure then called the *Old Mansion.*

In contemporary times, Monte Maria has become a refuge for individual and group retreats. The library, chapel and gardens are open for public visitation every Tuesday through Thursday and some weekends. Amidst the turbulent pace and pressures of modernity, it has become a welcomed destination for repose.

**A Delayed Posthumous Honor For A Merited Patriarch
George Washington Monument:
Capital Square, Richmond**

For all of the acclaim that later accompanied the life of George Washington, public monuments receded into an afterthought following his death in December 1799. The impetus to honor Washington's accomplishments and legacy screeched to a halt upon the presidential election of Thomas Jefferson.

Jefferson loathed Washington's rival Federalist Party and shared a contentious relationship with John Adams, the reigning president at the time of Washington's death. Jefferson and Washington ironically had worked together amicably. For most of their lives, they remained friends. Yet upon Jefferson's ascension to the presidency, past political grievances would re-surface. He would eventually reconcile with Adams and both men died on the identical day, July 4, 1826, precisely fifty years following the signing of the Declaration of Independence.

Publicly honoring Washington became a victim of petty political bickering. The Washington Monument located in Richmond became only the second equestrian statue of Washington to be unveiled within the United States. The first was unveiled in 1856 at Union Square, New York City.

The Richmond statue's cornerstone was laid in 1850, but not completed until 1869. The sculptural compilation features six other noted Virginians who impacted the American Revolution. They include Thomas Jefferson, Patrick Henry, Andrew Lewis, John Marshall, George Mason and Thomas Nelson, Jr. The lowest level of the monument features bronze allegorical figures that represent relevant themes and/or events.

Historically, the monument became the site for the February 1862 second inauguration of Confederate President Jefferson Davis and Vice-President Alexander Stephens. Elements of the monument were incorporated into the Seal of the Confederate States, where Washington became a revered honorary patriarch due to his Virginia birth and formation.

**The Origins of Collectible Trading Cards
Former Allen and Ginter Tobacco Company Site:
600 E. Cary Street NW, Richmond (Stemmery
Location)
Seventh & E Cary Street, Richmond (Factory Location)**

Collectible trading cards trace their origins to the tobacco industry and specifically Allen and Ginter, cigarette manufacturers formerly based in downtown Richmond. Their establishment was founded in 1865, eventually employing up to 1,100 individuals. The majority were young women who hand-rolled and packaged the cigarettes. The company became the first factory within the United States to hire predominantly women to manipulate cigarette production. Competitors soon imitated their labor practice.

Eighteen male commercial salesmen canvased the company's marketing territories elevating their product into international prominence. Allen and Ginter occupied three large brick buildings downtown, each five stories high providing them with 157,500 square feet of operating space. Two of the buildings comprised the manufacturing and shipping departments. One was used exclusively for the storage and preparation of tobacco leaves.

Beginning in 1875, the company became the first tobacco enterprise to issue colorful trading cards include inside each cigarette pack. Their initial intent was based on practicality. The rigid cards stiffened the soft packs making distribution and longevity easier. A collector craze for the printed cards soon followed that not only enhanced tobacco product sales, but stimulated competitor duplication.

One of the most eccentric card series issued by Allen and Ginter was entitled *Actresses* featuring *Omene*, an early practitioner of belly dancing on the American stage. The company released four trading cards featuring *Omene* that was later expanded in 1890 by the Kinney Brothers promoting *Sweet Caporal Cigarettes*. *Omene's* performances were viewed as too shocking for upscale theatre audiences. Burlesque shows and carnivals became her preferred showcase, offering an act featuring gyrating hips and corset-less costumes.

She evolved into a national media phenomenon. Few readers actually knew what she looked like. Her illicit reputation became further fueled by her rumored sexual and relationship liaisons. Keen towards self-promotion, her admitted affiliation with a press group in Chicago called the *Whitechapel Club* elevated her notoriety briefly to unprecedented heights.

The Whitechapel organization was founded by a group of Chicago based newspapermen in 1889. The designation was named after the district of London where the infamous *Jack The Ripper* prowled for victims. The anonymous serial killer was designated as the club's president. The jest was not fully understood or even appreciated by a puritanical shocked general public.

The organization was also informally named the *Suicide Club*. Interior walls of their meeting location were decorated with pistols and knives that had been employed in murders. Human skeletons were hung above the central table and skulls were fitted as shades for the gas-lit fixtures. Drinking goblets were reportedly fashioned from the skulls of deceased local prostitutes and tables created from coffins.

The eerie and macabre reputation attracted an exclusively male audience. Future American presidents William

McKinley and Theodore Roosevelt reportedly had visited the club. *Omene* became the sole acknowledged female to enter the confines during the club's abbreviated history. She was invited to dine there and afterwards suggestively dance, integrating skeletal bones into her routine. By today's standards, the display was more comical than sensual. She was sworn to secrecy, but offered her story anyway to the *San Francisco Morning Call* in the June 10, 1893 edition. She revealed what she had observed within the inner sanctum adding notable embellishments.

Her notoriety peaked following the article. The widely circulating tobacco cards provided a public glimpse of her appearance. Rather than flaunting her flesh, she dressed overtly modest draped either in her belly-dancing costume or inside a full-length hooded cloak. A veil often obscured her lips focusing on her heavily charcoaled eyes. This modest approach intended to accentuate her exotic and mysterious foreign appearance.

The novelty of the self-invented *Omene* withered rapidly. She would be arrested two years later in New York City for stealing valuable jewelry from her lover, Edmundo de Olivieri. Her identity was exposed upon her arrest as simply Nadine Osborne. She died in her late 20s or early 30s during 1899 in Montreal from cancer. Her celebrity status evaporated permanently.

Despite their own worldwide product recognition, Allen and Ginter would make a fatal strategic decision. In 1881, American inventor James Bonsack, 22, won a competition sponsored by the company to automate the cigarette production process. Bonsack developed a machine that rolled a single long cigarette that was then cut into separate units. The initial prototype was flawed with numerous design failures requiring constant attention to keep operational. Allen and Ginter decided not to employ the device and maintained their existing female hand-rolling process.

Competitor James Buchanan Duke understood the long-term benefits with automation. He immediately signed a contract with Bonsack for his machine's exclusive use. His company, the American Tobacco Company proactively worked with Bonsack to refine and address the machine deficiencies. His tactic ultimately propelled his company into industry dominance based on superior production capability.

Allen and Ginter recognized their error in judgment too late. By 1890 the company was reduced into one of five subsidiaries that formed the newly established American Tobacco Company Trust. That merger monopolized the tobacco industry.

The collectible card industry would proliferate following the tobacco industry consolidation. The T206 Honus Warner baseball card issued between 1909 until 1911 would become the most valuable example issued by the American Tobacco Company. Wagner was considered one of the most popular players of his era, but excessively conscious of his public image. He refused to grant extensive production of his tobacco collectible card because reportedly he did not want children buying cigarette packs to obtain it.

His high-minded ethical philosophy has developed later criticism for its inaccuracy. Wagner actively chewed tobacco and had appeared previously in advertisements for tobacco products. His true motive may have been predicated on baser motives...he simply wanted higher compensation.

Whatever his true intention, only an estimated 50 to 200 cards were distributed to the public. In 1933, one of the cards sold for an unprecedented $50. By 1991, the value had appreciated to $451 thousand. During 2016, the identical card sold for $3.12 million followed five years later at $6.6 million, elevating it into the world's most expensive sports card. In August 2022, a 1952 Topps brand Mickey Mantle baseball card eclipsed that record with an auction sale of $12.6 million.

Questions over provenance, doctoring and legitimacy have tainted the confirmation of authenticity for numerous Wagner card offerings. As long as its value continues to wildly appreciate, the fascination, deceit and insanity will continue.

**A Municipal Gothic Revival Architectural Marvel
Former City Hall Building:
1001 East Broad Street, Richmond**

The former Richmond City Hall occupies an entire downtown city block rivaling any municipally designed executive branch within the United States and Europe. Designed by Elijah E. Myers, the trophy Gothic Revival design features a unique symmetrical appearance. The 195-foot clock tower on the left side of the façade gives an impression of asymmetry. The completed masterpiece functioned as Richmond's City Hall from 1894 until the 1970s.

In architectural vernacular, the interior centers around a large skylit atrium surrounded by four levels of cloister-like arcades linked together by a grand staircase. The four principal levels are constructed in gray granite, extracted from quarries along the James River, near Petersburg.

Two historic buildings, the former 1818 city hall and the Edmund Randolph House, an 1800 octagonal-ended structure were demolished to prepare the site. The 1853-constructed First Presbyterian Church was relocated. Detroit based Myers was selected in 1884 following a design competition. The project was bid twice due to the lowest bids being significantly above the designated budget. A fresh competition was staged and a more cost efficient plan by the Boston firm of Wait and Cutter was selected. Working drawings were prepared during 1886.

Despite the Wait and Cutter's selection, the city council reversed their decision later that year and returned to the originally chosen Myers' project.

During his era, Myers was a well-respected professional

having designed the state capitol buildings in Colorado, Idaho, Michigan and Texas. The spectacular interior atrium completes the aesthetic package and over time would arguably justify the extravagance and cost overruns. Myers reportedly paid a bribe of $1,500 to ensure that his design would be fully adhered to. It was larceny well invested.

His completed version became the tallest locally until being surpassed by the First National Bank Building. Despite the extravagance and polish, the building's future became in jeopardy during 1915 upon the popularity of the Beaux-Arts architectural style. Proposals were submitted to demolish City Hall to create a mall aligned with the northern side of the Virginia State Capitol building. Renewed threat for demolition surfaced during the 1970s, but a solution became the restoration of the edifice in the early 1980s. The building is currently employed for office use. Any future attempts towards demolition would seem architectural heresy under the guise of contemporary idiocy.

TWISTED TOUR GUIDES.com

A Movable Feast To Understanding the Civil War
American Civil War Museum:
480 Tredegar Street, Richmond
White House of the Confederacy:
1201 E Clay Street, Richmond
American Civil War Museum:
159 Horseshoe Road, Appomattox

If writer Ernest Hemingway considered Paris a movable feast, Richmond's Civil War Museum is an equivalent with three exhibition sites dedicated to displaying and explaining multi-facets of the American Civil War.

The Civil War was a conflict that has eluded simplistic diagnosis and analysis. The struggle accompanying to unify the nation following exhaustive warfare still remains complex and polarizing. The three museum sites include the White House of the Confederacy coupled with two additional branches located on the historic Tredegar Iron Works grounds and the Appomattox battle site. Each site contains a comprehensive collection of militaria and artifacts.

The genesis of a Civil War museum began in 1894 with the Museum of the Confederacy located inside the former Confederate White House. The Ladies Hollywood Memorial Association raised funds to save the building from demolition. The residence maintains a collection of flags, weapons, documents and personal effects related to the Confederacy and features tours of the house restored to its 1861-65 appearance. Over 15,000 documents and artifacts are showcased. A newer building was built and opened in 1976 adjacent to the White House to better preserve and exhibit the museum's collections.

The historic Tredegar museum site traces its roots to 1836, the original iron works facility. The company manufactured an array of items including locomotives, train wheels, spikes, cables, ships, boilers, naval hardware, iron machinery, and brass items. A new building was constructed in 2019 featuring more than 7,000 square feet of gallery space for permanent exhibitions of items from the extensive Civil War artifact collection.

The Appomattox Museum opened in 2012, adjacent to the local Court House, site of the decisive battle. It's theme focuses on the closing days of the Civil War and beginnings of the Reconstruction era. The complex is situated on eight acres of land and contains 5,000 square feet for exhibits.

Far from glamorizing the war from a southern perspective, the intent of the three exhibitions is to provide a repository of historical memorabilia for research and continued discussion. The goal towards ultimate reconciliation may be distant, but a more informed public makes the inching forward process possible.

A Toppled Public Monument Representing A Lost Cause
Stonewall Jackson Monument:
1001 E. Broad Street, Richmond
Wickham-Valentine House:
1015 East Clay Avenue, Richmond

Despite serving as the capitol for the Confederate States of America, Richmond has wrestled profoundly with that distinction since the conclusion of the Civil War. Displayed public monuments of Confederate leaders have provoked strong emotions and reactions from Civil Rights protestors, particularly over the past decade.

Confederate General Stonewall Jackson's monument has remained unmolested within the tranquil confines of Capitol Square Park. Confederate President Jefferson Davis endured a violent toppling from his Monument Avenue perch on June 10, 2020 amidst public protests.

The two memorials share an important difference. Jefferson's memorial is owned by the city and Jackson's by the state. The sole impediment blocking Jackson's removal is state legislative approval. The current conservative political climate has cooled towards removing further historical monuments. This situation may change with a different political party in power. Strangely, Jackson's fate may have also evaded public desecration because the memorial inscription does not specify his popularly known *Stonewall* designation, instead only his birth name *Thomas*. He is dressed in his military uniform, but discreetly positioned away from major public traffic.

The offending sculpture might have simply become discarded or the bronze melted down for other uses. Instead, the disfigured work, originally commissioned in

1907, was laid on display horizontally inside the Valentine Museum in 2022. The edifice is recognized as an important piece of Richmond's history and represents an opportunity for open public discussion over the Succession movement and Jim Crow-era racism.

The Wickham-Valentine House was constructed in 1812 and considered one of the finest local examples of Federal period architecture. The house is a two-story structure covered by a shallow hip roof and surrounded by a low balustrade. The building was constructed for John Wickham and attributed to architect Alexander Parris. Wickham was the attorney who defended Vice President Aaron Burr during his trial for treason.

In 1882, Mann Valentine II purchased the property. He decorated the interior with artifacts including excavations of Native American earthwork mounds in the Southeast. Upon his death, he bequeathed the house and contents to the city to establish a museum. The focus of varied permanent exhibitions display, preserve and interpret Richmond's 400-year history. The context of the toppled Davis monument has become a perfect historical addition.

A bronze statue of Abraham Lincoln seated with his 12-year-old son Tad is positioned discreetly in the rear courtyard. The pair visited Richmond on April 4 and 5th, two days following the Confederate forces evacuation of the former Capitol.

The Valentine Museum was gifted the historic Decatur O. Davis House in 1988 to become included as part of the museum complex. Constructed during 1879 in the Second Empire architectural style, its original owner was a partner in a local wholesale grocery and liquor firm.

STONEWALL JACKSON MEMORIAL

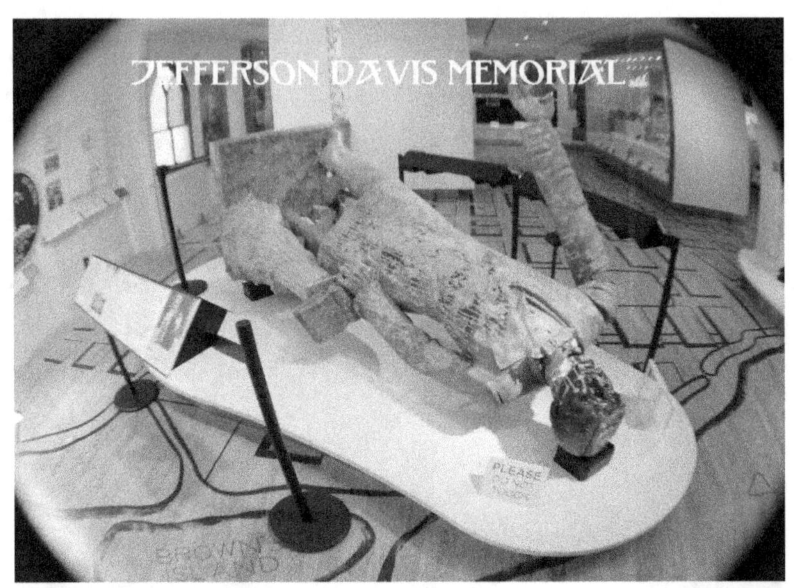
JEFFERSON DAVIS MEMORIAL
PLEASE
DO NOT
TOUCH
BROWN
SOUND

ENTRANCE
ENTRADA

DECATUR O. DAVIS HOUSE

A Commanding and Surrealistic Downtown Train Depot
Amtrak Main Street Station:
1500 E. Main Street, Richmond

Located in Shockhoe Bottom at the base of Church Hill, Richmond's Main Street Amtrak station remains a dominating and towering downtown presence. Its ornate, domed clock turret crowns the depot completed in the Renaissance Revival style in 1901. During that era, transcontinental train travel was an enchanting experience savored with indulgence and paced leisurely. Contemporary society has since altered that calm typified by a more frenetic speed.

The architecture firm of Wilson Brothers and Company, based in Pennsylvania, designed the station in extravagance and detailing. The station would accommodate train and later, city transit services. Locally called *The Clock Tower*, the depot has since been relegated into Richmond's secondary train outlet.

Transcontinental travel has changed markedly in affordability, speed and transport efficiency. Extended destination train service has become limited to those travelers unshackled by hectic time constraints and deadlines. Hub-encircled airports today rapidly stream and distribute passenger cargo. Their need for efficiency has displaced gilded chateau design. The striptease rituals enforced at airport security stations have likewise replaced civility and stately tranquil boarding rooms. The changes are necessary, but a poor commentary on modern existence.

Amtrak took over most intercity passenger train service within the United States during 1971, including the Main Street station. In 1972, Hurricane Agnes aggravated the

James River into flooding the depot. Three years later, Amtrak relocated its Richmond stops to Richmond Staples Mill Road, a much smaller suburban station, located five miles north of downtown. Fires plagued the Main Street station during 1976 and 1983.

Main Street station complex retains a distinctive mystique beyond simply a train depot. The complex is accentuated as a bizarre convergence of multiple overpasses and bridgeways spanning the adjacent parking lot. A surrealistic impression conveys travel passageways merging together into a collective denominator. The charisma of leisure transport may have become a forgotten legacy, but remaining icons like the Main Street station reinforce the memory of a former magnetism.

A Fitting Shrine to Edgar Allen Poe
Edgar Allen Poe Museum (Old Stone House):
1914 E Main Street, Richmond
Poe's Former Residential Sites: Corner of Second and
Franklin Street, Richmond (Demolished in 1883)
Ellis House, Fourteenth Street and Tobacco Alley,
Richmond

Edgar Allen Poe and his epic poem *The Raven* are frequently associated with Baltimore. Ironically he was born in Boston, spent most of his adult life in Richmond and completed his first draft of *The Raven* in Saratoga Springs, New York.

Poe was born on January 19, 1809, the second child of American actor David Poe, Jr. and English-born actress Elizabeth Arnold Hopkins Poe. He had an elder brother named William and a younger sister named Rosalie. His mother was an English stage actress who traveled from London with her actress/mother to Boston in January 1796. Her mother died two years following their arrival.

Elizabeth continued her acting career along the East Coast performing in over 300 roles. Baltimore born David Poe, Jr. saw her perform in Norfolk, Virginia and decided to join her acting troupe. He abandoned his family's wishes for him to study law and married her in 1806. She bore Edgar at a boarding house near Boston Common on January 19, 1809 where she had performed on stage only ten days before.

David deserted the family in 1810 due to his chronic alcoholism. He moved to New York and abandoned his stage career. He reportedly died in Norfolk, Virginia the following year. Poe's mother contracted tuberculosis in 1811 while residing in a Richmond boarding house. By

October, her condition and finances had worsened to such a significant degree that she could no longer perform. A benefit performance was staged for her behalf on November 29. She remained bedridden surrounded by her children. She expired on Sunday morning, December 8 at the age of twenty-four and was buried at St. John's Episcopal Church. A memorial marker designates her approximate burial site, as the actual location is unknown.

Throughout his mother's illness, fellow stage performers Mr. and Mrs. Luke Usher cared for the three Poe children. Their name likely inspired Poe's tale *The Fall of the House of Usher*. Each child was disbursed through adoption upon Elizabeth's death.

Edgar's own tragic fate would be heavily influenced by his mother's premature death. He was adopted into the home of John Allan, a successful Richmond merchant. Poe served as a lieutenant in the Richmond Youth Honor Guard and studied ancient and modern languages briefly at the University of Virginia. He dropped out after a year, the consequence of mounting debts.

He fabricated his name as *Edgar A. Perry* and age to 22 (he was 18) he joined the army as a private in May 1927. That year, he released his first 40-page book of poetry that eluded recognition and attention.

His military status floundered once he revealed his true name. His adopted father was unsympathetic towards his creative efforts and professional prospects. He did support Poe's effort to gain a discharge so that he might receive an appointment into the United States Military Academy at West Point.

He was accepted as a cadet on July 1, 1830. His West Point

experience was brief and disastrous. His adopted father disowned him when he was expelled. Poe purposely exited the program by getting court-martialed for *gross neglect of duty and disobedience of orders*. He refused to attend formations, classes or church. He pled *not guilty* certain that he would be condemned and dismissed.

Despite his dishonorable discharge, several of his West Point peers pooled their resources together enabling him to finance a volume of poetry entitled *Poems*.

Poe's brief residence in Baltimore followed and initiated an evolution from poet to serious author of imaginative short stories. He would also meet his first cousin Virginia there who at the age of 13 became his wife on September 22, 1835.

Poe was completely dependent on his writings for income. His published works and various editorial positions extended his name recognition throughout the publishing industry, but contributed little initially towards his financial stability. His alcoholism, erratic behavior and public accusation of plagiarism against Henry Wadsworth Longfellow alienated him from many peers. Longfellow never responded to his charges. In 1842, Poe's wife Virginia first became ill with tuberculosis. Five years later she would die from the disease at the age of 24.

Poe had a life pattern of pursing beautiful women who either rejected him or died young. He became devastated and despondent following Virginia's death. She has often been cited as his inspirational Lenore in *The Raven*. She however was still living upon its publication. It is equally probable that his mother was the model for the ill-fated Lenore.

The poem was first released in the *Evening Mirror* on January 29, 1845. The work was concurrently published in *The American Review: A Whig Journal* under a pseudonym. The response and acclaim launched Poe's reputation into international recognition

During the two years following Virginia's death, Poe had established his literary legacy. His life was an absolute shambles. He'd unsuccessfully attempted to court poet Sarah Helen Whitman and a childhood girlfriend Sarah Elmira Royster. His behavior and worsening drinking sabotaged both prospects.

At 40, his abrupt and mysterious death augmented his legend. On October 3, 1849, he was discovered delirious and semiconscious in the gutter of Gunner's Hall Tavern in Baltimore. Currently the location is a parking garage. He was dressed in another man's clothing and muttering incoherently.

Diverse suppositions speculated that he might have been severely beaten, drugged or self-intoxicated. Suggestions of a heart attack, terminal syphilis and even rabies were suggested as possible causes. He died four days later at the Washington Medical College during the early morning hours never regaining consciousness. His relevant medical records including his death certificate would vanish.

Posthumously, his extensive body of writings would find an expansive and appreciative audience. His style of writing was frequently replicated. His unique material and originality has never been competently matched.

The Richmond based Poe Museum was initially created in 1906 inside the former *Southern Literary Messenger* building. The location was where Poe began his journalistic career. Poe researcher and collector James Whitty along with a likeminded group of literary enthusiasts started the group. The state's first monument to the writer initially failed to generate enough public support and funding.

The city's building inspector decided to condemn the *Messenger* edifice and demolish it as part of a plan to widen 15th Street. Wiley was able to convince preservationist Archer and Annie Jones, tenants of Richmond's *Old Stone House* to relocate the museum inside the historic property. The structure is considered the city's oldest residential building. The bricks and granite from the *Messenger* building were employed to pave the garden path leading to a memorial park and construct a shine honoring Poe. The Jones allowed the location to be constructed upon an empty lot behind the *Old Stone House*. The Poe shrine was opened to the public on April 26, 1922.

There is no evidence that Poe lived or even visited inside the *Old Stone House* during his lifetime. Due to its historical significance, he would have been well aware of its existence. He reportedly stood guard as a youth cadet outside of the house and passed it regularly on his habitual walks down Main Street to Rockett's Landing. The house was constructed during the brief reign of English King James II from 1685-1688. A peculiar feature of the house is the insignia IR located to the right of the east window on the south side of the house.

During one of its later incarnations as a curio shop, a live bear was featured on display. Two black cats named *Edgar* and *Pluto* presently patrol and guard the premises. Both were discovered as tiny kittens in the *Enchanted Garden* section in 2012 and cared for by museum staff volunteers. Poe had a strong affinity for his beloved tortoiseshell cat named *Catterina*. She sat on his shoulder to watch him write and slept on his wife's chest to keep her warm during her fatal illness.

420

Public Bath Houses Before Indoor Plumbing
Branch Public Bath #1:
1801 East Broad Street, Richmond
Branch Public Bath #2 (Razed):
709 West Main Street, Richmond

Not until 1950 did most Richmond homes have indoor plumbing. Access to clean water for drinking and bathing periodically resulted in disease outbreaks ranging from cholera to polio.

During 1909, local banker John P. Branch opened the city's first public bath. He constructed the facility and then deeded title to the city. He stipulated that the city reserve $3,000 annually to operate it. Still standing Public Bath #1 employed coal-fired boilers to provide hot water for showers and tubs on the second floor. The success of the facility resulted in the construction of a second public bath since demolished.

Facilities were segregated and users would pay 10 cents to receive a bar of soap and sterilized towel. Admission for children was 3 cents. Time limits were imposed upon men of twenty minutes and for women, thirty minutes. At the peak of popularity in the 1920s, public baths serviced an approximate 80,000 residents. Winter became the most popular time as during the spring and summer, creeks and lakes became popular bathing options.

The Branch Baths remained in operation until 1950. By then the rise of indoor plumbing had deeply curtailed patronage.

**Richmond's First Modern Skyscraper
First National Bank Building:
827 E. Main Street, Richmond**

Leading the charge into a fresh era of Beaux-Arts architecture, the First National Bank Building became Richmond's initial skyscraper in 1913. Architect Alfred Bossom, an associate with Clinton and Russell of New York, designed the steel framed high rise that combined monumental scale with contemporary technology. The structure featured a base of Corinthian columns supporting a towering 19-stories of office space overlooking the financial district. The building's nine-story shaft has deep-set paired windows broken by balconies near the top. This distinction was considered unusual flair then for local constructions.

The exterior is clad in brick, limestone and granite with exquisite detailed ornamentation. The appearance would be altered when its Florentine-style cornice was removed. First National Bank was Virginia's oldest banking institution before eventually becoming Sovran Bank. The edifice would evolve into residential housing and office condominiums.

A Yuletide Season To Remember and Forget
Virginia Governor's Executive Mansion:
Capitol Square, Richmond

Virginia Governor Elbert Lee Trinkle was voted into office during the 1921 election by winning the Democratic primary with 57% of the vote and the general election with 66%. He had begun his political career in 1915, winning a seat in the state Senate. He was branded a *Moderate Progressive* for his support of Prohibition and woman suffrage. He opposed the establishment of a coordinate college for women at the University of Virginia, rationalizing that it might undermine four already operational educational institutions for women. He lost in a 1916 congressional race to unseat an incumbent.

Following his election as governor, Trinkle floated a bond plan to finance better roads intentioned towards rural residents. That voting contingent then composed two thirds of the state's population. He overestimated the popularity of his proposed financing plan portrayed by his own party as a vehicle to increase taxes. Party chairman Hal Flood and important influencer Harry Boyd obstructed his plan. Trinkle would compromise by approving a three-cent gas tax increase proposed to complete the road system within seven years.

Boyd would evolve into his political nemesis and barrier to higher office. The Virginia road network issue effectively ended Trinkle's political career. Boyd outmaneuver him on critical issues and consolidating power within the party.

Trinkle eventually broke ranks with Boyd concentrating on issues such as prison reform and the ill-fated Racial Integrity Act. The legislation condemned racial integration and even promoted forced sterilization. As governor, he became isolated as simply a figurehead and would be replaced by Boyd in the 1925 Gubernatorial primary. Boyd would win election to one term as governor before running for the U.S. Senate. He served 32 years afterwards while dominating Virginia politics. There was no space for Trinkle amidst his influential domain.

As the 1925 Christmas holiday concluded, Trinkle was only weeks from relinquishing the executive mansion. The family was planning and packing for a return to Wytheville, Virginia and his law practice. He would complete a distinguished two-decade career cultivating a stellar reputation for his oratorical and debating skills.

On January 4, 1926 while he was absent from the mansion, his wife Helen and their children were lounging leisurely on the property. Five-year old son Billy dashed through the ballroom with a lit sparkler. In his enthusiasm, he accidentally ignited a nearby dry and brittle Christmas tree. The blaze spread quickly. Billy and his mother were safely evacuated immediately. Helen realized that their 15-year-old son Lee was taking a nap upstairs. She dashed past restraining police and firefighters to re-enter the house and head towards his room.

She awakened Lee, but fire department ladders were unable to extend to the bedroom window. The pair jumped dropping into rescue equipment. Her heroics resulted in second-degree burns requiring weeks of recuperation at the Medical of Virginia Hospital. She was an accomplished violinist and her Stradivarius instrument was consumed in the fire.

Following his tenure as governor, Trinkle would support President Franklin Roosevelt's *New Deal* policies during the 1930s in contrast with Boyd. Trinkle refused to run for any subsequent elected office and became an executive, then president of the Shenandoah Life Insurance Company in 1933.

In 1939, a state investigation into the company's business practices resulted in the discovery of improper loans and investments. The investigation recommended that someone more knowledgeable with the insurance industry lead the company. Trinkle denied all wrongdoing and was stung by the accusations towards his integrity. He became distressed by the adverse publicity. Amidst the speculation and rumors, he died of a heart attack on November 25, 1939. Son Billy Trinkle would live until the age of 93, marry and become a great grandfather, dying in 2014.

An Uncompromising Agent of Change Against Discrimination
Oliver Hill Building:
102 Governor Street, Richmond

Oliver Hill challenged the status quo with regard to racial discrimination within Virginia. As a prominent black attorney and civil rights activist, Hill and his colleagues filed more legal challenges to segregation than any other lawyers in the South. He was the lead attorney for the Virginia State Conference of the National Association for the Advancement of Colored People (NAACP) and remained professionally relevant until his retirement in 1998.

He was born in Richmond and earned his law degree in 1933 at Howard University. There he met future NAACP lawyer and Supreme Court Justice Thurgood Marshall. The pair would collaborate on numerous high profile and landmark cases. He was one of the leading lawyers in *Davis v. County School Board of Prince Edward*, one of five lawsuits that were consolidated into the Supreme Court case *Brown v. Board of Education of Topeka, Kansas* in 1954. The Court's ruling became the first stride towards overturning an extended history of injustice.

The decisive victory declared that segregation in public education was unconstitutional. Hill believed that political activism was an important component in assaulting discrimination. He was the first African American elected to Richmond's city council in 1948.

On October 28, 2005, two years before his death, Virginia's State Finance Building was re-named in his honor. Constructed in 1894, the structure is a three-story Beaux Arts style building with a buff brick veneer and terra cotta detailing. It has served various functions including the State Library collections, Supreme Court and Attorney General's offices. It is currently the headquarters for the Lieutenant Governor and Virginia Department of Agriculture and Consumer Services.

**A Futuristic Icon Sustained Upon Church Hill
WRVA Building**

200 North 22nd Street, Richmond

In 1968, internationally renowned architect Philip Johnson designed a futuristic oddity that remains an important 20th century architectural landmark. His firm at the time, Budina and Freeman, oversaw the construction of a cubist structure to house WRVA (AM), one of Virginia's first radio broadcast stations. During the evening hours, WRVA could be heard across most of the eastern half of North America with a good radio.

Perched upon Church Hill, the minimalist two-story horizontal complex is accompanied by a vertical communications tower. The completed pair became the toast of modernism. Constructed in concrete, the iconic project followed Johnson's successful designs of the New York Pavilion at the 1964 World's Fair, a new wing for Manhattan's Museum of Modern Art and Washington D.C.'s Dumbarton Oaks Museum and Kreeger House.

The originally installed Western Electric transmitter was replaced during the 1980s with a 50,000-watt Continental transmitter. The Western Electric unit would serve as a back up. During the 1990s, a newer Harris transmitter replaced the Continental.

The formal dedication attracted Johnson, Virginia governor Mills Godwin and the radio station's owner, general manager and notable broadcasters. The completed development instantly became a cornerstone of historically staid Church Hill.

In 1974, the WRVA traffic helicopter lost a tail rotor at low altitude and crashed into a South Richmond house on West 31st Street. WRVA reporter Howard Bloom, the pilot and a young child were killed in the disaster.

The radio station would undergo numerous ownership changes before being acquired in 1992 by Clear Channel Communications, the forerunner to iHeartMedia. WRVA's departure from the location necessitated a major renovation between 2007 until 2008. The former radio station was converted into a clinic for the organization ChildSavers, an association entrusted with the recovery and health of over 6,000 children annually. Most of their clients are referred to the program via social workers, teachers, police, and the justice system.

The reconstruction project preserved the white concrete surface, cubist framework and enormous disproportionate windows. Colorful interiors were installed to create an upbeat and cheerful environment. Johnson, who passed away at the age of 99 in 2005, would not witness the restoration of his creation. Yet his futuristic vision remains as novel today as the when first introduced over a half-century ago.

The Reinventive Presence of Richmond's Tobacco Row
Former R. J. Reynolds Tobacco Building:

320 S 12th Street, Richmond
Former J. N. Boyd and Company Tobacco Warehouse Ruin:
544 E. Cary Street, Richmond

Tobacco has remained one of the largest industries in Richmond. Accompanying ethical issue behind such an acknowledged carcinogenic product has remained a contemporary issue, despite a decline in domestic consumption. In 1973, Philip Morris USA opened a 1.6 million-square-foot manufacturing center in South Richmond that then created half of the cigarettes sold in the United States.

At the time of the construction, 37% of American adults smoked, Marlboro was the world's top tobacco brand and television advertising for cigarettes had just been banned. Philip Morris was the region's largest private employer with more than 10,000 workers. The Capital One Financial Corporation would eventually surpass the company's lead position.

The Food and Drug Administration currently regulates the tobacco industry. One of the company's largest expenses is attributed to numerous payouts generated by successful lawsuits against them. American adult smoker levels have dropped below 20% according to the Centers for Disease Control and Prevention.

Despite the known hazards, cigarettes remain a profitable industry even if pricing has become elevated to unprecedented heights. Alternative products to conventional cigarettes have been introduced ranging from nicotine gum to devices converting nicotine-infused liquids into vapor. They sustain an addictive marketplace. Once cannabis becomes legalized federally, a resulting growth market will materialize

Within the historical downtown core and traditional Tobacco Row district along the James River and Kanawha Canal, a collection of warehouses and factories remain a reminder. The tobacco industry growers and shippers established facilities there due to the ease of river accessibility for export. During the Civil War, the infamous Libby Prison and nearby Castle Thunder detention center were established by the Confederate government.

The changing dynamics and demographics of the tobacco industry prompted a mass exodus of tobacco related commercial tenants during the late 1980s. The empty shell buildings ceased to make economic sense for an industry that could construct facilities upon cheaper suburban real estate. Following the completion of Richmond's James River Flood Wall in 1995, large-scale redevelopment projects repurposed the former warehouses into modernized commercial developments, lofts, condominiums, and retail space.

**Richmond's Gay Godfather's Mysterious
Disappearance
409 Club, 409 Broad Street, Richmond
Dial Tone Club, 3526 W Cary Avenue, Richmond
Smitty's Club (Lesbian Oriented Clientele), 310 S
Sheppard Street, Richmond
Cha-Cha Palace, 719 West Broad Street, Richmond**

Richmond's gay community during the early 1970s was a clandestine fraternity that straddled a fragile line between acknowledgement and persecution. The gay district was known as *The Block* and encompassed the boundaries of First, Franklin, Main and Foushee Streets.

The Alcohol Beverage Control (ABC) frowned upon granting liquor licenses for gay bars. The police vice squad became a familiar and unwelcomed presence, not conducive to attracting clientele. Harassment was standard policy and procedure. LGBTQ community service organizations were nonexistent.

Leo Joseph Koury was a heterosexual businessman raised in the restaurant business. He perceived alchemy within a community seeking lifestyle friendly outlets. He labeled himself *the Godfather of the gay community* and managed to briefly establish a cooperative environment with the ABC and law enforcement patrols. Discreet cash disbursements kept his clubs under the conventional community radar.

Koury had plenty of protective cash as his operations became very successful. He located his clubs inside *The Block* where real estate and rents were inexpensive. His lucrative holdings included the 409 Club, the Dial Tone and Smitty's Club, oriented towards a lesbian clientele. His operations became so profitable, that competition became inevitable.

Three business partners decided to open an afterhours club called the Cha Cha Palace in 1977. Their success was immediate. Clients converged from New York City, Baltimore, Washington D.C. and Norfolk. Koury's monopoly was severely threatened as his clientele shifted towards the more upscale and fresh location.

He offered to buy out one of the partner's share, but was rejected. Koury was considered generally very approachable and charming. Unwanted competition changed everything. Shortly after his offer was discarded, a bullet was fired through a front window of the Cha Cha Palace. The club employed a bouncer, Charles Kernaghan, who was murdered.

One year later, Koury's empire was near collapse. He was indicted by a federal grand jury in connection with Kernaghan's killing. His misdeeds revealed another attack conducted by a hit man that killed one man and wounded two others. He was also the alleged instigator of an abduction-for-ransom attempt of a local pharmaceutical heir.

Koury vanished completely upon news of the indictment and stayed gone. He would remain on the FBI's 10-most-wanted list for twelve years. His friends and acquaintances initially were shocked by the disclosures due to his perceived hospitable and charming demeanor. His business rivals were not surprised. Koury exhibited relentless and threatening obsession towards anyone challenging his livelihood.

His lengthy departure stimulated innumerable speculation and rumors. Erroneous sightings placed him in South America with implications that he had stashed over $1 million in cash for disbursement. He never contacted his wife or four children.

The truth was bizarrely revealed in June 1991, when a congenial part-time store clerk named William Franklin Biddle registered into a San Diego hospital. He died shortly afterwards from a brain hemorrhage. Biddle was the altered name for 56-year old Leo Koury. He had been living alone and destitute locally. He didn't drive or own a vehicle.

He had reinvented himself arguably as an improved version. He was regarded by store patrons *as quiet, simple and a devout Catholic fluent in Spanish and Arabic*. He reportedly often assisted those in need, lending or giving away money. Investigators, following a tip, discovered that he'd hidden $25,000 inside a safety deposit box. Before that revelation, he had been given a pauper's burial.

The Godfather had met a demise more incredulous than the Richmond bar empire he'd once presided over. None of his former properties or competitors remains in operation and the neighbor has not gentrified noticeably. Leo Koury, whose vanishing act once commanded extensive attention has completely receded from local history.

409
409 CLUB

CHA CHA PALACE
RALPH'S, INC.
TWISTED TOUR GUIDES.COM

A Perpetrator(s) Preying On Richmond's Elderly Population
Golden Years Serial Killer Acknowledged Murder Sites:
Kensington Gardens Retirement Home (Johnston-Willis Hospital):
2900 Kensington Avenue, Richmond
Homeless Victim: 640 West Broad, Richmond
Jane Foster, 4904 Monument Avenue, Richmond
Lucille Boyd, 2800 Block West Grace Street, Richmond

Beginning in 1990, a series of unsolved murders plagued the city's West End. At least thirteen women were murdered under similar circumstances. Investigators suspected the responsible perpetrator was a lone serial killer, although additional suspects would later emerge.

The victims were aged 55 to 89 and lived by themselves. The first six were black and stabbed to death. The remaining seven were white and strangled. The killings were labeled the *Golden Years Murders* due to the age of the victims.

In July 1996, 51-year old vagrant Leslie Burchart was arrested for trespassing. He unexpectantly confessed to killing three homeless men in Richmond. He was tried, convicted and sentenced to life imprisonment. Three years later, he confessed to killing four other the female victims on the official list of the Golden Years Murders. Was his admission truthful or a mere publicity stunt?

Shortly before his death in 2022, Burchart recanted his confessions and stated his innocence. His schizophrenic condition made his confessions questionable. Some of Burchart's originally claimed victims according to the Richmond Police Department did not die from foul play, rather from alcohol poisoning. Burchart's demise made closer follow-up impossible. A police detective that was involved in Burchart's arrest and interrogation disclosed publicly that Burchart had likely killed many more individuals than he claimed.

The majority of the murders persist unsolved and a lone suspect's guilt remains in question.

A Purported Nobleman Swindles Elite Richmond Society
Otto Von Bressensdorf's Former Residence:
1 Brockenbrough Lane, Richmond

During 1993, *Baron* Otto von Bressensdorf swept into Richmond society as a maelstrom brandishing honors and titles of family pedigree. During the 1980s, he had created an investment enterprise that he named Lyons Capital. The entity attracted entrepreneurs seeking venture capital to initiated or expand their existing operations. Lyons Capital required an upfront $10,000-$30,000 finders fee and boasted of a 70% success rate.

Richmond's elite embraced Otto and Elena von Bressensdorf socially and his optimistic promises. His investment house reportedly earned $1 million annually. The funds were deceitfully funneled into furnishing their 1920s Tudor-style mansion spread over 1.3 acres adjacent to Carillon Playground. The couple spent lavishing and ostentatiously. The interior opulence featured a classically painted ceiling, sumptuous artwork, chandeliers, inlaid decorative wood flooring, magnificent fireplaces, rugs and expensive furnishings. They drove around Richmond in a conspicuous 1964 Rolls Royce Silver Cloud and 1986 Jaguar Vanden Plas.

The *Baron* decorated his office with mounted military medals and framed historical honors heralding his claim of German nobility. He crafted stories elevating his family's heroic attempt to fight Hitler during the Nazi era. Conspicuously positioned on a wall was a photo of him posing with Ronald Reagan. He fabricated stories touting his film industry connections. To complete his profile, he hired individuals representing phony companies to write glowing reference letters falsifying his business successes.

He provided Dunn & Bradstreet with fraudulent financial statements resulting in an impressive credit rating for Lyons Capital.

A financial scam that pays out zero dividends is ultimately fated to public disclosure. Some of Lyons' investors went bankrupt awaiting a promised cash infusion that never materialized. They filed suit against Lyons Capital and began discussions with law enforcement agencies.

On January 1998, the FBI indicted the von Bressensdorf's on 209 counts of fraud, wire fraud and money laundering. The investigation raised serious questions regarding both of the perpetrator's origins, nationalities and heritage claims. Both were convicted and sentenced to 11 years and 3 months in prison.

Shortly after sentencing, the federal government seized the couple's belongings and staged an auction on the premises of their 18-room mansion. Over 500 bidders converged upon the grounds including the couple's 18-year-old son Michael. Bidders devoured the carcass of the former opulent estate that included paintings, jewelry, antiques and combined lots of household items. The 7,000 square foot brick mansion sold for $590,000.

Years following the grand disbursement and scandal, the residence has appreciated significantly, despite or due to the notoriety. In November 2021, the house sold for $1.1 million. The property currently remains unoccupied, stripped of its former luxurious trappings. The latest offering price is listed at $1.9 million.

The *Baron* and Elena vanished from local and national headlines upon their incarceration. There has been no published record of their release or any attempt at reinvention. Richmond society will never forgive or entirely forget their duplicity.

**A Late Night School Board Eviction Attempt Taints The Legacy of a National Political Figure
Richmond City Hall:
900 E Broad Street, Richmond**

L. Douglas Wilder became one of Virginia's most nationally renowned administrators, serving as the country's first elected black governor. He left office in 1994 and began working in the private sector over the next decade. In 2004, seemingly missing the limelight, he ran for mayor in Richmond winning 80% of the vote in a four-candidate race.

He didn't hesitate long before flexing his newly acquired power. He fired department heads, publically criticized public officials, and initiating secret investigations. In August, he awoke the wrath of the local school board by opposing a City Council ordinance. The ordinance enabled the school administration to remain in their historic headquarters within City Hall for an additional five years. Wilder wanted the board to vacate the premises to make room for the city economic development department. During the same power grab, he attempted to obtain the authority to hire and fire the superintendent of schools.

Wilder didn't view the necessity for due process to slow his ambitions. On September 22nd, accompanied by local police, 150 movers from three separate companies dismantled the school board offices on the top six floors of City Hall. The movers relocated the contents into transport vans. The eviction was halted abruptly at midnight after school board members, hearing of Wilder's action, rushed to their offices. A circuit court judge simultaneously issued a temporary restraining order instructing the movers to return everything. The aborted transfer cost the city an estimated $1 million.

Wilder was defiant regarding his actions. He had already blazed a brushfire of controversy by firing the police chief and a dozen of long-term city employees claiming that they had not been hired properly. Each was allowed to reapply for their positions. One chose not to. The reapplying candidates were each rehired. The fruitless exercise resulted in a thwarted waste of intimidation.

Wilder's initial election priorities were targeted towards cleaning up local corruption, lowering crime statistics and stimulating economic development. One of his *cost cutting* polices was to remove the metal detectors at the entrance of City Hall. During this same period, he established a detail of 8-10 police officers to serve as his personal bodyguards.

During his tenure, constant infighting tainted and distracted from his attempted objectives. His popular support steadily dwindled until he opted not to seek a second four-year term in 2008. He continued as a professor in public policy at Virginia Commonwealth University (VCU), lecturing inside the governmental and public affairs building named after him.

His declining professional years were plagued by controversy. He founded the United States National Slavery Museum in 2001, a non-profit organization based in Fredericksburg. The institution endured numerous tax related controversies before filing for Chapter 11 Bankruptcy protection in September 2011.

Wilder would extend his public spats prompting the resignation of the VCU dean of the governmental and public affairs department. He harshly criticized the Library of Virginia's for limiting access to his gubernatorial administration's documentation. He refused to endorse Barack Obama for a second presidential term. In March 2019 he was accused of sexual harassment, which was rebuffed by the claimant. In October, he was cleared of wrongdoing by a review panel although an investigator confirmed that he had kissed the woman without her consent. The culmination of charges and negative publicity resulted in an anticlimactic and disheartening political career finale.

The Richmond School Board continues to be housed within the City Hall structure. Any lingering whispers towards their future relocation have become silenced. Wilder remains living into his 90s and one day will lionized for his unprecedented accomplishments. His four years as Richmond's mayor will not likely be prominently included within his citations.

CITY HALL

**A Week Of Governing Dangerously
Virginia State Capitol Building:
1000 Bank Street, Richmond
Attorney General of Virginia Office:
202 N. 9th Street, Richmond**

During a single week of February 2019, a succession of embarrassments plagued the Executive Branch of the State of Virginia. The string of calamity began when a photo publicly surfaced from governor Ralph Northam's 1984 Eastern Virginia Medical School yearbook. On one page of the yearbook, an individual (presumably Northam) wore blackface paint and another (unidentified), a Ku Klux Klan outfit. Northam's yearbook appearance controversies continued to plague him when his 1981 Virginia Military Institute (VMI) yearbook pictured him with a corresponding nickname of *Coonman*, widely interpreted as a racial slur.

Before the questionable listings were publicly confirmed as him, Northam apologized. He lamely explained that he had darkened his face with shoe polish as part of a Michael Jackson costume for a party. He confessed that only two people at VMI referred to him as *Coonman*. As the negative disclosures were being revealed, a photograph surfaced from a prior political event, depicting him ignoring a black rival attempting to shake his hand.

Amidst this shrouded forest of accusation and idiocy, the circus concluded with a 55-page report confirming the inability of anyone to identify the costumed individuals shown in the Eastern Virginia Medical School yearbook pages. Collective amnesia had dimmed the recollection of over 80 people interviewed connected to the school and/or yearbook staff. They could not remember *anything*, *no one* or even *when* or *if* the photograph was actually taken.

The mounting scandal prompted Northam to seriously consider resigning. Unfortunately his successor, Lieutenant Governor Justin Fairfax abruptly became unavailable due to accusations of his own past impropriety. On February 3rd, Vanessa Tyson, a current university professor surfaced publicly claiming that Fairfax had sexually assaulted her fifteen years before inside a hotel room during the 2004 Democratic National Convention in Boston.

Fairfax insisted that their encounter was consensual. He claimed that her timing coincided opportunistically with his imminent elevation to governor. As Tyson began to publicly detail her allegations, Meredith Watson emerged four days later alleging that Fairfax had violently raped her in 2000 when the two were undergraduate students at Duke University. Both governor and lieutenant governor faced impeachment charges. Their fellow Democratic state legislators halted any ensuing proceedings.

As if the political buffoonery couldn't worsen, Attorney General Mark Herring, who had earlier called upon Northam to resign, voluntarily issued a statement admitting that he had once worn blackface as a 19-year old University of Virginia student. His intention was an attempt to resemble rapper Kurtis Blow at a party. His admission officially tainted the entire Virginia executive governmental branch.

Despite widespread national demands for all three men to resign, each waited out the maelstrom and did nothing. Northam was term-limited and simply served out his remaining days in office. Republican Glenn Younkin would defeat former governor Democrat Terry McAuliffe in the subsequent election. Both Fairfax and Herring would lose in their bids for reelection during 2021.

The sins and folly of their formative years would betray all three men. As with many early indiscretions or errant social media postings, few individuals imagine that their past will ever intrude upon their future. Amongst the dubious trio of Virginia's 2019 Executive Branch, their questionable and foolish actions derailed their political ambitions.

ATTORNEY GENERAL'S OFFICE

The Removal of Remembrances Past
Former Robert E. Lee Memorial Site:
Intersection of Monument Avenue and Allen Street, Richmond

The removal of Richmond's city owned Confederate monuments was completed officially in December 2022. The statue of General A. P. Hill that once towered above a busy intersection proved the most complicated. His remains were interred beneath it. The location was also problematic because the statue was situated in the middle of a busy intersection where traffic accidents were frequent.

With yellow straps positioned under its shoulders and a rope around its neck, the statue was lifted off its base in mere minutes before being laid on a flatbed truck lined with tires. Removing the base became more delicate since city records didn't indicate precisely where Hill's remains were located. His skull, bits of cloth and a few bones were eventually discovered under a mound of earth near the monument's foundation.

Four of Hill's indirect descendants agreed to transfer his remains to a cemetery in Culpeper, near his birthplace. They requested control over the future placement of the sculpture. Their preference was either a battlefield site or within the city of Culpeper. A federal circuit judge ruled that Richmond city officials, not the descendants, had the right to determine the subsequent destination. The statue was given to the Black History Museum and Cultural Center of Virginia.

The shedding of Confederate historical reminders was nearly concluded. The city could not legally remove monuments within its boundary owned by the Commonwealth. The removal was addressing an inglorious and awkward past for a progressive community. During 2020, approximately 160 Confederate symbols were removed following the Civil Rights protests following George Floyd's killing in Minneapolis.

Within Richmond, Monument Avenue is a famous tree-lined grassy mall dividing eastbound and westbound traffic. Starting in 1890, Monument Avenue evolved into a celebrated and picturesque residential boulevard extending fourteen blocks. The route features prominent mansions, churches, and apartment buildings. Five bronze Confederate leader statues were installed originally depicting Jefferson Davis, J.E.B. Stuart, Stonewall Jackson, Matthew Fontaine Maury and Robert E. Lee

Four of the sculptures were removed following years of debate and indecision from their memorial pedestals during July 2000. Robert E. Lee's statue, the largest, was handled differently as it was property of the Commonwealth. The 21-foot bronze weighed 12 tons and was positioned on a 40-foot granite pedestal. It was officially removed on September 8, 2021 and the circular roundabout grounds repurposed with the planting of more than 6,000 plants and 28 trees.

The lone remaining memorial along Monument Avenue is inoffensive, inspiring and appropriate. Black tennis legend Arthur Ashe was born in Richmond and became renowned for his pioneering sports exploits and commitment to Civil Rights. The statue was erected in 1996 without controversy.

Monument Avenue today retains an altered appearance with the absence of the towering and offending icons. The times have changed and polarizing memorials are no longer welcome.

FORMER ROBERT E. LEE MEMORIAL GROUNDS

Author, photographer and visual artist Marques Vickers was born in 1957 in Vallejo, California. He graduated from Azusa Pacific University in Los Angeles and became the Public Relations and Executive Director for the Burbank, California Chamber of Commerce between 1979-84.

Professionally, he has operated travel, apparel, wine, rare book and publishing businesses. His paintings and sculptures have been exhibited in art galleries, private collections and museums in the United States and Europe. He has previously lived in the Burgundy and Languedoc regions of France and currently lives in Western Washington.

He has written and published over one hundred books spanning a diverse variety of subjects including true crime, international travel, social satire, wine production, architecture, history, fiction, auctions, fine art, poetry and photojournalism.

He has two daughters, Charline and Caroline who reside in Europe.